THE PIONEER FARMER AND BACKWOODSMAN

VOLUME ONE

James Pattison Cockburn

WALKING ON THE KINGSTON-YORK ROAD, 1830

It is recorded that two of 'the old pioneers' of Norfolk County, Timothy Culver and his wife, walked in 1795 from New Jersey to Norfolk and back, over 1000 miles. It was Timothy's second trip on foot, and they returned a third time by ox-cart with their possessions.

THE PIONEER FARMER
AND BACKWOODSMAN

EDWIN C. GUILLET

VOLUME ONE

Toronto THE ONTARIO PUBLISHING CO. LTD.
Distributed by UNIVERSITY OF TORONTO PRESS

BOOKS BY EDWIN C. GUILLET

Early Life in Upper Canada (1933)
Toronto: From Trading-Post to Great City (1934)
The Great Migration: The Atlantic Crossing by Sailing-Ship
    since 1770 (1937)
The Lives and Times of the Patriots (1938)
Finding New Homes in Canada (1938)
    (in collaboration with Jessie E. McEwen)
The Pathfinders of North America (1939)
    (in collaboration with Mary Elizabeth Guillet)
Toronto Illustrated (1939)
Pioneer Arts and Crafts (1940)
This Man Hanged Himself! (1942)
Pioneer Life in the County of York (1946)
Life Insurance Without Exploitation (1946)
Cobourg, 1798-1948 (1948)
Pioneer Inns and Taverns:
    Volume One (1954)
    Volume Two (1956)
    Volumes Three and Four (in one) 1958
    Volume Five (1962)
The Valley of the Trent (1957)
In the Cause of Education (1960)

IN PREPARATION

Pioneer Religious Life
History of the Ontario Secondary School Teachers' Federation
Sir John A. Macdonald

Printed in Canada by T. H. Best Printing Co. Limited

TO

THE HONOURABLE LESLIE M. FROST

PRIME MINISTER OF ONTARIO

1947-1961

UNDER WHOSE ADMINISTRATION

THE RECORDING OF THE PROVINCE'S HISTORY

TOOK ON NEW SIGNIFICANCE

FOREWORD

by the Honourable Leslie M. Frost, P.C., Q.C., LL.D., D.C.L.
Member of the Legislative Assembly for
Victoria-Haliburton since 1937
Prime Minister of Ontario 1947-1961

To his long series of studies about the early history of the
Province of Ontario, Dr. Guillet has added his latest work,
dealing with the settlers of what was then a wild frontier region.
Earlier volumes in his wide-ranging works on pioneer life include *Early Life in Upper Canada, The Great Migration,
Pioneer Arts and Crafts, Pioneer Inns and Taverns, The Lives
and Times of the Patriots, In the Cause of Education,* and local
histories of Toronto, Cobourg, and York County. In the
Ontario series of books on early life in this Province published by the Champlain Society on behalf of the Government
of Ontario, the first volume *The Valley of the Trent* came from
the author's pen.

This work aims to present, for the first time, a history of
pioneer settlement and farming from contemporary sources
and, as well, a social history of those times. The author begins
with the immigrants to our wilds, including the United Empire
Loyalists and the arrivals from overseas, setting out the
troubles they encountered on their way to their new home,
and then describes their life in their settlements in the New
World. The problems faced by the pioneers are ably presented.
Included are the many details of their daily life, the food they
ate, the clothing they wore, and the homes in which they lived.
Not forgotten are the varied aspects of the social life of those
early days. The many illustrations, most of them from contemporary paintings, sketches, steel engravings, and woodcuts,
add immeasurably to our knowledge of pioneer times and of
the ways of life of our early settlers. Many of these pictures
were obtained by Dr. Guillet during his work as Research
Historian for the Ontario Department of Public Records and
Archives.

Here too, for the first time, is a detailed coverage of pioneer farm processes. Quotations from a vast array of contemporary records—diaries, letters, emigrant guidebooks, travel literature, newspapers, and farm journals—describe vividly the immigrants' settlement in the woods, the methods of clearing away the forest, of constructing primitive homes, barns, and fences, the first crude farming, and the progressive changes down through the years that gradually altered the crops, the farm tools and machinery, and the arts and crafts of the men and women whose indomitable courage laid the basis of Canada's richest province. It is a colourful record.

As we draw farther and farther away from the days of our pioneer settlements, it is important to have works such as these which set out the lives and stories of our pioneers who opened up this new and shining land. Without such histories the measure of their accomplishments, the hardships they endured, and the courage with which they persevered would gradually be largely forgotten and lost to memory.

The author is to be congratulated on the finished product resulting from the wide research he has carried out, the diligence with which he has investigated the various sources concerned with the first days of our province, and the readability of the language in which he has set out his material. This is indeed a work which adds much to our knowledge of early Ontario and which will be treasured in the years to come.

LESLIE M. FROST

October 31st, 1962
Sturgeon Lake,
   near Lindsay, Ontario

PREFACE

THIRTY years ago, when I wrote my first book *Early Life in Upper Canada* for the Department of Education of the Province of Ontario, I stated that other volumes on the same general topic would follow as the years passed. These have appeared, and the present work is intended to extend the series further. *The Pioneer Farmer and Backswoodsman* has been a long time in mind, and research for it has gone on intermittently for many years. The sources, in fact, were too extensive to be assimilated quickly, and over a long term much material has been added and a much more comprehensive work is the result. The two volumes published herewith supplement *Early Life in Upper Canada*. Farm processes, unmentioned or referred to in a few sentences in that volume, are now given the detailed attention they deserve, and they are described largely by those who actually saw them—the farmers themselves, or the more observant of the numerous travellers who visited Canada.

Many types and classes of people—in a day when social divisions were emphasized—participated in the settlement and development of Ontario. The poor and the destitute came in great numbers, but there were as well the wealthy and exclusive, the 'gentleman farmers' and the half-pay officers, many of whom contrived, for a time at least, to experience in 'the backwoods' the pleasures and amenities of contemporary life without the hardships. Life in 'the Bush' was very different, then as now, from life in towns or along 'the Front'. It is often a story of extremes.

'Fame,' it has been said, 'is the spirit of a man surviving himself in the minds and thoughts of other men, undying and imperishable, . . . the recompense not of the living but of the dead.' The spirits of innumerable pioneers will, we hope, live again in these pages, and the life and liveliness of their times be revived. Whether they were writers, travellers, or observers, or were farmers, townsmen, or backwoodsmen, or were craftsmen, inventors, or artists, great numbers of them now seem to the author like old friends, from long-continued reference to their activities and work. To some extent at least they are commemorated here, as they must eventually be on a larger scale in historical biography of the future.

Nostalgia, whether real or adopted for a purpose, is an important element in human life. But people are usually careful not to carry nostalgia too far. It is the rare enthusiast for the simple life who will imitate Thoreau, build a log hut in the woods, and live there for a couple of years at a net expenditure of $6.10 for beans and a few other seeds. The labour of pioneer blacksmiths and metal-workers was arduous and tiresome, even if the work was creative. Only those who were used to nothing better would care to live in the pioneer log houses described by Susanna Moodie—'dens of dirt and misery that would shame an English pig-sty'—or to work long hours by candlelight at exhausting crafts like spinning, weaving, or straw-plaiting, much less to cut a field of grain with a sickle or work day and night at meat-packing or potash-making. In indulging our nostalgia, we sometimes do not reckon on the suffering and misery that accompanied primitive life; we refer to 'the little red schoolhouse' in terms of endearment, oblivious to the barbarity of corporal punishment and other crudities that often went with it; we ignore, while glorifying life in the woods, its frequent sordidness: the drunkenness, the barbarous and obscene conduct, the maiming of oxen and horses, the incendiary burning of farmhouses, and the destruction of the farm machinery of those seeking to make progress. We should avoid indiscriminate admiration of our ancestors without the qualification that there were numerous rascals and scoundrels among them. Many protagonists of the glory of 'old times' ignore the unfortunate and vicious, preferring distortion to candour, fiction to fact, hypocrisy to honesty, euphemism to truth.

For several generations, in fact, the inhabitants of Ontario lived in an age of comparative violence. The wild life of clearing the land was often carried over into human relations, and fighting and brutality were characteristic of many regions. Emotional thinking in politics and in religion (though our pioneers were not quite as intolerant as in earlier centuries when torture and death were often the penalty of dissent) frequently led to personal and mob violence, to bitterness between friends, and to the disruption of family relations. Arguments led to fights, not to peaceable disagreements, and rivalry was usually expressed in feats of violence and endurance rather than in skill at sports. Religious differences, usually the most disturbing influence in new settlements and often a source of bitter animosity and snobbery down to recent times, were frequently intensified by riots, not softened by rational controversy. Only the slow progress of education gradually brought tolerance.

Yet it was above all else an age of independence and achievement. People were valued for their ability to work hard and long—'the pith o' sense, an' pride o' worth'—not for their rank, or inherited or adventitious wealth. Those who were rewarded by eventual prosperity were the admiration, if sometimes also the envy, of the district. Many had inner resources of artistic skill and intellectual interest, and were not—as so many of us are today—dependent upon commercialized entertainment to occupy spare time. Some were isolated and lonely, but there is no evidence that the pioneers were ever bored with themselves. With all our progress we have lost some pleasures that a slower, less noisy way of life had in abundance.

There was a pride in skill and workmanship that has largely disappeared in a machine age. Ploughing matches brought participants and spectators from far and near; field trials of reapers and binders were held with enthusiasm; and 'Delivery Day', when all the sales of farm implements in a region paraded the nearest town before entering upon farm work, was a colourful event. The exhibits at local fairs and the Provincial Exhibitions were eloquent examples of the skills and crafts that are now a comparative rarity in town or country.

In describing the lives and labours of the early settlers, however, we must prefer the factual to the lyric; and if our own laziness suggests that our ancestors' exertions were heroic by comparison, we must keep in mind that to them these exertions were just the daily round. To obtain a more considered and objective view we turn to travel books, which are both the meat and sauce of social history. The literate pioneer may have faithfully described his activities in diaries and letters, but it is the traveller whose comments relate them to what was better or worse, more primitive or more advanced, both in his own country and elsewhere. But there is a qualification even here, for it is the well-to-do who travel and their reactions were different from those of the miserable and destitute of the Old Land to whom the worst privations of the New would have been an improvement over what they had daily experienced. *The Pioneer Farmer and Backwoodsman* aims to present the progression of the farm and farmer from the primitive to the machine age; and since few details are too trivial to be significant, or variations too unusual to be omitted from the picture, the widest research has been necessary. In the pageant of social life the broad democratic view—since that is the way of life that survived—has been taken.

Americans and Canadians flock in droves to museums, and there may see anything from collections of alligators and snakes to restorations, archaeological remains, antiques, and the fine arts. It is said that the 'spectator quotient' (if that is the correct jargon) of the museums outruns even that of professional baseball. Ontario's Upper Canada Village near Morrisburg ranks high among restorations. The expenditure of some $3,000,000 upon this memorial to early settlement, together with the excellent work of preservation and restoration undertaken by the Conservation Authorities Branch of the Department of Lands and Forests, has encouraged local groups and individuals to enter the field. Two Brantford teachers, D. G. Kilmer and G. L. MacDonnell, are bringing together near that city typical early buildings which will form the Westfield Pioneer Village. Near Markham is being reassembled the log house erected by one of the sons of Christian Reesor, who rode horseback from Pennsylvania to the region in 1794. The furnishings will form a museum of authentic survivals of old times in the township. Numerous similar projects have been completed or are under way in various parts of Ontario. We live in a day of pioneer memorials.

There are, however, many private collectors of relics of the past who await a provincial historical museum—or several museums in different parts of the province—as repository for their treasures. Such official collections will be of prime importance. The Sigmund Samuel Canadiana Gallery has done much to prevent our best historical art from crossing the border, but it has self-imposed limitations and its collection is not restricted to Ontario. The National Gallery of Canada does not limit its collection to Canadian works. What we need is the encouragement of a broad historical sense, unfettered by artistic snobbery which imposes current personal tastes and refuses what posterity might readily accept. We knew one discriminator who would have nothing by Paul Kane, another no work of Arthur Heming's, and a third who could see no value in a historic portrait unless it was of a politician, a financier, or an aristocrat. Some galleries are being filled with the abstract or non-representational to the exclusion of anything tangible or realistic. The province is full of historical art and innumerable other memories of the past, and it is to be hoped that comprehensive collections will be preserved before it is too late. The 450 illustrations in this work include many never previously reproduced, the result of five years' travel in search of them for the Department of Public Records and Archives. A few are of the folk art or primitive variety, but what they lack in artistry they frequently make up for in picturesque vividness.

The same may be said with reference to literary source materials. I make no apology for including a few examples of those 'hapless poets', who, in William Hazlitt's words, 'have sighed out their souls to the Muse in vain, without ever getting their effusions farther known than the Poet's Corner of a country newspaper'. While their inspiration, as well as their abilities, is strictly limited, they add to the humour of nations, to our appreciation of how our forefathers thought and felt, and to our knowledge of the minutiae of existence long ago.

The credits for assistance in a work of this scope, and particularly for illustrations, are many and widespread. The great collections, and notably those of the Public Archives of Canada, the Sigmund Samuel Canadiana Gallery, the Toronto Public Library, the University of Toronto Library, the Legislative Library of Ontario, the Archives of Ontario, the Royal Ontario Museum, and the National Gallery of Canada, have been indispensable and the author's thanks are extended to their staffs. Some rare materials have been obtained from the Coverdale Collection, Manoir Richelieu, Murray Bay; the New Brunswick Museum, Saint John; the British Museum, London; Cambridge University Library; and the Burton Historical Collection, Detroit.

There are several other extensive contributors to *The Pioneer Farmer and Backswoodsman*. The International Nickel Company has given permission for the reproduction of a set of excellent illustrations drawn by Russell Taber, descriptive of Canadian life at the period when pioneering was drawing to a close. The Massey-Ferguson Company has similarly made available the fine illustrations by T. W. Maclean on the progress of farm processes and machinery, which originally appeared in *Harvest Triumphant* by Merrill Denison. Permission to reproduce four illustrations from the set *Pioneer Days* has been granted by the Informative Classroom Picture Association, Grand Rapids, Michigan.

Government agencies, both Federal and Provincial, have assembled in various departments collections of historical illustrations. In Ontario unique photographs were obtained through instructions to forest rangers to collect or copy items of value in their districts. The co-operation of V. B. Blake has enabled the inclusion in these volumes of excellent photography on historical aspects of river valleys where conservation and development of natural resources are carried on under the direction of the Conservation Authorities Branch of the Department of Lands and Forests. The Archives of Manitoba has many early photographs of sections of Northwestern Ontario that were once part of that province.

Collections of photographs assembled by individuals in various parts of Ontario are represented in these volumes, and credit notes designate the source under those used. Particularly important have been the companionship and photography of George M. Douglas, Lakefield, whose enthusiastic interest in the local history of the valley of the Trent has greatly enriched this work.

In the course of the last five years my wife and I have visited most of the public libraries, historical museums, newspaper offices, and antique shops of Ontario in search of information, historical illustrations, and other materials for the Archives of Ontario. The series, *Old Times in Ontario*, published in the *Toronto Daily Star*, is in part a report upon these researches, but they are also extensively reflected in these volumes. Appendix C, the journal of Captain Charles Gifford, is printed for the first time by permission of Leon Konorowski of Oshawa. Similarly reproduced for the first time are the full set of paintings in the Ware sketchbook in the Toronto Public Library. Representative sketches and paintings of Charles Davy Brown are reproduced by courtesy of Caroline Brown of Haysville and Mrs. John Patterson of Brampton; those of Captain George Downes by courtesy of Gordon Walmsley of Picton; those of Sarah Ann Carter and John J. Dalton by courtesy of Winifred Dalton of Weston; the large collection by W. Edgar Cantelon in the Eva Brook Donly Museum, Simcoe, by permission of the president, George Bramhill; those of Reginald Drayton (grandson of a prominent early settler, Captain Charles Rubidge) by courtesy of his son Nigel Drayton, Gore's Landing, and the Ontario Archives; those of Anne Langton by courtesy of the family; those of the Reverend Michael Farrar by courtesy of Helen Marryat, Hastings.

Individual illustrations reproduced in these volumes are included by courtesy of those in charge of the public libraries of Hamilton, Orangeville, Kingston, Peterborough, Paris, Kitchener, Picton, and Fenelon Falls; the Haliburton Municipal Hall; the Women's Canadian Historical Society of Toronto; the Thunder Bay Historical Society and Museum, Fort William; the Dundas Historical Society; and the Head of the Lakes Historical Society, Hamilton. To these should be added from the point of view of achievement and inspiration the local history collections of many other communities, and of private individuals in these communities, in which the past is depicted authentically and colourfully. Northern Ontario collections in general fall outside the scope of the present work, but the co-operation of the following, largely in the southern sections of the province, has greatly extended the field of historical illustration: Nila Reynolds, Oshawa (formerly of West Guilford, Haliburton); Charles H. Williamson, Omemee; Orrie Vail, Tobermory; R. O. Jennings, Smooth Rock Falls; C. H. Hale and Teefy Mulcahy, Orillia; Mrs. R. B. McWilliams, Lakefield; Mrs. Frankie MacArthur, Lindsay; Mrs. George Downey, Tiverton; Mrs. Roy Lunney, Bowmanville; Margaret Smyth, Mount Pleasant; Henry Holland, Sarnia; Bertha Shaw, South Porcupine; Agnes Turcott, Wawa; Grace Schmidt, Kitchener; Mildred and Irving Nattress, Port Arthur; Norman Greene, Timmins; Olive Newcombe, Dundas; Clara Benson, Port Hope; B. K. Van Buren, Hope Township; Blodwen Davies, Markham; Phyllis Denne, Bridgenorth; Lloyd Davy, Mrs. Lloyd Davy, and Mrs. C. W. Dickson, Grafton; Claude Snider, Gravenhurst; Edith Macklin and Russell Foster, Peterborough; Neil F. Morrison, Windsor; Genevieve Muir and Frank Inksater, Paris; J. A. Bannister, Port Dover; Mrs. R. S. Lambert, Creemore; Frank C. Taylor, Cobourg; John Ostler, Pakenham; Jeanne Minhinnick, Upper Canada Village; Harold Wills, Cochrane; Leon Wright, Kinmount; Ronald Curry, Haliburton; Mrs. Frank Harris, Wellington; E. C. Bigley, Fenelon Falls; Mrs. G. M. Irwin, Gore Bay; Mrs. D. Clark,

Little Current; Mrs. Ernest Batten, Dummer Township; A. A. Silcox, Shedden; Alice Pilant, Brantford; Robert McKnight, New Liskeard; Helen I. Cowan, Baltimore (Maryland); Florence Hayward, New York; C. C. Johnson, Parry Sound; Richard Dean, Norwood; Mrs. William Staples, Burleigh Township; and J. M. McCrea, Harold McCrea, Edith Firth, Mrs. Everett Drake, W. Perkins Bull, W. C. Givens, B. Napier Simpson, Jr., Mrs. E. Wilkins, David McFall, Charles McFaddin, Hazel Anderson, Hugh McKanday, Jerrine Kinton, J. C. Duff, G. H. Needler, Mrs. J. E. Laughlin, V. X. McEnaney, George A. Smith, Edith Fowke, Anthony Adamson, and John Rempel, all of Toronto. Many of these have supplied historical information as well, as have a number of others, particularly Mrs. Marie Berrill, Port Credit; Mrs. Dorothy Angus, Erin; Richard Pilant, Brantford; R. S. Lambert, Creemore; Francis J. Petrie and Arnold Sherman, Niagara Falls; Mrs. Ralph Preston, Bethany; and Michael Foran and Norman Found, Toronto.

The table of contents, like that of *Early Life in Upper Canada*, has been extended in detail to facilitate the location of processes of farming and elements of social life; these may be found also in the extensive index, along with persons and places and all sorts of interests and activities mentioned in the work. My wife has aided in the preparation of the index, and by proofreading and suggestion throughout.

Special appreciation is extended to the Honourable Leslie M. Frost, long a friend to history and historians, for the Foreword he has written for this work, and for encouragement which has not only increased the scope of the subject matter but enriched it immeasurably.

Edwin C. Guillet

736 O'Connor Drive
Toronto, March 1, 1963

CONTENTS

VOLUME I

Contents

Contents

Contents

Contents

ILLUSTRATIONS

VOLUME I

Illustrations

Illustrations

Illustrations

Illustrations

THE PIONEER FARMER AND BACKWOODSMAN

The weapons with which we have gained our most important victories, which should be handed down as heirlooms from father to son, are not the sword and the lance, but the bushwhack, the turf-cutter, the spade, and the boghoe, rusted with the blood of many a meadow, and begrimed with the dust of many a hard-fought field.

— HENRY DAVID THOREAU

CHAPTER I

INDIAN AND FRENCH AGRICULTURE

WITH variations of some three weeks in the commencement of
the growing season in southern and northern parts of 'Old'
Ontario, and a similar difference in the time, frequency, and
intensity of snow and frost, it may yet be said that the entire
region from the Essex Peninsula to the south shore of Lake
Nipissing has a climate suited to agriculture. But the success
of individual crops varies according to the soil and the length
and intensity of the growing season. In the Niagara fruit-belt
the average period of growth is 212 days per year, and 158
days are frost-free, while in Algonquin Park the figures are
176 and 93, respectively, with the other regions somewhere
between.

Not all of southern Ontario was covered with an aboriginal
forest. Sandy stretches of thinly timbered land called oak-
plains were found in the Long Point district, the valley of the
Grand River, in Northumberland County, in York County east
of the Humber, and in Ancaster, Burford, Dumfries, Niagara,
and Stamford townships. Though easy to clear, these lands
were at first not popular among settlers except as pasture land,
particularly, perhaps, from their lack of timber for buildings,
fences, and fuel. Not until about 1850, for example, were the
Rice Lake Plains north of Cobourg utilized for wheat.

The great explorer Champlain first described Indian agriculture. He wrote in 1613 that while the Algonkins of Allu-
mette Island and vicinity were largely hunters and fishers, they
yet grew some Indian corn, squashes, and kidney-beans. Two
years later he found other tribes growing similar crops in the
Nipissing-Georgian Bay region, where they planted Indian
corn and other cereals and dried wild fruits for winter use; and
when he passed south to Huronia, in modern Simcoe County,
he found the land largely cleared and thickly settled, with the

3

T. H. Ware

INDIAN CANOE AT COLDWATER

INDIAN PETROGLYPHS, PETERBOROUGH COUNTY
These rock carvings were discovered in 1954 near McGinnis Lake.

same crops plus sunflowers for the seeds, which they used for both soup and hair-oil.

The Indian women carried on the laborious maize culture, even to the extent of chopping and clearing with their primitive stone axes. The corn was planted in hills, two feet apart and ten kernels in each, and the same hills were used year after year. The Indians always grew more than their needs, for it was essential to provide for years of poor harvests. Wooden shovels and pointed stakes were their only farm tools, and with these it was difficult to remove heavy grass from the corn patch. It was often easier to move somewhere else, village and all.

In addition to dried fruits the Indians gathered nuts— acorns, chestnuts, and walnuts—and grapes, plums, cherries, cranberries, crab-apples (sometimes preserved in maple syrup), strawberries, blackberries, raspberries, gooseberries, and blueberries. Of the blueberry, which seems to have been their favourite, Lahontan wrote:

These Berries serve for several uses after they are dry'd in the sun or in an Oven: for then they make Comfits of 'em, or put 'em into Pyes, or infuse 'em in Brandy. The North-Country Savages make a Crop of 'em in the Summer, which affords 'em very seasonable relief, especially when their hunting comes short.

Indian sugar-making was an ancient and very primitive process, and the resulting sugar poor and dirty. Relays of red-hot stones were originally their only means of boiling sap, for at first they had only wooden kettles or troughs. The Tobacco Indians, west of the Hurons, and the Neutrals along Lake Erie, differed from the other tribes only in that they cultivated tobacco, and it was the men who worked at this crop, not the women.

The Reverend George Playter's *History of Methodism in Canada* is among the finest source-books of Indian life in the period of settlement. He gives an account of 'the great annual feast of the offerings of the first fruits of the earth', which corresponded closely to the settlers' Thanksgiving. The Indian missionary Peter Jones saw the ceremony at an Indian encampment on the lower Muncey River in 1825, and his description is quoted by Playter:

They brought a little of all that they had raised, such as Indian corn, potatoes, pumpkins, beans, melons, and squashes, together with twelve deer. The Indian women were busily engaged cooking their

5

provisions. Previous to the commencement of their exercises they invited us strangers into a long Pagan Temple prepared for such purposes. There is a door at each end, one opening to the east and the other to the west. On entering we observed all the Indians seated on the ground round two fires. In the centre of the temple was a large post, round which was suspended a number of deer skins and wampum. I was also informed that wampum is kept buried at the foot of this post.

Near the post sat two Indian singers, each with a large bundle of undressed deer skins which served as drums. There were two young men appointed to watch the doors and keep the fires burning. The doors being closed, the young men brought each of them an armful of hemlock boughs, which being thrown on the fires smothered them and caused a great smoke, in order that the smoke might fill every corner of the temple. Each man waved his blanket over the fire. This was done with the idea of purifying the temple and driving out the evil spirits.

After the smoke subsided an old chief rose up who was the master of the ceremony, with a turtle shell in his hand which he began to rattle; he then delivered a speech to the people telling them the object of their meeting, that they had come together to thank the Great Spirit for the growth and ripening of their corn, &c. When he finished his speech he began to dance, sing, and rattle the shell—the two singers sang with him, beating on their skins: when he took his seat he handed his shell to the next person, who performed in the same way. Thus it went on from one to the other all night. The purport of their speeches was recounting the mercies of the Great Spirit to them during the past year, and telling any remarkable dreams they had had. In the course of the night a number of them went out at the west door, making a wailing noise to the moon; they came in again at the east door. In the morning the meat and soup were divided amongst the people. These feasts often last several days. No drinking or improper conduct is allowed; the utmost solemnity prevails.

When the French arrived in America they imitated some of the Indian methods, particularly in maple sugar manufacture; and having iron kettles they could make it better. The first agricultural products at Quebec were Indian corn, squashes, and kidney-beans, grown Indian fashion. By 1624 the Récollet missionaries were growing vegetables in Huronia, and by 1645 they had taken young cattle there. Such beginnings of Indian and French agriculture were destroyed by the Iroquois invasions at the middle of the century, and the gathering of wild rice was long almost the only pursuit approaching the agricultural. In threshing it, we are told,

They take it to their camps and dig a hole in the ground, put a deer-skin into it, then so pour the rice into it; boys are set to trampling the chaff out with their feet, after which they fan it, and it is then prepared for use.

A large granite pot-hole between Stoney and Cedar lakes, Peterborough County, is said by the farmers in the vicinity to have been used by Indians for threshing wild rice,* but they have the mistaken impression that the Indians had made it for the purpose, a thing quite impossible with their primitive tools.

Motion Picture Bureau, Ontario

INDIAN SUGAR CAMP

Among the lakes noted for wild rice was Rice Lake, known in the French period as *Folle Avoine* (Wild Oats), the two plants being quite similar. When Charles Fothergill visited Rice Lake over a trail from Smith's Creek (Port Hope) in the winter of 1816-17 he found that many Indians harvested as much as 60 to 80 bushels annually and were glad to sell three bushels for a dollar. He wrote that 10,000 bushels might at that time have been harvested on the lake, and that wild ducks often ate so much of it that they were unable to fly and could be easily speared**

*The Indians sometimes used a hollowed stump for the purpose, and the idea was imitated by settlers who had no access to a grist mill.

**The volume of Fothergill's journal quoted here is in the possession of Douglas S. Robertson, Toronto. See Appendix to Volume Four of the author's *Pioneer Inns and Taverns* for a transcription of the greater part of it. The department of ornithology of the Royal Ontario Museum has sixteen of the twenty volumes of the journal.

Wild rice, now an expensive delicacy at $1.50 to $2.00 a pound, was used in early times in soup, and with wild duck, partridge, or venison. When boiled it was (and is) delicious served with maple sugar and cream. Other appropriate accompaniments to a 'wild' meal include wild-grape jelly, wild cranberry sauce, and wild-grape juice.

An example of the agriculture practised by French missionaries among the Indians, in both the East and far West, is the gardening at Fort Frontenac between 1676 and 1679, in La Salle's day, as described by Father Louis Hennepin:

The Ground which lies along the Brink of this Lake is very fertile. In the space of two Years and a half that I resided there in discharge of my *Mission* they cultivated more than a hundred Acres of it. Both the *Indian* and *European* Corn, Pulse, Pot-Herbs, Gourds, and Water-Melons throve very well. It is true indeed that at first the Corn was much spoil'd by Grasshoppers; but this is a thing that happens in all the Parts of *Canada* at the first cultivating the Ground, by reason of the extream Humidity of all that Country. The first Planters we sent thither bred up Poultry there, and transported with them Horned Beasts, which multiply'd there extreamly.

There were also thirty-five head of cattle at Fort Frontenac at the time, and some 500 acres had been cleared; but agriculture had been abandoned and the land become wild again long before the end of the French period.

In the vicinity of Detroit agricultural developments were more permanent. On the west side of the river a settlement called the Petite Côte had fifty families by 1760. James Smith, who was there a few years earlier, observed that wheat and peas were the principal crops, and that the lots and dwellings were laid out in the fashion characteristic along the St. Lawrence. But the people, if picturesque, were not good farmers, for they were more concerned with the fur trade. Without much labour they could grow poor but sufficient crops of wheat, barley, oats, peas, buckwheat, Indian corn, and potatoes.*

Their chief implement was a crude plough of a type common along the St. Lawrence, with a wooden mould-board, short and almost perpendicular handles, and an almost straight beam resting on an axle supported by two small wheels. A plough of this kind was still being used in the locality in 1818.

*Lieutenant-Colonel Hamilton, commander at Detroit in 1761, described the colony on both sides of the river in idyllic terms, stating that every farmer had his yoke of oxen, his calash (*calèche*) for summer driving and his carriole for winter, and everywhere were blossoming shrubs and fruit trees.

Courtesy Henry Holland

SARNIA'S FIRST STORE AND TRADING-POST

Kept by the settlement's first postmaster, George Durand, the store was located at the southwest corner of Christina Street and the London Road.

It was drawn by two yoke of oxen and a team of horses, with three men conducting the work, the whole 'making as much noise as if they were moving a barn', as an eye-witness put it. The French usually yoked their oxen by the horns rather than the necks.

In the French period the Detroit settlements had few cattle and no sheep, but by 1776 there were some 3000 cattle and

Eighty Years' Progress in British North America

HABITANT DRIVING A CALÈCHE

9

2000 sheep and about 2500 settlers along the shores of the river. Great numbers of horses were used for pleasure driving rather than for ploughing or farm activities. They had also swine to fatten for salt pork, but in general all stock were left unprovided for in winter and had to forage for themselves.

The French [observed Patrick Shirreff in the early eighteen-thirties] seem to have little system in their farming, growing wheat, Indian corn, and grass. They plough with oxen and a driver. The sheep are similar to those of the lower province, many of them being black-coloured with a little white on the face and neck. The oxen are of different colours, somewhat larger than those of Lower Canada, and many of them are without horns. The horses are small, and perhaps not equal to those of Montreal.

But in one respect these French settlements were distinctive —in fruit-growing—for from very early times every farm had peaches, plums, apples, and pears. Some of the original seeds, and even small trees, are said to have been brought to the region by the first French missionaries. The coming of the Loyalists speedily reduced these French pioneers to a position of secondary importance; in fact there were probably only a few dozen families left on the Petite Côte when the first Loyalists arrived. There persisted, however, a considerable French settlement on the Canadian side of the Detroit.

CHAPTER II

THE UNITED EMPIRE LOYALISTS

THE difference between patriots and rebels in this world is always closely related to success or failure, and the point of view from which they are regarded is all-important in forming public opinion. Even before the Declaration of Independence in 1776 there were Loyalists in the American colonies, but they were usually known as 'Tories' and 'enemies of their country';* and the separatists or revolutionists were often called 'damned rebels' by those whose sympathies lay in the direction of Britain or were not given to change of any kind. Fortunately modern historians have been able to come to general conclusions on these pioneer settlers of early Canada who have at times been unreasonably and uncritically venerated in a sort of ancestor worship; though of course no objection can be taken to bona fide descendants keeping green the memory of ancestors distinguished by their loyalty and public spirit.

In 1789 Sir Guy Carleton (Lord Dorchester), Governor-General of British North America, proposed to put a mark of honour upon the families who had adhered to the unity of the Empire and had 'joined the royal standard in America before the Treaty of Separation in the year 1783', but he did not specify what the mark should be; subsequently it became 'U. E.'

The listing formed at that time was henceforth called 'the old U. E. list', and its names are obviously of those who were

*Here is the logical attitude of an American historian relative to those who opposed the Revolution which founded their nation: 'Thousands of American settlers denounced the Revolution as treason and subversion, fought it, retreated to Canada or took ship to England, leaving behind the men of faith, who went on to build a continent.' ('In Time of Trial', by Barbara Ward, *The Atlantic,* February 1962.) In other words the Loyalists were to the winners reactionary imperialists—an unpopular group when the Republic was in process of formation, and at least equally a term of reproach among the emergent nations of Asia and Africa in our own day.

11

the real and unqualified Loyalists. Later governors authorized additions to the list in the interest of attracting settlers. These are sometimes called 'late Loyalists',* but contemporary settlers from Great Britain and Ireland and the writers of travel books describe them variously as American Loyalists, Americans, United English Loyalists, and Yankees. In 1822 Robert Gourlay referred to them as 'loyalists of the United Empire', but others used terms of opprobrium such as 'Yankee land-grabbers' and 'skedadlers', and charged that many of them left the United States to evade their debts or, a little later, to avoid service in the War of 1812. But it must be remembered that many of these charges were levelled against them by those used to British aristocratic government, to whom they were democrats, republicans, or (in the fashion of our day) communists.

The official class in the American colonies provided one section of loyalists who acted from a mixture of duty, fidelity, bias, and self-interest; and there were a few large landed proprietors who were loyal because they were aristocratic, who were not rebels because the established order best served them. Of the professional classes but few were Loyalists, and scarcely any of these came to Upper Canada. There were as well wealthy traders who found revolution bad for business, and conservative farmers who saw no reason to complain. The great mass, however, were none of these, but as one writer put it, 'of no trades and all trades, of all grades of wealth, education and social position . . . not known outside of their respective localities.' These made up the opposition to rebellion and independence, and many of them became soldiers and sailors in the British forces of resistance to revolution. Of the total of some 2100 families who settled in what is now Ontario the greater part were humble farmers from the rear concessions of New York State. A few of more intellectual type, and some with college degrees, settled first in New Brunswick and then removed to Upper Canada.

Having supported the losers, the Loyalists were, in many instances, forced by persecution and ill-treatment to leave their homes, and it matters but little what proportion of the others sought to come to Canada to remain under British rule or merely as adventurers seeking free land. And though, officially, claimants to the name and land-grants might have set-

---

*Many of these were people with British sympathies, who tried unsuccessfully to live under the Republic; others were interested in obtaining free land.

Ensign James Peachey

ENCAMPMENT OF THE LOYALISTS AT NEW JOHNSTOWN (CORNWALL), ST. LAWRENCE RIVER, 1784

tled in Upper Canada as late as July 28, 1798, great numbers who came prior to that date were, as one put it, neither more nor less than 'pioneer farmers whose only motive was the traditional American search for better lands and a perfect home'.

Two Loyalist corps are of special interest to this province—the King's Royal Regiment of New York (Royal Greens) and Butler's Loyal Rangers—for they carried on their campaigns and activities from Canada. But the settlers from these regiments were preceded by a number of others who, if we omit the few French, may truly be called Upper Canada's pioneer settlers. In December 1780 five families were building houses for themselves in the Niagara district, in what was to be called the County of Lincoln, and they would have planted a crop of fall wheat had the supply arrived in time. Peter Secord subsequently claimed to have been the province's first settler, but Michael Showers of the Rangers has at least as good a claim to the honour.

A year later considerable land had been cleared and prepared for spring sowing, and Colonel Butler reported that for the previous three months the settlers had maintained themselves and had had only half rations from the beginning. In August 1782 sixteen settlers, all married and thirteen with children, were on the land. Corn and potatoes were their chief crops, but some wheat and oats had been harvested. One settler had a negro slave, and the number of horses, cows, sheep, and hogs suggests that some had been able to bring stock with them from New York State.

There was a great rush, of course, after the treaty of peace in 1783, and most settlers trekked north on foot or in boats by the Mohawk River, Lake Champlain, and the Oswego River, or their tributaries. Susanna Moodie obtained firsthand the details of one Loyalist family's experience:

Wait a while; you know nothing of a Canadian winter. This is only November; after the Christmas thaw you'll know something about cold. It is seven-and-thirty years ago since I and my man left the U-ni-ted States. It was called the year of the great winter. I tell you, woman, that the snow lay so deep on the earth that it blocked up all the roads and we could drive a sleigh whither we pleased, right over the snake-fences. All the cleared land was one wide white level plain; it was a year of scarcity and we were half starved; but the severe cold was far worse nor the want of provisions. A long and bitter journey we had of it; but I was young then, and pretty well used to trouble and fatigue; my man stuck to the British government. More fool he! I was an American born, and my heart was with the true cause. But his father was English, and says he, 'I'll live and die under their flag'. So he dragged me from my comfortable fireside to seek a home in the far Canadian wilderness. Trouble! I guess you think you have your troubles; but what are they to mine? (She paused, took a pinch of snuff, offered me the box, sighed painfully, pushed the red handkerchief from her high, narrow, wrinkled brow, and continued): Joe was a baby then, and I had another helpless critter in my lap—an adopted child. My sister had died from it, and I was nursing it at the same breast with my boy.

Well, we had to perform a journey of four hundred miles in an ox-cart, which carried, besides me and the children, all our household stuff. Our way lay chiefly through the forest, and we made but slow progress. Oh! what a bitter cold night it was when we reached the swampy woods where the city of Rochester now stands. The oxen were covered with icicles, and their breath sent up clouds of steam. 'Nathan,' says I to my man, 'you must stop and kindle a fire; I am dead with cold, and I fear the babes will be frozen.' We began looking about for a good spot to camp in when I spied a light through the trees. It was a lone shanty, occupied by two French lumberers. The men were kind; they rubbed our frozen limbs with snow, and shared with us their supper and buffalo-skins. On that very spot where we camped that night, where we heard nothing but the wind soughing amongst the trees and the rushing of the river, now stands the great city of Rochester. I went there two years ago,

O'Reilly, *Sketches of Rochester*, 1838

LOG HOUSES OF ISAAC AND ENOS STONE, ROCHESTER, 1812
Enos is shooting a bear caught in his cornpatch.

to the funeral of a brother. It seemed to me like a dream. Where we foddered our beasts by the shanty fire now stands the largest hotel in the city; and my husband left this fine growing country to starve here!*

By July 1783 Loyalists in process of settlement in thirteen townships along the St. Lawrence and the Bay of Quinte num-

Courtesy Gordon Walmsley   Capt. J. P. Downes

WELLINGTON, PRINCE EDWARD COUNTY, IN 1847

bered 3776. There were in the group 1568 men, 626 women, and 1492 children, and 90 servants; and of the servants a half dozen were negro slaves. In 1784 a small group of Loyalists under Captain Michael Grass drew lots for the new townsite, Kingston. In the whole province these early Loyalists numbered about 6000.

The settlement of Loyalists was effected at government expense, and on that account their experiences were in general less arduous than those of later settlers; certainly there would at least be much less urgency in the securing of food, for rations were provided for three years. Nor could it be said that they were modest in pressing claims for other aids, for those near Cataraqui (Kingston) petitioned for boards, shingles, nails, window glass, arms and ammunition, and a list of tools, implements, clothing, and other supplies that would have done

*For other details of Loyalist trails, routes, and experiences see the author's *Early Life in Upper Canada*, Section II, Chapter I, and Section IV, Chapter I.

credit as stock for a pioneer general store; and in addition to seed of various types, they asked for two horses, two cows, and six sheep 'to be delivered at Cataroque to Each Family at Government's Expence'. They did, however, in pleading poverty and inability to purchase, suggest a moderate tax by which at the end of ten years the government might be reimbursed 'if required'.

It was speedily apparent to officials that these requests were so extravagant that the expense would be 'enormous', and apart from provisions, only an axe and a hoe were in general provided to each man. The food rations per day were calculated at

two thirds Allowance to the 1st May, 1785, and from that period at one third Allowance to the 1st day of May 1786, estimating the whole Ration at one Pound of Flour and one Pound of Beef or twelve ounces of Pork, and the children under 10 years of age to have a moiety of the Allowance made to grown Persons.

There was considerable confusion in effecting both settlement and the provision of necessities, and especially among those farthest from the base of supplies. In July 1784 there was still 'great disorder' at Cataraqui, the settlers 'not having yet got upon their Land, many of them unprovided with a Blanket to cover Them, scarce any Turnip seed and neither Axes nor Hoes for Half of Them'. But as far as possible and without paying too much attention to the red tape of the day, those in charge provided the Loyalists with such necessaries as the government stores contained, and to an extent well beyond official intentions; in spite of which some of them were found to be 'uniformly discontented and troublesome' and their demands 'vexatious'.

The provision of seed proved difficult both at Niagara and along the St. Lawrence, for supplies had to be forwarded by bateaux.* A few bushels each of Indian corn, wheat, buckwheat, oats, and peas, some small seeds and a forge, dressed leather, and grindstones were at Coteau du Lac in April 1781 awaiting transport to Niagara at the first opportunity after the opening of navigation; and the same difficulties were experienced three years later along the St. Lawrence and in the Bay of Quinte region. Eventually 1000 bushels of seed wheat had to be obtained from the Mohawk Valley, as well as turnip,

*See *Early Life in Upper Canada,* Section IV, Chapter 3, for details of this type of travel.

carrot, cabbage, onion, celery, radish, and parsley seed in small quantities.

The land grant to Loyalists was 100 acres to each head of a family, and 50 to each member; while a single man was given 50 acres. Non-commissioned officers received 200 acres, and for higher ranks the grant was much larger. Many of the earliest Loyalists received 200 acres of bush land in the rear as well as 100 acres along the St. Lawrence. Due probably to their nearness to the base of supplies those in Glengarry were given much more equipment than those farther up the country. In general all sons of Loyalists were granted 200 acres on coming of age, and daughters received the same on marriage. But because they were called Loyalists it was not assumed that they were necessarily loyal to the Crown, and the Land Board's duty was to investigate each case and to administer the oath of allegiance to all applicants. Twelve months' occupation entitled each settler to a permanent deed.

Except insofar as they were different or exceptional, the experiences of the Loyalists in clearing the land and establishing themselves will be described in due course with those of later settlers. The 'Hungry Year' of 1788-89, following a poor harvest because of unusual weather conditions, is well authenticated, though most accounts of settlers' experiences are reminiscences in old age, or second-hand stories of children and grandchildren who did not personally recall the hardships. Perhaps the best account is one very near to the event, recorded by Jacob Lindley in a description of a journey to Detroit in 1793:

Joseph Moore and myself went four miles to see Jeremiah Moore's family. They related the dreadful circumstances they were reduced to in this country by scarcity of bread and provisions of all kinds in the year 1789, when they came to an allowance of one spoonful of meal per day for one person, eat strawberry leaves, beech leaves, flax seed dried and ground in a coffee mill—catched the blood of a little pig—bled the almost famished cow and oxen—walked twelve miles for one shive of bread, paid twelve shillings for twelve pounds of meal. One of the lads who was hired out carried his little sister two miles on his back to let her eat his breakfast, and they gave him none till dinner. The children leaped for joy at one robin being caught, out of which a whole pot of broth was made. They eat mustard, potato tops, sassafras root, and made tea of the tops. The relation was deeply affecting. The case being general, one could not help another: which brought to my mind the many thankless meals enjoyed in the land of plenty.

18

THE PIONEERS

Arthur Heming

Bad crops did not provide the sole cause, for the poor harvest coincided with the end of government rations. Many settlers would have been self-sufficient after three years, certainly under ordinary conditions, but there were some whose wartime habits were detrimental to industry, and when 'Old George' (the King) failed to feed them indefinitely their suffering was acute. Reminiscences refer to the time as 'the scarce year', 'the hard summer', and 'the starved year', describe the killing of horses and dogs for food, the use of 'what roots the pigs ate' and of 'leaves, ground nuts, herbs, and fish', the passing of 'a beef's bone' from house to house to be reboiled for soup, and the eating of bullfrogs, dandelion, pigweed, and the buds and bark of trees. 'Men willingly offered pretty much all they possessed for food. I could show you one of the finest farms in Hay Bay that was offered to my grandfather for half a hundred of flour and refused,' said Canniff Haight. William Kirby describes nature's sufferings in his long poem *The Hungry Year*:

> *Corn failed, and fruit and herb. The tender grass*
> *Fell into dust. Trees died like sentient things,*
> *And stood wrapped in their shrouds of withered leaves*
> *That rustled weirdly round them sear and dead.*
> *From springs and brooks no morning mist arose;*
> *The water vanished; and a brazen sky*
> *Glowed hot and sullen through the pall of smoke*
> *That rose from burning forests, far and near.*

The population of Upper Canada was about 10,000 in 1791, the year of the creation of the province, and of these some 7000 had been given land as Loyalists. Though grants continued to be made under that head until 1798, the later arrivals were decreasingly Loyalist and increasingly Americans who, as the Duc de la Rochefoucauld-Liancourt put it, 'falsely profess an attachment to the British Monarch and curse the government of the Union, for the mere purpose of thus wheedling themselves into the possession of lands.'

The name Loyalist might, with reason, continue to be used until the period of the War of 1812, though those who came were neither more nor less loyal than other inhabitants in resisting the American invasion. After that time their fusion with other settlers makes it inaccurate and confusing to use the term at all. Their descendants were as prominent in the opposition as among followers of the 'Family Compact', among

Frances Hopkins

THE ARTIST AND HER HUSBAND IN A HUDSON'S BAY CANOE

Earlier publications using this illustration named the pair in the centre as Viscount and Lady Monck.

Mackenzie's Reformers as in the Tory party; but almost half of the members of the Legislative Assembly elected in its first half century, 1791-1841, were Loyalists or their direct descendants, which is not remarkable considering their prominence in the establishment of representative government and the beginnings of democracy.

The Loyalists, however, and partly for these very reasons, were not generally highly regarded by their contemporaries, nor by British travellers, who included them with other 'Yankees' settled in the province. Referring to the Niagara region, which he visited more than once in the period 1818-1820, John Howison wrote:

A great majority of the individuals who are owners of these farms came to the province twenty or thirty years ago in the character of needy adventurers, and either received the then unimproved land from government or purchased it for a trifle. . . . Many of them possess thirty or forty head of cattle and annually store up two or three thousand bushels of grain in their barns; but this amelioration in their condition, unfortunately, has not produced a corresponding effect upon their manners, character, or mode of life. They are still the same untutored, incorrigible beings that they probably were when, the ruffian remnant of a disbanded regiment, or the outlawed refuse of some European nations,* they sought refuge in the wilds of Upper Canada, aware that they would neither find means of subsistence nor be countenanced in any civilized country. Their original depravity has been confirmed and increased by the circumstances in which they are now placed. . . . It is indeed lamentable to think that most of the improved part of this beautiful and magnificent Province has fallen into such 'hangmen's hands'; and to feel convinced that the country will retrograde in every thing that is truly great and desirable, and remain detestable to persons of liberal ideas, as long as these boors continue to be the principal tenants of it.

Reference to the lives of a few prominent Loyalists will exemplify the influence of many. Stephen Burritt drew lot 29 on the first concession of Augusta Township, and he and his family were the first settlers 'who went back and settled on the Rideau'. There he took his father, who lived to be nearly a hundred.

After the exciting life of the Revolutionary War, Burritt

*This reference is to mercenary soldiers brought from Europe to fight against the colonists, for these also ranked as Loyalists. Dr. Howison's opinions are called 'scandalous' by Robert Gourlay, the noted reformer, who said these farmers were a mixed lot but that the Family Compact ruling clique was responsible and its members characterised by 'depravity of the most odious kind'.

found it hard to settle down. He tried fur-trading, exploring the Rideau, and the adventurous life among the Indians. Building a raft at Cox's Landing he floated down to what came to be called Burritt's Rapids where, after a fight, he was accepted as a friend by the Indians.

Carrying in supplies thirty miles through the wilds, he and his wife were shortly near death by fever, but the squaws nursed them back to health while their men harvested their small crop of corn; there, too, in 1793, their son Stephen was the first white child born on the Rideau. They always kept open house for the Indians, even when they became important and prosperous.

ROBERT LAND'S LOG CABIN   COLONEL ROBERT LAND

Colonel Land, a Loyalist from New York, is believed to have been the first settler in Wentworth County.

Another Loyalist whose experiences seem to be well authenticated is Joel Stone, founder of Gananoque. He opened a store and a lumber business and built a boat, after earlier losing all his possessions while staying on a nearby island with a French trader.

His wife having died some years earlier, Stone was looking for another and in that day they were not easily obtained. Hearing that one Mrs. Dayton, who had been a neighbour in Connecticut, was now a widow in Brantford, he wrote her a guarded letter with matrimony in view. But in those days of great travel difficulties even Cupid did not co-operate with any speed, and he was constrained to write again that if she had a good offer from another he would not expect her to wait for his visit.

Finally she became his wife as well as a noted benefactor in and around Gananoque, where in a radius of forty miles she rode her horse to help the needy and tend the sick; while her own home always gave a hospitable welcome to travellers and a special entertainment for Indians on New Year's Day. The Stones were prominent Methodists and practical exponents of social justice; and as Justice of the Peace, Joel Stone was a force for law and order in innumerable ways.

In general, Loyalist reminiscences do not add greatly to our knowledge of pioneer life. In many instances it is apparent that references to very early conditions are, if not based altogether on hearsay, at least garbled by an intermixture of later events; and the result of the desire of old people to tell a good story is often something rambling, incoherent, and exaggerated. Here, for what they are worth, are some of the reminiscences that seem to point to variations from the experiences of later settlers.

Susan Greeley, Haldimand Township, granddaughter of Loyalists, observed that log houses usually became uncomfortable when the logs began to settle: 'Ours was made of hardwood—yes, any kind of wood would do if you could get logs perfectly straight—maple, basswood, poplar.' She was referring to the period a few years after the War of 1812, when iron hinges and latches could sometimes be obtained; 'but none of these things could have been procured by the first settlers 35 years before,' said she; 'all were of wood.' She describes the Loyalist 'stick chimney' in considerable detail, stating that when the sticks, plastered inside and out with a very adhesive clay, were built up to a safe distance above the roof the chimney was perfectly safe as long as the clay was unbroken; but, she observes, 'We had a brick chimney and regular fireplace, which lasted much longer than the house did.'

James Dittrick, as the son of a Loyalist, was granted land in 1808 in the vicinity of St. Catharines. He refers mostly to his parents' experiences, some of which he may have shared as a boy. At first, he says, it was a Robinson-Crusoe life in Indian 'tents' of poles and brush.

My father [he continues], who had naturally a mechanical turn, amused himself of an evening in making spinning wheels, a loom, and a variety of useful things for farming purposes. Time passed, and having grown some flax and obtained some sheep, my mother set to work to prepare the same for some cloathes in which we were greatly in need of. She had not any thread, so my father, which doubtless he learned from the Indians, stripped off the Bass Wood Bark, saturated it in water like Flax, and obtained a fine strong and useful thread. . . . We none of us had any shoes or stockings, winter or summer, as those we brought with us were soon worn out. At length my father tanned some leather, and I recollect the first pair of shoes he made which fell to my lot; I greased, and putting them too near the fire, on returning to my grief found that my shoes were all shrivelled up, so that I could not wear them. It was twelve months before I obtained another pair. . . . I was singularly unfortunate, for the first pair of trousers my mother made me from the proceeds of her flax were burnt by putting them too near the fire; all that remained of my old ones was similar to a pair of breeches, the leg part having been torn off, bit at a time, in going through the bush—so I was obliged to remain twelve months barelegged and barefooted through all the various changes of the weather.

Amelia (Ryerse) Harris of the Long Point country adds something to the solution of the clothing problem when she says that it was 'flax, the Pedlar's pack, and Buckskins' that

John Ross Robertson Collection   Mrs. J. G. Simcoe

KING'S HEAD INN, BURLINGTON BAY, 1796

the early settlers had to depend upon for clothing when their first supply was worn out. Deerskins were carefully preserved and dressed, and the men had trousers and coats made of them. Though not very becoming, they were said to be

very comfortable and strong and suitable to the work they had to do. . . . After the [flax] seed was in the Ground the culture was given up to the women. They had to weed, pull, & thrash out the seeds and then spread it out to rot. When it was in a proper state for the Brake it was handed over to the men who cracked & dressed it. It was again returned to the women, who spun and wove it, making a strong linen for Shirts and plaid for their own dresses. Almost every thrifty farm house had a Loom, and both wife and daughters learned to weave.

The Pedlar's pack supplied their little finery, the pack generally containing a few pieces of very indifferent Calicos at 8 and 10 shillings New York Currency a yard, and a piece of Book muslin at 16 & 18 shillings a yard, a piece of check for aprons at a corresponding price; some very common shawls and handkerchiefs, white cotton stockings to match, with two or three pieces of ribbon, with tape, needles and pins, and horn combs. This with very little variation used to be the contents of the Pedlar's packs. Opening the pack caused much more excitement in the family then than the opening of a fashionable shopkeeper's showroom does at the present day.

More characteristic of Loyalist days than later, because of the scarcity of grist mills, were the grain mortars or hominy blocks. They were usually hollowed-out hardwood stumps in which corn was ground by a pestle, attached perhaps to an overhanging branch as a sweep to lessen the work of the pounder; but Susan Greeley describes a variation:

Well, they were logs of hard wood, generally maple, three or four feet in length and about two feet in diameter, one end hollowed out mortar shape, the deeper the better consistently with the length and strength of the arms which were to use it, and made as smooth as possible, a pestle-shaped mallet fitting the cavity. It was very efficient to pulverize corn, but I do not think that wheat flour could be made with it.

For the 'precious white flour' there were long trips to the nearest mill. 'Several', says Susan Greeley, 'would join to get their grain ready, and then whoever could best afford the time would take it down [to Kingston], often hindered by rough weather.' Some Loyalists made a trip each summer down the St. Lawrence to Montreal to procure a year's supplies.

Doctors, lawyers, clergymen, and teachers were few and far between in Loyalist days, and it was many years before the services of these professional classes—however defective—were

From *Pioneer Days*   Creigh Collins

PLUMPING MILL OR HOMINY BLOCK

From *Pioneer Days*   Creigh Collins

THRESHING WITH A FLAIL AND WINNOWING GRAIN

readily available. 'We may say', recalled Thomas Anderson, son of a Loyalist, 'that the first generation born in Upper Canada were without book learning, but they labored like slaves to render their children more fortunate.' Dentistry was strictly an amateur occupation at the time, and there were many more quacks than doctors.

In addition to the medicine chest [recalled Amelia Harris] my Father purchased a pair of Tooth Drawers and learned to draw teeth to the great relief of sufferers. So popular did he become in that way that in after years they used to entreat him to draw their teeth in preference to a medical man—the one did it gratuitously, the other, of course, charged.

Only magistrates and the few clergymen of the Church of England could legally perform marriages, so it resulted that most couples were united by magistrates. 'I think David Secord performed more ceremonials and united more happy young people than anyone else', said James Dittrick; and he recalled that 'dress was the last thing thought of', and that 'the women all wore their linsey-woolsey, and the men and lads homespun cloathes, far more suitable to the rude log house and rough country than those of a finer material'. But as Dittrick, in his 75th year, added that he had for years spent his life in retirement and had no wish 'to mix much with the world', we may assume that the Loyalist women were a bit more worldly than he had grown to be, and that they gloried in some fine feathers on special occasions.

Historically the Loyalists, and American settlers in general, formed a highly important element of the province's population. They were experienced settlers, and in general a tough breed whose mere presence was an encouragement to those who came after. If they had furnished among their descendants no other leader than Egerton Ryerson no one could disparage their contribution to Ontario; but they were as well among the first fighters against despotism, the earliest champions of representative government, and the most uncompromising proponents of equal rights to religious freedom and the liberties of the subject.

CHAPTER III

EMIGRATION ACROSS THE ATLANTIC

THE causes of the emigration of millions of people from the British Isles to America in the 19th century were many and varied. Extreme poverty in Ireland, the passing of the clan system in Scotland, the discharge of officers and men after the Napoleonic Wars, and unemployment resulting from great changes in agriculture and industry in the whole Kingdom forced the greatest mass emigration in the world's history.

The experiences of emigrants as they crossed the Atlantic in the days of the sailing-ship were never-to-be-forgotten. In the early period it was usual for the traveller to go down to the nearest ocean port and investigate until he found a ship sailing for Quebec or New York; but in the eighteen-forties and -fifties, when emigration became a grand rush for the New Land, there were larger emigrant ships which were packed to overflowing with men, women, and children, many of them ill and destitute.

Many emigrants tramped from their homes to the seaport, perhaps hiring a wagon to carry their small possessions. Arriving with their bundles they had often to put up at an inn for a week or more before arrangements could be made for a passage. At the great ports, like Liverpool, there were numerous ships leaving more or less on schedule, but in the others it was usually a matter of making a bargain with a captain. People of wealth could travel cabin class and avoid most of the hardships.

Many were fooled and cheated at the seaports. Assuming that innkeepers, storekeepers, and ships' agents were honest like themselves, they were frequently disillusioned. Their small fund of cash might be stolen, or sadly depleted in the purchase of useless utensils or bad supplies that they were told were necessary for the voyage. Some were even sold tickets on boats that did not exist, and had to return to their old home to save anew for the great adventure; but most were soon aboard ship.

29

ENGLISH EMIGRANTS ON THE WAY TO THE SEAPORT

THE PRIEST'S BLESSING

LOADING BAGGAGE ABOARD, LIVERPOOL

For many years there was no medical examination whatever. The only one, in fact, that any of them had was not even of use in keeping cripples from boarding the ships, for the procedure consisted of passing before an official who, without looking up and in one breath, shouted 'What's your name? Stick out your tongue! Are you well? All right!'

When Robert Louis Stevenson crossed the Atlantic to America he was disillusioned as to the type of people who were with him on the voyage. He had expected that he would be participating in a hopeful and adventurous sally to the New Land, but he quickly found with respect to emigration that 'nothing is more agreeable to picture or more pathetic to behold'. He had expected that the typical emigrant would be some bold, eager, hawk-nosed type of humanity, but his companions on the voyage were very different:

Now those around me [he wrote] were for the most part quiet, orderly, obedient citizens, family men broken by adversity, elderly youths who had failed to place themselves in life, and people who had seen better days. Mildness was the prevailing character; mild mirth and mild endurance. In a word I was not taking part in an

Illustrated London News

THE STEERAGE

Spirits were usually highest at the start of the voyage.

31

impetuous and conquering sally, such as swept over Mexico or Siberia, but found myself, like Marmion, 'In the lost battle, borne down by the flying'.

The steerage passage, which alone the vast majority could afford, proved a most miserable experience in sailing-ship days, and many never recovered from the hardships of the voyage. On some ships hundreds of wooden bunks in long rows, two or even three tiers high, provided the emigrants' accommodations, and people were packed in five and six together—men, women, and children. In the aisles between the rows they often had to eat, exercise, and store their goods, and it can readily be imagined how dirty and crowded they were; for the water supply was doled out in pitifully small quantities, and there was never enough for adequate washing. Some captains refused to allow the steerage passengers to come on deck during the entire voyage, which might be twenty days or three months, and even in ordinary non-epidemic years fever and cholera frequently caused the death of large numbers, especially children.

We had the misfortune [wrote John and Harriet Veness upon arrival in Canada] to lose both our little boys. Edward died 29th April and William 5th May. The younger died with bowel complaint, the other with rash fever and sore throat. We were very much hurt to have them buried in a watery grave. We mourned their loss—night and day they were not out of our minds. We had a minister on board who prayed with us twice a day. He was a great comfort to us on account of losing our poor little children. There were six children and one woman died in the vessel.*

Most of any ship's passengers, as one emigrant put it, had,

like ourselves, all their earthly belongings to see to; not merely light portmanteaus and compact bags of the tourists but with beds and bedding, huge chests, and even pianos and farming implements, all jumbled together, to say nothing of Durham calves, Dorking fowls, hedgehogs, ferrets, Leicester sheep, and even full grown bulls and cows . . . a combination of a Pickford & Co.'s warehouse, a small menagerie, and a farm-yard.

In sail-and-steam ships of later days much of this conglomeration was in the hold below the steerage, but in sailing-ships there was often deliberate overcrowding to increase profits.

*See the author's *The Great Migration,* where the emigrants' experiences are described in detail from hundreds of diaries, letters, emigrant guidebooks, newspapers, and other contemporary sources. Two diaries not referred to in *The Great Migration* are printed in a short Supplement published in 1962: (1) the cabin passage of John Howard, 1832; and (2) the steerage passage of John Roberts, 1847.

EMIGRANTS ON THE SAILING-SHIP *CAMBRIDGE*

The artist, T. H. Ware, was an English lawyer who emigrated to Upper Canada to see what it was like. The crudities of backwoods life near Lake Simcoe impressed him unfavourably and he returned home, but not before he had enriched our records immeasurably by his sketches and paintings.

SAILORS ON THE *CAMBRIDGE*, 1844

T. H. Ware's sketches of sailors and emigrants, preserved in the Toronto Public Library, appear to be unique.

If the ship provided food, as some did, it was generally small in quantity and low in quality. The entire lack of fruit and vegetables made the diet unbalanced, and the bad results were aggravated by lack of exercise and proper sanitation, foul air and overcrowding. The water, too, was seldom even clean. It was customary to fill the ship's casks from the river in which she set sail, and if some was left over it was used on the next crossing. Frequently the supply was so dirty before the voyage was over that vinegar or quick-lime had to be put into it to kill the smell. One passenger reported in his diary that the supply given the emigrants on his ship was 'quite foul, muddy, and bitter, and resembled nauseous ditch water'.

The better ships had two grates on deck, fore and aft, but no fires were allowed for cooking in windy or stormy weather; and where so many wanted to use such limited facilities many a quarrel took place over their use. Some guidebooks advocated taking a supply of brandy along to bribe cooks or other officers. Many emigrants subsisted on oat bread or oat cake which had been baked hard for the voyage, or perhaps they had—as some Scots did—sixty pounds of oatmeal, one pound for each day of the voyage. The poorest Irish were known to come aboard with a few herrings and a bag of potatoes*—which usually rotted long before they were half way across; these destitute people were even known to mortgage their lives, agreeing to work for years for sea-captains as payment for their passage.

The worst ships almost beggar description. It is said that emigrant vessels could sometimes be identified by their smell even half a mile to windward. In the 'ship fever' year, 1847-48, more than a hundred died at sea on some Irish emigrant ships. Rats so overran the hold and emigrant quarters that on one ship 400 were caught in an organized hunt, without any perceptible diminution in their ravages; but at least one captain allayed fears that they might sink the ship by gnawing through the outer boards— 'They have too much intelligence for that', said he!

*The Irishman and his beloved 'praties' have been the subject of many a joke, but when there was a crop failure, or for other reasons a scarcity of potatoes, hundreds of thousands of Irish emigrated to America. More food was there almost invariably to be had—even if it were not much more diversified than the addition to potatoes of fat pork fried for dinner and supper, and the same warmed up for breakfast. Joseph Abbott thought it 'very odd' that potatoes and salt would not do in America as it had in Ireland, and he asked an Irish labourer on his farm just why it was: ' "An' sure, and doesn't the *hate* of the climate require stronger food?" Well, but in the winter, I rejoined; "An' troth, and don't ve *thin* want something substantial to keep the *cauld* away from your heart?" ' (Abbott Diary, June 17, 1819.) The complete diary is reprinted in Volume II, Appendix A.

DENNIS O'BRIEN   'YANKEE CAPTAIN'

Sketches by T. H. Ware on the sailing-ship *Cambridge*, 1844.

Storms often created untold misery in the steerage, and at the end of the voyage even the strongest passengers were sometimes more dead than alive. Shipwreck off Newfoundland or Nova Scotia was not infrequent. There were, however, many well-regulated vessels and considerate crews, and where good conditions and fair weather prevailed the voyage provided much of interest to landsmen. Natural phenomena, quaint sailors' customs, and resourceful passengers who organized games and amusements might render the voyage pleasant. It was usual, too, to anchor a day or so off Newfoundland, where fine fish could be caught with the crudest of equipment. Below Quebec was the quarantine station at Grosse Isle where there was some pretence, at least, of inspection before admittance to the country. As the sick were taken off and the others proceeded to Quebec, it occasionally happened that parents and children were separated, and in some instances they never saw one another again.

EMIGRANT SHEDS, QUEBEC, 1873

WOMEN'S BEDROOM, EMIGRANT SHEDS, QUEBEC, 1873
The woodcuts are from the *Canadian Illustrated News.*

A great many, of course, were fortunate in securing passage on ships of the better class, and reached America after four or five weeks' sailing; and when steamships become common the emigrants' sufferings were shortened to twelve or fourteen days.* No doubt 'Bridget Lacy', whose 'master', the Reverend

---

*As soon as steam-and-sail packets were introduced those who could afford them found conditions very different. Regular meals were served in both saloon and steerage, steerage passengers were invited to religious services in the saloon, and a clean and speedy voyage was usual. (See the Mickle family book manuscript, Toronto Public Library, for an Atlantic passage of this type in 1852.)

Illustrated London News

DEPARTURE FROM WATERLOO DOCKS, LIVERPOOL, 1850
'The spectators on shore took off their hats and cheered lustily, and the
emigrants raised a shout that must have been heard in Liverpool.'

James Magrath, had taught her reading and writing, was exceptional among pioneer servants—even fictitious ones—but her
racy account of her ocean voyage was probably paralleled by
many less literate but equally loquacious:

If you were only to have seen how smooth we floated down the
River, and out of the Bay, and away to Wicklow, where I was born
at the back of the murrough near Tinnakilly, you would have said,
Away you go eating and drinking, and laughing, and cracking jokes;
but, my jewel, before the second day was over we were all knocked
of a heap; and then if you were to hear all around you as I did,
groaning, and raching, and willy wombling, and calling for water,
and nobody to bring them a sup, and wishing themselves at the
bottom of the sea; in troth, Mary, you would have pitied a dog in
the same taking.

The hold was full of people, mighty snug and decent, with money
in their pockets, going out to make their fortunes; and most of them
Protestants that found home growing too hot for them; and that
they had better save their four bones and their little earnings before
it was too late, and sure enough I believe they're right. There are
mighty good people among them, and mighty pretty girls, that when
they arn't sick sing psalms in the evening, very beautiful; and there's
one Jenny Ferguson, from the north, that I am very thick with, and
she has a voice like an angel. In troth there are none of them
bad, and it's mighty sweet upon the sea.

Well, my dear, when the singing is over they're all very merry; and there are some gay lads, and great fun, and a little courting, but all in a civil way; and I sometimes make one, and between you and I, Mary, but don't say a word at all at all, I think there's a servant-boy of a Mr. Jackson's, one Benson, that's throwing a sheep's eye at me—but nothing *certain,* barring a sly pinch here and there, and other tinder tokens that may end in smoak after all.

There must, indeed, have been many instances of highly satisfactory voyages like that described by a Waterloo veteran, Captain George Arundel Hill, who sailed in 1831 in the cabin of the brig *Agness* from Limerick, in charge of Captain D. Gorman.

There were [he wrote in that rarest* of guidebooks, *A Guide for Emigrants from the British Shores to the Woods of Canada* (Dublin, 1834)] rather more than 200 souls on board, all of whom arrived in Quebec except an 'old woman of eighty' and an infant. Previous to landing, the passengers drew up an address highly complimentary to their Captain; and though, for aught I know, such a proceeding may be usual on occasions of the kind, it was in this instance well and truly merited. I believe Captain G. to be a good seaman, and am confident of his being a good and kind-hearted man: one who will not only feel a warm interest in the safety and comfort of every person on board his ship, but who will take the best and surest means to secure both. I shall only add that if I knew of any of my friends in Ireland who were coming over to Canada I would say to them, 'Endeavour to secure a passage with Dan Gorman'.

---

*Widespread search in the great libraries of Britain, Ireland, the United States, and Canada yielded no copy, nor even a listing of this 56-page booklet, but F. G. Ketcheson of Richmond Hill, authority on Canadiana, had in 1952 one in his outstanding collection, now widely scattered. The author borrowed it for photostating, and copies are now in the Public Archives, Ottawa, and the Toronto Public Library.

CHAPTER IV

ASCENDING THE ST. LAWRENCE

THE immigrant was well-advised not to loiter in Quebec or Montreal, but to push westward at once. 'The Journey up from Quebec', recalled Archibald McKinnon of Markham Township, 'had to be performed with Durham boats drawn by oxen and guided by pilots who walked on the tow-path along the shore and with pike-poles kept the boats at a certain distance from shore.' This was a usual means of ascending the St. Lawrence before the days of canals and steamships, and as it was cheaper it continued long after the introduction of stagecoach and steamboat.

Bateaux were heavy flat-bottomed rowboats, thirty or forty feet long and six to eight in width, much smaller than the Durham boat. The means of navigation varied with the conditions. In quiet water they were rowed, with poles and sails used at times, and in swift water they had to be hauled over portage roads or dragged by men or oxen walking along the shore. Durham boats were large half-decked barges, sometimes 100 feet long and capable of carrying 350 barrels of merchandise as well as numerous travellers. Setting-poles and sails were used to propel them. Three or four men on either side placed their long iron-shod poles in the shallow water and walked the length of the boat as they laboriously pushed it along against the current. Six or eight oxen hauled them up the chief rapids.

Our travelling this way is very tiresome [wrote one immigrant] and took us eight days to get to Prescot. The first night we reached a village and after begging hard we prevailed with them to let us lay on their floor. . . . The others made a large fire and sat or slept by it. . . . In the night I was taken ill with spasms, and a fever followed. We at last came to Prescot, *sleeping on the ground every night but two*. . . . When we came to Prescot we were all very wet with rain and went to a tavern, hoping to dry ourselves; but we were so many,

Public Archives of Canada   Lieut. Philip Bainbrigge

QUEBEC FROM POINT LEVI, 1836

The Dominion Illustrated

MEMORIAL, POINT ST. CHARLES, MONTREAL

Erected by workmen on the Victoria Bridge, 1858, in memory of 6000
immigrants who died of ship fever, 1847-8, and were buried near by.

standing in their way, they did not want us there, so we was forced to remain as we was.*

Sometimes a steamship could be hired to tow a group of bateaux in the more open stretches. A well-to-do traveller, Patrick Shirreff, sympathetically describes the sad plight of the immigrants:

At Coteau-du-Lac our steamer took seven bateaux in tow, in one of which I counted 110 immigrants of all ages, who were doomed to pass the night on board. Men, women, and children were huddled together as close as captives in a slave-trader, exposed to the sun's rays by day and river-damp by night, without protection. It was impossible to look upon such a group of human beings without emotion. The day had been so intensely hot that the stoutest amongst them looked fatigued, while the females seemed ready to expire with exhaustion. Conversation was carried on in whispers, and a heaviness of heart seemed to pervade the whole assemblage. Never shall I forget the countenance of a young mother, ever anxiously looking at twin infants slumbering on her knee and covering them from the vapour rising from the river, and which strongly depicted the feelings of maternal affection and pious resignation. Night soon veiled the picture, and, I fear, brought no relief to the anxious mother.

At Prescott, west of which there are no rapids, most travellers took a steamship for Kingston, Cobourg, or York. Crowded in without decent accommodations, perhaps standing on the deck all night, the immigrants suffered almost as severely as in earlier stages of their epic journey; but it was not for long, for they usually reached their destination the following morning.

At York (Toronto) they were dumped off, and it was a common sight in summer to see hundreds of immigrants clustered about on the old rotting wooden wharves.** But the sick and destitute were perhaps aided by the Stranger's Friend Society, and in 1830 an Emigrants' Asylum sheltered the most unfortunate. Many thousands, especially in the great cholera and 'ship-fever' (typhus) years—1832 and 1847—died on the threshold of the Promised Land. At worst the conditions were unspeakable. An investigator wrote:

I have seen small, incommodious, and ill-ventilated steamers arriving at the quay in Toronto after a 48-hours' passage from Montreal,

*Many other accounts of experiences are given in the author's books *Early Life in Upper Canada* and *The Great Migration.*

**Many thousands of immigrants came to Upper Canada without funds, and could hardly have moved westward from Quebec if the Canadian Government had not paid experienced settlers to arrange transportation and effect their settlement or their employment on roads and other public works. The best general history of immigration is Helen I. Cowan's *British Emigration to British North America* (Revised Edition, 1961).

Willis, *Canadian Scenery*   W. H. Bartlett

MAITLAND'S WHARF, TORONTO, 1840

freighted with fetid cargoes of 1100 or 1200 'Government emi-grants' of all ages and sexes, the healthy who had just arrived from Europe mixed with the half-recovered convalescents of the hospital, unable during that time to lie down—almost to sit. In almost every boat were clearly marked cases of actual fever, in some were deaths, the dead and the living huddled together. Sometimes the crowds were stowed in open barges and towed after the steamer, standing like pigs upon the deck of a Cork or Bristol packet. A poor woman died in hospital here in consequence of having been trodden down when weak and fainting in one of those barges. I have, myself, when accompanying the emigration agent on his visit of duty to inspect the steamer on her arrival, seen him stagger back like one struck, when first meeting the current of fetid infection exhaled from be-tween her decks.*

Settlers for York and neighbouring counties were fairly close to their destination, but many others had still arduous experi-ences to face before seeing their land. Perhaps the lively letter of John Climie, Dalhousie Township, dated February 8, 1821, gives the most representative experience, and at the same time

*This highly public-spirited man was Stephen E. De Vere, who travelled in the steerage of an overcrowded ship to see conditions at first hand. See *Evidence before the Select Committee of the House of Lords on Colonization from Ireland, 1847*, pp. 45-8. He deserves to be included among the great philanthropists of history.

Public Archives of Canada

James Gray

BROCKVILLE FROM UMBRELLA ISLAND, 1828
A Durham boat may be seen in the foreground.

Willis, *Canadian Scenery*   W. H. Bartlett

APPROACHING MONTREAL, 1840

Willis, *Canadian Scenery*   W. H. Bartlett

TIMBER RAFTS, JUNCTION OTTAWA AND ST. LAWRENCE RIVERS, 1840

BATEAU RUNNING LACHINE RAPIDS, 1843

At the bow may be seen a black bear, mascot of the 83rd Regiment.

IN THE THOUSAND ISLANDS

Public Archives of Canada Artist unknown

'KINGSTOWN, JUNE 15, 1844'

tells the folks back home what they may expect—from the decision to emigrate until they have become established and are on the way to independence:

Indeed, there are a good deal of hardships to overcome before obtaining the prize; such as selling our articles for half-nothing—leaving our country and friends we held so dear—crossing the Atlantic—meeting with gales of wind—sometimes sea-sick—too much choked up in our berths—sometimes loathing our food, though good and wholesome—wearying for a sight of land, but, with bad navigators and contrary winds, going faster back than forward—and, to crown all, associating with profane swearers and Sabbath-breakers. Then landing in a strange country, and if you are not on your guard you will be taken in in making merchandise—jogging in waggons—going up the river in small boats—landing at night at the side of a wood—kindling a fire—cooking our victuals—making our beds—every one running faster than another to find the low-most spot—then hurried up by the break of day by the conductor crying 'Get into the boats!' Scarcely giving us as much time as to collect our children and bed-clothes (for there is no casting off body-clothes on these occasions) together, till the boats are off—then plying and rowing with oars till coming to the strict running of the rivers, which they call rapids, on which poles and oars have no effect—then the male passengers with all the sailors but one who is left to guide the boat through whilst we are pulling with ropes, till we get it through the stream, which is sore work: indeed, you must understand that the boats sail by the sides of the river, so as that we are on land while pulling the same.

Then after water-passage the land-carriage, which is about 60 miles, which they accomplish in about two days with four-wheeled carriages with two horses, load ten cwt. The road is very rough, and they go with such fury that sometimes, going down a hill, all is upset; however, the driver is forthcoming for any damage. The families are left in a village while the husbands are sent away to view their land, at a distance of 15 or 30 miles farther up the country; and the most of the road no other thing to guide us than a spole off the side of the trees, and, if not properly attended to, are sure to wander. . . . Robert F——was about five days lost in the bush, and your cousin Peacock was two days and lost his watch while wandering among the trees. Lying in a wigwam, and nothing but a blanket about you, and perhaps not a change of clothes for two or three weeks, and all this time absent from your wife and children until our houses are up; and carrying provisions on your back for about three months; and worst of all separated from religious society.

You will be saying after reading this catalogue, 'Oh! America is not for us!' but hooly, hooly, stop a wee, I am not done yet. Do you know that I have got up my house, which is 16 feet by 20, and two stooped beds of my own making, and a case for my library, and a shelf for the dishes. . . . We have got about two acres of our land chopped, and we hope to get twice as much by seed-time; and you know that the house, and rent, and fire are free, along with a well-furnished house, and plenty of provisions in it, without the fear of a grocery balance coming on, or a laird to say, 'It is Martinmas!'*
. . . And to tell you more of our comforts, we in this Concession have formed ourselves into a religious society, and two of our number are appointed to lead the worship; and we intend to meet in our several houses till we get a house built for the purpose.

The unwary immigrant was imposed upon not only in the great seaports. A favourite trick of sharpers was to claim to represent forwarding companies and so obtain travellers' baggage. The best-dressed might prove the most dangerous, for among people to be seen about the streets of Toronto, says the *Journal of a Wanderer* (1844), were numerous

half-pay officers with their noses in scarlet uniform, . . . strutting about the town and lounging about the hotels. They are chiefly from Ireland, and talk about their *cousin Lord this* and their *uncle Lord that*. There are another class *called* gentlemen who also frequent the hotels and the coffee-houses for their victims. This class prey upon the poor emigrants on their arrival. They are up to all sorts of tricks to defraud the new-comer out of his dollars; and so sure as a settler has any transactions with them, so sure is he taken in—something is certain to be wrong. All emigrants ought to avoid them.

*St. Martin's Day, November 11th, when rents were usually collected in Britain.

CHAPTER V

THE PIONEER HOME

Our occupation was to make
*   The lofty forest bow;*
With axes good we chopped the wood,
*   For well we all knew how;*
We cleared the land for rye and wheat
*   For strangers and ourselves to eat,*
And from maple trees we gathered sweet
*   In the New Country.*

Our roads were winding through the woods
*   Where oft the savage trod;*
They were not wide, nor scarce a guide,
*   But all the ones we had.*
Our houses, too, were logs of wood,
*   Rolled up in squares and caulked with mud;*
If the bark was tight the roof was good
*   For a New Country.*

—'One of the earliest settlers in Darlington Township'.

A settler's first home—usually a log, slab, or board shanty—was commonly erected with the aid of people earlier settled in the district. In conducted and assisted emigrations it was sometimes ready to receive him when he arrived, but more usually a raising bee was the method of getting the work done cheaply and quickly, at a total cost of a few dollars for materials other than those supplied by the forest. Sometimes two or three acres, and often much less, was cleared first to enable immediate planting of seed, while the settler's family lived with friends or neighbours.

As the years passed, the shanty was usually superseded by the log house, and it in turn by frame, roughcast, brick, or stone, whichever was most readily available. These stages were often visible on one farm, the earlier structures being left for use as barns, sheds, or pig-sties as the owner's prosperity made pos-

48

The Pioneer Home

Eighty Years' Progress in British North America

BEGINNING A HOME

Nationality played a prominent part in shaping the settler's first home. In rural Ireland in the eighteen-forties nearly half the population lived in windowless mud cabins of one room, and some Irish immigrants tried to adapt the same type to Upper Canada in spite of the great difference in climate.

sible their replacement; and in after years many a pioneer had a sentimental attachment for these evidences of his success.

There was, indeed, a temporary shelter cruder than the log hut—cruder even than the Indian's wigwam of poles. A manuscript, 'Advice to Settlers in Canada', by an anonymous inhabitant who appears to have lived north of the upper St. Lawrence, includes a crude sketch of a man lying in a hammock, with a fire burning almost under him. Beneath is the following description:

Temporary hut made of branches with a standing tree at each angle, the roof poles to be bound to the cross rails with wythe rods, birch bark strands, or strong twine previously provided for the purpose —the lower ends of the roof poles having a fork to rest on and bound at the top will answer very well—the roof is finished by spreading broad pieces of bark on it, which may be cut with the ax from the hemlock, spruce, or birch trees, whichever grows nearest —each piece as large as a calf's shin if possible.*

*The late J. G. Ketcheson of Richmond Hill had this manuscript booklet in his fine collection of Canadiana.

49

The log shanty* was a rude structure about 10 feet by 8, raised to a height of 6 feet at the front and sloping to 4 feet at the rear. Bark or rough boards and slabs usually formed the roof, but the split basswood troughs common on log houses were sometimes found. Adam Scott, first settler on the site of Peterborough, used black-ash bark as roofing for the shanty he erected there in the spring of 1820. Since the roofing material was almost invariably green and unseasoned, the concave-convex troughs might be more satisfactory than other varieties after the warping and cracking that always followed as sun and

Toronto Public Library   T. H. Ware

TWO SHANTIES ON THE COLDWATER ROAD, 1844

water exerted their force. Occasionally a shallow cellar was dug under a part of the shanty, and proved useful for storage.

Sometimes shanties had no windows, and in place of a door they were frequently merely open on one side, where a fire was kept going; and settlers are known to have spent the winter under such primitive conditions. The fittings were as crude as the building. For sleeping there was the floor itself or rude bunks on the walls, with hemlock boughs for mattresses; and a few pegs were put in the wall upon which to hang the settler's few possessions. The surroundings were no better, at least to the eye of the average traveller:

*The settler's shanty is not to be confused with that of the lumbermen, which A. C. Buchanan describes as 'a temporary hut and grog-shop in the Forest, made of logs or the branches of trees formed like a tent covered with bark or grass, and is the headquarters of a gang of Lumberers, perhaps from twenty to thirty, and their only bed is a bear-skin and a pair of blankets; their food is salt pork, peas, and flour, and a liberal quantity of rum. The principal or head of these lumbering parties is a sort of itinerant Yankee.'

There is not much of the picturesque [wrote Dr. John Bigsby as he passed through Upper Canada] near the usual home of the working emigrant. A clearance in the woods is very offensive to the eye, being a dismal scene of uncouth log-huts, blackened stumps, leafless scorched trees, and awkward zig-zag fences.*

The home of one of the more enterprising of the Irish settlers brought by the Honourable Peter Robinson to Peterborough County in 1825 was visited two years later by Captain Basil Hall. The family included some ten children and lived in a log hut twenty by twelve feet and seven feet in height. Two great chests, four feet long and nearly a yard high, formed a large part of the furnishings of the house. In these the family had brought such crockery and other possessions which it had been possible to carry from Ireland. As to the sleeping arrangements Captain Hall observed that

on the side of the room, fronting the door, three beds were placed in a line, touching one another and occupying the whole length of the establishment. But I did not push my inquiries any further as to the principles of stowage at night by which a dozen souls were lodged in three such cribs.

John Langton, who eventually rose in the scale of human activity to become Auditor-General of Canada, describes the shanty on Sturgeon Lake in which he spent the first six weeks as having a piece of canvas for a door and a hole in the roof to serve as a chimney. The spaces between the logs obviated the construction of windows. So numerous, in fact, were these openings that 'when you were outside at night and the fire was bright, the shanty bore a striking similitude to a tin lantern'. The furnishings were just as crude: 'My bed consisted of two buffalo skins, one above and the other below; and empty barrels, chests, etc., served the purposes of chairs and tables.' But the log house he shortly moved into was comparatively luxurious:

A table [he wrote] had been manufactured out of a door and two empty barrels, a table cloth was airing by the fire, silver forks, mustard, and such-like almost forgotten luxuries were ready to grace it, and last—not least—we were almost longing for bedtime to luxuriate once more in the novelty of a pair of sheets.

Where boards were readily available the frame shanty replaced the log, and in the later period tar-paper was frequently

---

*Dr. Bigsby, from whose book *The Shoe and Canoe, or Pictures of Travel in the Canadas* (1850) this description is quoted, was an eminent geologist and a commissioner representing Canada in the settlement of boundary disputes with the United States.

used as a covering. James Simpson, from near Penicuik, Scotland, arrived in Downie Township in May 1834. 'And when he came, while his family were living in a temporary shed or shanty of boards on his lot', we are told, 'he set about the planting of potatoes, of which he had a good crop, sufficient nearly for the use of the family during the winter.'

The 'common' log house might be but little larger than the shanty, and with but one room. It was usually almost square, with the sides averaging 22 by 18 feet.* The 'improved' type was of squared logs, about 20 feet by 18, with a height of 10 or 12 feet, the roof sloping both ways from the peak. Sometimes elaborate two-storey log houses with numerous rooms were built by those who had romantic notions of their warmth and comfort and the money to gratify their whims, but in general they were not the best long-term dwellings. A woman who had lived in both log and brick houses found that the logs 'would settle and thus draw all the casings, doors, and floors apart, and thus render them very uncomfortable'. Many, on the other hand, found log houses quite satisfactory, though it was usually considered a sign of prosperity—or in our jargon a 'status symbol'—to replace them as soon as circumstances permitted.

Considerable finesse was sometimes used in the building of the log house, and of barns as well. 'Ex-Settler', the author of *Canada in the Years 1832, -33, and -34*, advised that care be taken in selecting both the timber and the right time to cut it:

You must choose [he wrote] the proper time for cutting building logs, which is when there is least sap in them, for they then last longest; people say this takes place in the depth of winter—I would be inclined to think it is in August.

He recommended cedar as the lightest and most durable wood, having observed that heavier logs settle so much that they are quickly out of square. Experienced settlers sought to avoid this settling by leaving the building a year unoccupied, and then

---

*This average is computed from statistics of eighteen houses erected in 1816-1817 in the Westminster New Settlement, London District, as recorded by Robert Gourlay. The houses ranged in size from 18 by 16 to the largest, which were 30 by 14 and 28 by 20. At that time the fees per 200-acre farm had recently been increased to a peculiar combination of two currencies given as '41 dollars and 1s.'. There were, of course, great variations in log construction, as well as many technical details which cannot be described here. John I. Rempel has written extensively about them and taken many photographs to illustrate his material. The Archives of Ontario has copies of his photographs. For his description see 'The History and Development of Early Forms of Building Construction in Ontario', *Ontario History*, Volume LII, No. 4, and Volume LIII, No. 1.

Hall, *Forty Etchings . . .* (1829)   Capt. Basil Hall

EARLY LOG BUILDINGS, PETERBOROUGH
As recorded by the Camera Lucida in the late 1820's.

cutting out doors and windows. The foundation logs, too, should never be placed on the ground, where they will speedily rot, but upon sills or small walls of stone.

Oak, cedar, and pine logs were most commonly used, and the settler and his family or hired men sometimes had the site cleared and the logs ready before calling a bee to erect the house. Then a few gallons of whiskey might be almost the sole cost of raising the framework and setting the rafters in place. It was usual for the roof to be put on later, and there were various finishing touches to be added by the settler himself. If the logs had not been mortised or fitted at their joints, any openings were filled with a mixture of chips, lime, mud, moss, and sand, and the same 'chink-and-plaster' filler was rammed in between the logs with the help of a wooden trowel.

As most early houses were made of unsquared logs this *chinking* or *stubbing* had to be done before winter set in; but many of the later square-log structures were closely fitted during the raising, though cracks would still appear as the wood dried. Logs nearly two feet in diameter when squared were sometimes used for the improved log house. In Brant County, Muskoka, and occasionally elsewhere, the double log house was sometimes built for large families. Two cabins under the same roof, with a 12-foot space between them as a shed or storage room, provided double the amount of living space.

Doors and windows were commonly cut out by hand-saw, or

even with an axe; in fact it was perhaps the trouble of doing this that made it almost characteristic to do without windows. 'One would imagine', one writer puts it, 'judging by their log houses, that there was a heavy window-tax in Canada, or else that people deny themselves glass in their houses in order to put it all in their churches.' American glass of a brittle type was earliest used, and where glass was not available oiled paper or old clothes were substituted. A packing case often provided the wood for window-frames, and door hinges and locks, if any, were at first of wood or leather, and hand-made. Even 'aristocratic' settlers did much of their own carpentry work, and found that, as one said, 'We are neither degraded in our own estimation nor in that of the most elevated of our acquaintances by thus earning the bread of independence'.* A handy settler could effect numerous improvements and refinements in his log house.

The floors were often merely of packed mud, but strips of bark were sometimes laid on top until something better could be obtained. Roughly hewn logs, or half-logs smoothed off with axe or adze, were satisfactory until they dried out, whereupon the floor had to be relaid or a great deal of roughness tolerated. Sawn lumber, at first laboriously prepared by hand-saw or whip-saw, was a subsequent improvement, and people of wealth often painted or carpeted the floor. Those who had the time and means sometimes panelled the walls with cherry, butternut, or walnut.

The roof of the log house was sometimes of rough boards or slabs, but, as occasionally in the shanty, a concave-convex alternation of split basswood logs called *scoops* provided a more satisfactory covering, the concave troughs carrying off the rainfall. A writer of the time admired

the neatness and dispatch with which they were manufactured with no other implement but a common axe. A straight clean-looking basswood tree was selected and felled, the part free from knots and branches was cut into logs of such length as would, when laid upon the shanty, project beyond the front and back walls sufficiently to form an eave. These logs were then, with the aid of iron wedges, split as nearly through the middle as possible; and upon the flat side thus produced the axeman immediately commenced operations. The heart of the log is in a very short space almost entirely hollowed out, leaving only a comparatively thin shell of wood inside the bark. . . . The largest and heaviest were first selected and laid on the top

*The writer of a diary in 1852 recorded that he found on farms near Guelph 'two or three relatives of Lord Berners', and saw an English admiral's son ploughing his own fields. (Mickle family Book, Toronto Public Library.)

Courtesy Phyllis Denne

SGT.-MAJOR WILLIAM McCRACKEN'S HOUSE, STONEY LAKE
Erected 1832 at McCracken's Landing.

Conservation Authorities, Ontario

BRICK FARMHOUSE OF 1851 NEAR ORANGEVILLE

Conservation Authorities, Ontario

ROBB HOUSE, NEAR ARMADALE, BUILT 1853

of the building with the bark downwards almost touching each other, while the smaller and lighter ones were reversed and placed over the openings that intervened between each of the lower tiers.

Shingle roofs replaced the more primitive types as circumstances permitted, the shingles being split by hand-frow or axe from 3-foot blocks of cedar or pine; but for barns still longer shingles were frequently used.

Curtains or other makeshift means were more common than partitions in log houses—in fact there was seldom much effort to obtain privacy. The larger houses had partitions, however, and in early times when sawn planks were not available rough slabs were split by axe and wedge. Samuel Strickland saw some crudely cut from black ash, and made more exact planks from white pine with the aid of cross-cut saw and wedges. An American *slabber* could produce planks of varying thickness with surprising exactness.

In the most primitive houses there was an open fire on the earth, probably backed by a few large stones; and a hole in the roof served until a chimney could be made. Field stones were later used to build a better fireplace. A chimney of small laths or wicker, covered with clay both inside and out, surmounted the stone and formed a smoky and unsatisfactory outlet; because of its component parts it was sometimes called a 'stick-and-slab' chimney. Fires in the roof were so frequent that it was good policy, though not too often followed, to build ladders on the roof to enable a quick climb in an emergency. A picture of log buildings of the early garrison at York shows these ladders. One settler noticed that the chimneys collected soot so quickly that 'every two weeks, on the average' there would be an alarm of fire, and while some of the farm-hands would hasten to the roof others would obtain buckets of water and pass them upwards. Some settlers, who had experienced or observed the ravages of fire, put out their fire every night before going to bed, even in the severest winter weather.

Unforeseen difficulties often upset the best of plans. The Traills' supply of lime that was to plaster the chinks between the logs froze 'to stone' one cold night, with the work hardly half completed; and attempts to thaw it out by fire and hot water were rendered worse than useless when the water froze before it could take effect. A workman hewing the inside walls with a broad-axe injured himself badly, and though flooring-boards were eventually cut by a man who charged the high

Conservation Authorities, Ontario

DRESSED LOG HOUSE, GWILLIMBURY

wage of 6s. 6d. a day, they had to be relaid, jointed, and smoothed the following year when the green timber had become seasoned.

Interior arrangements of log houses were sometimes similar in most of the homes of one nationality. Along the Rideau Sir James Alexander found that the pioneer log house had usually 'a but and a ben', or an outer and an inner room. 'In the outer was the kitchen, parlour, and bedroom', he says in his *Transatlantic Sketches* (1833); 'in the inner was a loom or the tools and bench of a carpenter, with pork, flour, and salt barrels.'

Many settlers continued to live in cabins of unhewn logs longer than they might otherwise have done because of the tax on improvements. A house of this type with one fireplace went untaxed, but the square-log house, second storeys, and additional fireplaces did not escape the tax-collector. Many, consequently, considered themselves fined for making improvements, and were sufficiently penurious or obstinate to avoid taxes, however small,* even at the expense of continuing their

*E. S. Abdy, who travelled in Upper Canada in 1834, noted that the proprietor of a long-cleared farm near Niagara paid a tax of only $3 on his farm and six days' statute labour on the roads, which could be commuted at 50 cents a day. Fifteen years earlier the usual tax was a penny an acre on cleared land only.

crude living conditions. In 1834, somewhat more than half way through the pioneering period, one-fifth of the land was listed as cultivated, and there were the following taxable improvements in addition to 267 carriages and 1170 pleasure wagons:

> 3568 one-storey square-timber houses, with 122 additional fireplaces.
> 482 two-storey square-timber houses, with 169 additional fireplaces.
> 9968 framed, brick, or stone houses, with 3880 additional fireplaces.
> 2962 framed, brick, or stone houses, with 2686 additional fireplaces.

The log house, then, varied from a crude structure more like a stable—'dens of dirt and misery which would be shamed by an English pig-sty', as Susanna Moodie put it—to an improved square-log home which *could* be kept neat and comfortable, though Samuel Strickland considered log buildings 'the dirtiest, the most inconvenient, and the dearest'. The third of the Stricklands, Catharine Traill—always quick to see the best in her adopted country and to seize upon all possible means to render the crudities tolerable and even beautiful—advised newcomers that there were many ways to improve the log house:

Nothing contributes so much to comfort and to the outward appearance of a Canadian house as the erection of the verandah, or stoup as the Dutch settlers call it, round the building. It affords a grateful shade from the summer heat, a shelter from the cold, and is a source of cleanliness to the interior. It gives a pretty, rural look to the poorest log-house, and as it can be put up with little expense it should never be omitted. A few unbarked cedar posts, with a slab or shingled roof, costs very little. The floor should be of plank; but even with a hard dry earthen floor, swept every day with an Indian broom, it will still prove a great comfort. Those who build frame or stone or brick houses seldom neglect the addition of a verandah; to the common log-house it is equally desirable; nor need any one want for climbers with which to adorn the pillars.

Among the wild plants of Canada there are many graceful climbers which are to be found in almost every locality. Nature, as if to invite you to ornament your cottage-homes, has kindly provided so many varieties of shade-plants that you may choose at will. . . .

The commonest climber for a log-house is the hop, which is, as you will find, an indispensable plant in a Canadian garden, it being the principal ingredient in making the yeast with which the household bread is raised. Planted near the pillars of your verandah, it forms a graceful drapery of leaves and flowers, which are pleasing to look upon and valuable either for use or sale.

Catharine Traill, *Canadian Wild Flowers*   Agnes Fitzgibbon

SHOWY LADY'S SLIPPER ... WILD ORANGE LILY ... HAREBELL

The Fitzgibbon flower arrangements are typical of the 18th
and early 19th centuries.

The Canadian Ivy, or Virginian Creeper, is another charming
climber, which if planted near the walls of your house will quickly
cover the rough logs with its dark glossy leaves in summer, and in
the fall delight the eye with its gorgeous crimson tints.

The Wild Clematis or Traveller's Joy may be found growing in
the beaver meadows and other open thickets. This also is most ornamental as a shade-plant for a verandah. Then there is the climbing
Fumatory, better known by the name by which its seeds are sold by

the gardener, 'Cypress vine'. This elegant creeper is a native of
Canada, and may be seen in old neglected clearings near the water,
running up the stems of trees and flinging its graceful tendrils and
leaves of tender green over the old grey mossy branches of cedar
or pine, adorning the hoary boughs with garlands of the loveliest
pink flowers. I have seen this climbing Fumatory in great quantities
in the woods, but found it no easy matter to obtain the ripe seeds
unless purchased from a seedsman: it is much cultivated in towns
as a shade plant near the verandahs.

Besides those already described I may here mention the scarlet-
runner, a flower the humming-birds love to visit. The wild cucumber,
a very graceful trailing plant. The Major Convolvulus or Morning
Glory. The wild honeysuckle, sweet pea, and prairie-rose. These
last-named are not natives, with the exception of the wild or bush
honeysuckle which is to be found in the forest. The flowers are pale
red but scentless; nevertheless it is very well worth cultivating.

I am the more particular in pointing out to you how you may
improve the outside of your dwellings because the log-house is rough
and unsightly; and I know well that your comfort and cheerfulness
of mind will be increased by the care you are led to bestow upon
your new home in endeavouring to ornament it and render it more
agreeable to the eye. The cultivation of a few flowers, of vegetables
and fruit, will be a source of continual pleasure and interest to yourself and children, and you will soon learn to love your home and
cease to regret that dear one you have left.

The mud or mud-brick house is a type popular in parts of
Upper Canada prior to 1850, wherever the clay was heavy
enough for the purpose. York County was the location of most
of them, and they were usually of a simple and severe type due
to the nature of the material used. In 1843 the *British American
Cultivator* published two articles advocating houses of mud
bricks, and William Beason of Yorkville was mentioned as a
contractor who would build them for £1 per 100 bricks supplied and erected. For £22 he would construct the walls of a
house 38 feet by 28 and 14 feet high.

Among the largest mud houses is that of William Helliwell,*
two storeys high, erected in 1837 near Pottery Road and the
one time Circle of the Don, west of old Todmorden village.
Remaining until 1949 was the Van Nostrand mud house, York
Mills, an excellent example of early Ontario architecture. In
1838 St. Thomas' Anglican Church at Shanty Bay was built of
mud bricks. Its simple lines and magnificent setting in deep
woods, writes B. Napier Simpson, Jr., 'tends to enhance its

---

*He was for many years proprietor of a brewery. In 1896 he recalled his long
life in the Toronto region for John Ross Robertson, and his interesting
reminiscences are found in *Landmarks of Toronto,* Volume 2, pp. 1035-9.

Courtesy Caroline Brown   Charles Davy Brown

GALT IN 1857

Courtesy Caroline Brown   Charles Davy Brown

LOG HOUSE SITTING ROOM

Courtesy Caroline Brown   Charles Davy Brown

LOG HOUSE KITCHEN

Courtesy of the Artist   B. Napier Simpson, Jr.

J. C. VAN NOSTRAND MUD-BRICK HOUSE

architectural beauty and to make it one of the loveliest places of worship in the province'.*

The frame house, particularly popular among settlers of American origin, was frequently found in both towns and rural regions along 'the front', even in the first quarter of the nineteenth century. Thomas Fowler, whose travels made him especially familiar with the Lake Ontario townships in 1831, describes in his *Journal of a Tour through British America* the many refinements found in the homes:

A handsome frame building, such as is common among farmers, has a sunk flat for cellars, built with stones to the level of the ground, which contains the potatoes, fruit, and other provisions. The frame work commences immediately above ground. This floor generally contains two handsome parlours, a bedroom, and the staircase. The upper flat contains the dancing hall and one or two neat bed-rooms. Buildings of these dimensions are frequently forty feet long by thirty deep, and sometimes more. Almost every house of this description is carpeted with beautiful carpeting, which they get from the States or from Montreal; and the ordinary price for a pretty pattern is four shillings per yard. The rooms are handsomely furnished with chairs, tables, sofas, and mirrors; the walls are either painted or papered, while the flowing drapery of the windows reaches the carpet. As the sun is very strong here in summer they use thick window blinds, and also shutters made of splits, which

*See his pamphlet *Mud Houses in York County*. Napier Simpson has photographed several thousand early Ontario homes of distinction and is an authority on their architecture and construction.

open to the outside like folding-doors; but the windows are of the Scotch fashion through the Upper Province, and by drawing up the lower half they can open or fasten the shutters without leaving the room. The kitchen is generally attached in rear of the building, and besides the necessary accommodation for cooking, it contains the servants' apartments and an eating hall. There is also a brick oven in the kitchen, and they bake their loaf bread themselves, which is the kind daily used; also biscuit and tea bread when they want it. There are no double windows in Upper Canada, for, the winter being milder than in the lower provinces, these are not required. Stoves are also little used here except in churches and stores. Grates are sometimes used in rooms, but these are not very numerous.

In kitchens the fire-place is about four feet broad, and the blocks of wood are cut the length, while an iron bar in each side of the chimney, with feet about four inches high, supports the wood and lets in the air below to cause it burn, and the out end of each bar is about one foot high to keep the wood from rolling off. The ashes are clean swept up and put into a cask, which, with the refuse of the hog's lard, makes the family soap. All the kitchens I have seen in the country are floored with wood, as are also the shades, stables, and cow houses. A considerable number of the farm houses are pavilion roofed, with one tier of chimneys and generally covered with shingles, that is, wood cut very thin in the form of slates and put on in a similar manner. The interior of a frame house is finished with plaster or lath, but the outside is done with fine dressed boards and painted white or yellow. The window shutters are generally grass green and varnished, and the roof slate colour. Now these elegant mansions, with the verdant fields and the dark green woods, have a light and graceful appearance; and one of these fine frame buildings will cost from ten to fifteen hundred dollars.

Still among our most beautiful homes, the 'respectable' frame house painted white, with its verandah and green shutters was, says J. B. Brown, 'the family's ambition'. Sometimes ox-yokes and other pioneer implements were hung on the verandah to indicate how far the family had come from pioneer days,* and wild grape or other vines were often trained up the sides and posts.

The Magrath frame house on the Credit River may be taken

---

*Many a settler took great pride in his farm and home. A colourful example of one instance was verified by the writer by a visit to lot 24, concession 14, of Burleigh Township, just south of the village of Apsley. Here in 1862 came Robert Clifford. 'Believing,' says a biographical history of some 80 years ago, 'in the good old scripture adage that the house founded upon a rock would stand the storms of life, [he] determined to test the truth of the maxim.' Clifford chose the side of a hill rising 100 feet for his foundation, and built his log shanty and later a frame house just west of the old Burleigh Colonization Road. At a distance the site of the Clifford house resembled a snowbank, for the quartz was, we are told, 'white glittering surface . . . polished by the suns and storms of many a century' and 'admired by every traveller over the government road'.

THE ZACHEUS BURNHAM HOME, NEAR COBOURG
Built of 3-inch upright planks and then clapboarded.

as an example of an elaborate type of that construction. It was 44 feet by 33 and of three storeys, the lowest being a 12-foot basement of stone and lime. Its erection was efficiently arranged. First of all the *framer,* having been supplied with the dimensions and general plan, cut out the mortices and prepared the frame. Then a bee was called and a *boss* took charge. Using a *following* or raising pole the men gradually elevated the bents or perpendicular parts of the frame. Seventy men were at the bee all day, but the finishing touches, especially inside the house and the 12-foot verandahs on three sides, were effected subsequently by the settler and his sons.*

In general, however, the pioneer home was not a work of art. 'We build very ugly houses in Canada', wrote Dr. William Dunlop in 1832, 'very ill laid out and very incommodious'; but he noted that the people were willing to learn, for if one man

---

*The importance of co-operative bees in raising houses is seen from the fact that in 1817 it cost £25 to have a log house erected by hired men, and from £75 to £250 for a frame house. Yet in some districts so much food and liquor were used up, so many dishes broken, and so much drunkenness, swearing, and profligate conduct offended the more refined that bees were considered an abomination.

introduced neat improvements he was speedily imitated by his neighbours. The hope, consequently, was that better designs, plans, and elevations would be brought from the Old Land, and anyone who did so, he considered, would be a public benefactor.*

'The torments of the insect tribes', as Mrs. Traill calls them, were not confined to the mosquitoes** and black flies of summer. Log houses attracted other insect pests, particularly crickets, ants, and *sawyers,* as they were popularly called. Crickets were a nuisance not only for their continual chirping but because they were destructive of clothes, especially woollens; the ants were large black ones that infested the pantry and supplies of food; while the sawyers were wood-beetles who ate and creaked and grated their way into the logs, especially at night, and left heaps of fine sawdust as proof of their prowess.

Settlers in every stage of material prosperity sometimes built and furnished for display. The Reverend A. H. W. Rose observed in many farm homes in the eighteen-forties a characteristic which is in one sense almost as prevalent today. It was

a curious taste for building a considerable-sized two-storied brick or stone house for a show, putting curtains or blinds, the latter, figuratively as well as literally, to the windows, and then living in the kitchens, furnishing none of the upper portions of the house, into which, if you take a pilgrimage, you will probably find one room full of dried-apple shreds, another of Indian corn, another of pumpkins, and so on.

In more recent times many a farmhouse is fully furnished but the best parts of it used only on rare occasions like a wedding or funeral; and you can still see such incongruities as an upstairs door opening upon the space where a verandah had been planned but never built, or a front door for which steps were never made, presumably because the family had accustomed themselves to using the back door exclusively.

The inside of the pioneer home varied in appearance as much as the people themselves. Backwoods homes were usually fur-

*A book on early domestic architecture in Ontario is in course of preparation by Anthony Adamson and Marion MacRae.

**T. H. Ware, a prospective settler near Orillia who returned to Britain after a few months, included a recipe in his diary 'To drive away Mosquitos'. The cure sounds worse than the disease: 'When you have pitched your tent in the Bush for the night, place some dried buffalo or cow dung in a small heap on each side of your bed; set a light to it & it will smolder all night, & the smoke which arises from it in a pyramidical form will keep off all Mosquitoes.' He had another equally difficult problem: 'To Purify the Air in Stables'.

Photograph by the Author

ALPHEUS JONES HOME, PRESCOTT

A good example of an early stone house of Georgian architecture. Such homes are found along the St. Lawrence where stone is plentiful, and elsewhere of brick or clapboard, whichever was most readily available.

nished in a primitive manner, with hand-made tables, chairs, and beds—if they were not mere boards, sections of trees, benches, and bunks. Even in towns the wind often whistled through the houses and blew out candles, and the cold penetrated sufficiently to freeze solid any water in bedroom pitchers or basins. A prominent pioneer lieutenant-governor, Sir Francis Bond Head, noticed that the typical small English fireplace was being introduced in many town houses, but the general coldness of Canadian homes may be gauged from his statement that

though mine at Toronto was warmed with hot air from a large oven, with fires in all our sitting-rooms, nevertheless the wood for my grate, which was piled close to the fire, often remained till night covered with the snow which was on it when first deposited there in the morning; and as a further instance of the climate I may add that several times, while my mind was very warmly occupied in writing my despatches, I found my pen full of a lump of frozen stuff that appeared to be honey but which proved to be frozen ink.

The Pioneer Home

The ink freezes in your pens [said John Langton], the lather in your shaving brush; the latch of the door sticks to your hand, and the water has occasionally frozen in my glass at dinner. . . . I had nothing but iron pens, in which the ink froze so fast as to render the writing even of a short note a work of considerable time and labour.

By far the best description of the difficulties of the pioneer farmer due to 'the dreadful Canadian WINTER', as the Reverend George Playter calls it, is his own summary in *The History of Methodism in Canada*:

The winter in Canada . . . usually sets in suddenly, on the third or fourth week in November. One day the weather is fine, the sun shining, cattle and horses grazing, the plough is going, springs are running, gloves nor overcoats are wanted. But the wind at sun setting wears northerly and increases hour by hour, and the cold comes pouring down all night with a sprinkling of snow, changing by morning the whole face of nature and the employments of the people. The plough is frozen in the ground, sheep straying over the fields return to the barns, cattle and horses no longer graze, travellers put on their thick coats, and all employed without the house require a cover for the hands.

Cold continues: stagnant waters are frozen, next small running streams, and soon the great bays and lakes have solid ice for a covering, and even rapid rivers have the spray and upmost water congealed by the powerful cold. Intense cold does not prevail, yet occurs. Two or three days of such cold, and the weather moderates. Yet, while it lasts, the roads and streets are forsaken except by great necessity. But the cold pouring down from the northern quarters,

Willis, *Canadian Scenery*   W. H. Bartlett

WINTER, ORFORD LAKE

bringing down the thermometer to 30° or 40° below zero, makes the long dark night terrible.

The stove fires seem to give not half the usual heat, and yet burn away the fuel faster than the usual rate. Should the fires go out, the cold pours in at every hole and crack, so that each sleeper wakes up with cold biting his feet, requiring more covering for his bed. As the dreadful night passes along, the foundations of houses lift, making a cracking noise in verandahs, clap-boarding, and shingles on the roofs. The noise is sometimes as the report of a gun.

Morning reveals the terrible cold. A glass of water by the bed-side, or a wash bowl half full of water, is frozen to solid ice. The windows are covered with thick frost from the vapors of the room, and hinder all looking out as if a curtain fell. Outside, before sun rise, sky clear, no wind, but cold intense, drawing tears from the eyes and quickly touching the nose and ears.

In such cold, turkeys and fowls keep on the roost, cocks have their head combs frozen stiff, ducks and geese lie on their feet to shelter from the cold, pigs hide down deep under their strawy beds, and cattle and horses tremble as they stand in the stables or the sheds. Every creature having life keeps in the shelter, afraid of the mighty cold. Even the trees suffer, the cold freezing and splitting the bark with a noise as an explosion. Pumps are frozen and use-less, the cold even going down through the opening to the water beneath, coating with ice.

Snow always covers the ground in winter, but not always with the same depth or the same duration. The first snow storm may bring six inches of snow; the next a few inches more; the third six inches more; and so storm after storm will increase the depth, unless warm weather intervene and thaw the snow to water. The depth is usually from two to three and four feet on a level. The roofs are covered with snow, and the fields show a level surface, with stumps of felled trees scarcely appearing. Gardens are covered up: goose-berry, currant, and raspberry bushes hardly shew even the tops. The snow when above two feet is inconvenient for travelling and labour-ing in the woods; otherwise the snow is a great advantage, making smooth winter roads for sleighs; covering wheat and rye from the terrible cold, as well as the roots of tender garden bushes and plants; protecting cellars stored with vegetables and fruits, wells from freezing and denying water to man and beast, and foundations of dwellings and public edifices. . . . The snow and frost retire in April, with occasional returns in May and even in June—to the terror of gardeners and horticulturists.

Candles were cheap and in general use, while oil—sometimes only whale oil that burned in tin lamps without chimneys—was prohibitive at 9s. a gallon. Matches were unknown, flint and tinder being the usual method of striking a light. Every back-woodsman carried as tinder a piece of *punk* from the sugar

International Nickel Ltd.   Russell Taber

LAMP OIL

Niagara Historical Society

PIONEER LIGHTING EQUIPMENT
Sconces, snuffers, moulds, holders, and lanterns may be seen.

maple.* Some settlers kept for the purpose a supply of finely-split pine sticks tipped with brimstone, which were effective lighters if a coal remained; and if not, live coals were borrowed from a neighbour. As 'carrying fire' was necessarily a speedy matter, a short visit was so designated—'Why! you must have come for a coal!' Lucifer matches and coal oil provided a revolutionary advance. 'Lamp-oil' was then peddled from door to door, especially in or near the towns, and was stored in cans, wooden containers, or large demijohns.

Travellers often noted the general appearance of the interior of settlers' homes. Spinning wheels for flax and wool were commonly seen, with spun yarn hanging on wooden pegs. Snowshoes, a powder-horn, a bullet-pouch, and one or more of the old flint-lock guns hung on the walls, with perhaps a churn in that part of the room used as a kitchen. In older settlements these evidences of bush life tended to be replaced by pictures and other refinements, and a Franklin stove, as well as a cook-stove, was often seen. Peddlers brought around grandfather clocks, usually American; or perhaps the works only were purchased, and the farmer made his own box of rough pine or a fancier wood. Pianos were occasionally found even in the woods, some settlers going to the trouble and expense of bringing them across the ocean and up the country. Many farmhouses had Currier and Ives prints and religious precepts worked in coloured wool on canvas and still to be seen—*God Bless Our Home, God Is Love, What Is Home Without a Mother to Love*.

Admiral VanSittart, who expended £20,000 on an estate four miles east of Woodstock, where the village of Eastwood now is, had an establishment** that astonished Anna Jameson.

His house is really a curiosity [she wrote], and at the first glance reminded me of an African village—a sort of Timbucto set down in the woods, . . . and looked as if a number of log-huts had jostled against each other by accident, and there stuck fast: . . . odd galleries, passages, porticos, corridors, saloons, cabins, and cupboards; so that if the outside reminded me of an African village, the interior was no less like that of a man-of-war.

*'All our punk being wet in our pockets', wrote John Langton, . . . 'we were half an hour in getting a light. . . . At last with the assistance of gunpowder we lighted a fire, but to me as flint and steel bearer, it was at the expense of one whisker and both eyelashes.' John Mactaggart describes a similar method: 'Having a gun with us, we succeeded in lighting a good fire.' The first matches were merely thin strips of wood to light candles from the fireplace.

**He, and his son, also had one in the wilds of Bexley Township. For interesting details of this ménage see the author's *The Valley of the Trent*, pp. 65-6.

CAMPBELLTON POST OFFICE AND GENERAL STORE, IN THE 1890's

PARLOUR, O'HARA HOMESTEAD, MOIRA

The enterprising and ingenious pioneer could make all sorts of furnishings and equipment for home and farm, but perhaps the following description of Mrs. Traill's furniture would indicate the average in long-settled districts, and well above it in 'the Bush':

Our furniture consists of a brass-railed sofa, which serves upon occasion for a bed, Canadian painted chairs; a stained pine table; green and white muslin curtains; and a handsome Indian mat which covers the floor. One side of the room is filled up with our books. Some large maps and a few good prints nearly conceal the rough walls and form the decoration of our little dwelling. Our bed-chamber is furnished with equal simplicity.

With some allowance for his characteristic rancour, the description Edward Talbot gives of the furnishings of a log house is probably fairly accurate, certainly in the early period and for bush settlers:

For the first five or six years the primitive log-hut affords him an asylum, and he seldom manifests much anxiety to multiply its external decorations. His furniture is never of the most costly description and is seldom cumbersome. A bedstead, roughly hewn out with a felling-axe, the sides, posts, and ends held together in screeching trepidation by strips of basswood bark; a bed of fine field-feathers*; a table that might be taken for a victualler's chopping-block; four or five benches of the same rude mechanism; and the indispensable apparatus for cooking and eating, compose the *tout ensemble* of a Canadian's household furniture. He seems to have no idea of cottage comfort, and seldom evinces any inclination to make his hut even tolerably pleasant.**

*The German settlers (usually called Dutch) often used the feather bed as a covering, lying upon a straw or chaff one underneath. Travellers usually considered feather beds warm but unpleasant, and if there were any other covering to be had they would kick them off on to the floor.

**Further details of the more primitive house furnishings, utensils, and tools, and how they were made, are given in Volume II, Chapters IX, X, and XI, pp. 167-199.

CHAPTER VI

FOOD AND CLOTHING

Food in the pioneer period was as crude as other aspects of the life. Flour and pork formed the basis, for both could be easily transported in barrels. In winter most farmers ate salt pork three meals a day, but other meat, game, and fish provided variety in summer. A frying-pan full of grease was a characteristic sight at mealtime, for many a food was prepared in it. Potatoes provided some balance for the pork—if not saturated with grease in the cooking.

Bread, always homemade, was generally baked in outside ovens, which were sometimes hollowed buttonwood trees. In many instances it was as much steamed as baked, and for economy the flour was often mixed with crushed boiled potatoes. For yeast or barm to raise the bread various fermentations of salt, flour, water, milk, and boiled hops were used. While wheat bread was more usual, rye, corn, and buckwheat flours were also used for bread, doughnuts, and cakes; and especially was cornmeal Johnny-cake a favourite. Cornmeal porridge, usually called *supporne* or *mush*, was often the main part of an evening meal, and especially for children. The 'accustomed tip-top fare' for special visitors to the best farms, says a traveller, the Reverend James Dixon, was a sucking-pig.

Vegetables other than the potato did not usually grow well in 'the Bush', probably because of the fierce competition of wild life and insufficient attention and care. Turnips, cabbages, and many other vegetables were consequently luxuries, but became more common as the land was cleared and roothouses were constructed for their storage. Pumpkins, almost always grown in the cornfield, formed a staple food. They were sliced, dried, and kept over the winter, forming the base for pies, puddings, and even soup. Considerable use was made of cranber-

An early postcard

THE BERRY-PICKERS

ries* and many other wild fruits, and of hickory nuts, walnuts, chestnuts, and butternuts; and a visitor might be surprised by being served pickled butternuts prepared from nuts picked early in July when they are young and tender. The apple, often called the principal fruit of Upper Canada, was widely used. A characteristic pioneer activity was the preparation of dried apples in slices, to store for the almost universal apple pies, and there is more truth than poetry in this verse-description of the result of many an apple-paring bee:

> *First they don't take half the peeling off,*
> *Then on a dirty cord they're strung,*
> *Then from some chamber window hung;*
> *Where they serve as roosts for flies*
> *Until they're ready to make pies.*

Though with all these faults, old-timers like G. H. Green of Colborne Township considered the home-made dried apples 'had more apple flavour than the new-fangled evaporated brimstone-dried apple of today.' In the later period the season

*Perhaps the province's most noted cranberry marsh was one 18 miles in length by about 2 in width, through which the Rideau Canal was built. Hundreds of labourers died of ague and malaria during the work in that region in 1828. 'The berries are very plentiful,' wrote John Mactaggart in 1829. 'They are globose, transparent, of a yellowish colour sometimes marked with little black spots; they something resemble sparrow eggs and may be gathered in *bushels full* at the close of summer. Settlers will go ten miles to gather them; but as the mist of the marsh is extremely noxious to life, people prefer staying at home instead of visiting the abode of the ague.' (*Three Years in Canada*, 1829.)

for preserving fruits in jars was always a busy time for the women, who often made a bee of the work.

At times, and notably in 1835-36, the harvests were very poor because of early frosts, and prices of staple foods increased to four and five times normal. Many settlers were consequently in great want. Because cattle were usually allowed to fend for themselves, even in winter, milk was at first scanty and poor—if the bush settler had any at all—and butter was consequently of low quality. Various types of tea were used, but green was more common than black, and all that had not been smuggled in was expensive. Many settlers used hemlock, sweetfern, and New Jersey tea to mix with it, and a traveller, Anna Jameson, described what she was served as tasting 'for all the world like musty hay'. Sometimes whiskey or brandy was added to tea, but milk was seldom used with it. 'Coffee' of burnt corn, dandelion, or burnt bread was often used in place of anything better. Maple sugar usually sweetened tea and coffee, but an expensive loaf-sugar from which the grains were scraped off with a knife was available in later years. Good apple cider was made by some farmers, but in most districts whiskey was the standard drink. One traveller refers to it as 'the sole drink of all classes' and 'universally in use'.*

The best cider I ever tasted was on Yonge-street [wrote the Reverend Isaac Fidler]. A gentleman had been turning his apples into cider; after he barrelled it the casks were left so exposed as to be reached by the frost, which congealed the aqueous part of the liquid. The strength of the cider, the very essence and spirituous portion of it, was detached thereby from the water. He bored holes in the barrels and drew off the unfrozen part into bottles; this was the cider of which I am speaking, which in strength and goodness more resembled wine than cider.

Earlier settlers sometimes used juniper berries in making gin, and both essence of spruce and its boughs to make 'a healthy beer' and other concoctions. Wild raspberries, in such abundance around the stumps as to be a nuisance to the farmer, were often made into wine or raspberry vinegar; and currants and other fruits at times used to make drinks.

In towns, of course, greater variety in food was always to

*John Mactaggart considered 'potatoe whisky' to be 'the absolute poison of Upper Canada', and was pleased that its distillation was prohibited by law in the late eighteen-twenties. He said it was made of 'frosty potatoes, hemlock, pumpkins, and black mouldy rye', and that 'no hell broth that the witches concocted of yore can equal it'. It was sold, he said, by Yankee peddlers.

be found. Those in York who could afford luxuries were able to buy fancy cheeses, seafood, candied fruit, numerous vegetables, and even 'ices'. Breakfast, whether in urban or rural regions, was much like the other meals, and while the times of meals did not greatly differ from those at present, farmers were in the habit of working an hour or so before breakfast in summer, and of continuing in the fields until sunset before having supper.* In towns hours of work were similarly long, varying with the season. A workmen's protest in Cobourg in 1836 stated that 'the number of hours which we now work is nothing better than domestic Slavery,' and stipulated that thereafter 6 to 6 in the summer and 7 to 6 in winter should be the hours, with intervals of an hour each for breakfast and noon dinner in the former season and for dinner in the latter.

Clothing was often as crude as food, but in general the settler's wardrobe depended upon his stock of clothes when he arrived, for but few had money to buy any for several years. Dull brown or gray homespun was common, and *linsey-woolsey*, a cotton-wool mixture, was popular in the Loyalist period. As the years passed, various cottons and calicoes, some of them imported, were available. The Petworth Emigration Committee, which supervised the removal of many Sussex farm tenants and labourers to Canada, recommended that in addition to what he had in England, each male emigrant should bring 'a fur cap, a warm greatcoat, a flushing jacket and trowsers, two jersey frocks, four shirts, 4 pairs of stockings, and 3 pairs of shoes,' but the average Canadian settler had no such wardrobe. Captain George A. Hill, after experience in backwoods life, recommended

round jackets of strong thick cloth . . . for general wear during the winter season. . . . Cloth breeches I prefer to trowsers; and in place of putting on leather boots or strong shoes I advise a pair of the latter made very slight, and to draw over them strong woollen stockings, either *knit* expressly for the purpose or made of very close stout cloth. Thus dressed, your feet may bid defiance to the snow and will continue dry and warm. A few pair of strong Wellington boots will, however, be advisable, as the cloth hose are not the best to be used during a thaw. Plenty of warm woollen stockings will be an acquisition.

John Mactaggart, famous Scottish author of *The Gallovidian Encyclopaedia,* a rare, comprehensive, and humorous

*The reader is referred to the author's *Early Life in Upper Canada,* where pioneer foods and cooking are treated in great detail in Section III, Chapter 2.

Anne Langton   Anne Langton

JOHN LANGTON   BACKWOODS COSTUME
The Langtons were early settled on the shores of Sturgeon Lake.

account of the customs of the Lowlands, was for three years an
engineer on the Rideau Canal. The Irish labourers in and
around Bytown, he observed, were a tough lot with respect to
clothing.

You cannot [he wrote] get the *low Irish* to wash their faces, even
were you to lay before them ewers of crystal water and scented
soap: you cannot get them to dress decently, although you supply
them with ready-made clothes. . . . Blankets and stockings they
will not purchase; so the frost bites them in all quarters.

But there are other pioneer authors who are equally uncom-
plimentary to *his* nationality.

From Loyalist times flax was grown and processed, and with
wool was woven into homespun, which was dyed with the use
of butternut or walnut bark, among many other native dyes;
hanks of yarn were often seen hanging out to dry. Many country people—men, women, and children—went barefoot all
summer—'altogether from choice' one writer naïvely states.
Perhaps Joseph Pickering's reference to a girl of nineteen,
'smart and lively,' comes closest to the general practice. He observed that she wore no stockings when he saw her at a tavern,
but had them on when she accompanied her mother to a par-
ing bee later in the day. He notes that 'stockings are hardly

77

ever worn by the settlers in the woods in summer, either by males or females. In winter the latter wear stockings and the former socks.' Some rural girls no doubt tried to follow city fashions, one of which was the wearing of numerous petticoats and other 'unmentionables';* so much so that this verse was considered appropriate by the author of *Journal of a Wanderer*:

> *Thus finished in taste while on her you gaze,*
> *You may take the dear charmer for life;*
> *But never undress her, for out of her stays*
> *You'll find you have lost half your wife!*

Shoes were commonly home-made; or, if money was available, ordered from an itinerant shoemaker or one established in the nearest town. Especially because of their drab and primitive surroundings, women yearned for bright colours and trimmings, and one of their great pleasures was to survey what was available in a peddler's pack or the nearest general store; while a journey to Toronto might well be the event of a lifetime.

So great was the scarcity of clothing that in bush settlements it was not unusual to attend church in ordinary working clothes. Many farmers and lumbermen, both early and more recent, were, to put it mildly, not given to frequent change of clothing; it was not uncommon, in fact, for them to go for months without even removing the greater part of their clothes. Washing, whether of clothing or the body, was equally infrequent, and the fact, of course, was not hard to detect even at a distance.

Characteristic clothing at various periods is perhaps best described in travel books. It must not be thought that the Upper Canada Indians looked much like the Hollywood version of the riders of the Western Plains, for they much more resembled backwoodsmen.

The red men who wander about this part of Canada [writes Sir James Alexander] wear the blanket coat winter and summer, and a piece of printed cotton twisted round their long black locks like a loose turban; their legs are cased in blue or crimson leggings. The women wear the blanket wrapped round them from the head to the heel.

*For an excellent historical-humorous treatment of the subject see Robert Cortes Holliday, *Unmentionables: From Figleaves to Scanties* (New York, 1933).

Toronto Public Library   T. H. Ware

INDIANS AT COLDWATER, NEAR LAKE HURON, 1844

In Loyalist days calico frocks and sunbonnets were usual for young women, with flannel frocks and woollen hoods for colder weather. Those who did not go barefoot wore tan-coloured cowhide shoes. Young men wore 'hickory' shirts, older men flannel; and occasional coonskin caps were seen. One set of buttons commonly lasted for five or six successive suits of clothes. For winter journeys, then and later, and especially among Scottish settlers, a shawl covered the head like a hood and was pinned under the chin; while a silk gown or broadcloth suit was for very special use and intended to last a lifetime.

As the years passed and all sorts of people arrived from the Old Land the clothing became more varied. Dr. William Dunlop, who at times ranks with Thomas Haliburton among pioneer humorists, wrote that in Upper Canada

for four months of the year you were up to the neck in mud; for four more you were either burned up by the heat or stung to death by mosquitoes; and for the other four, if you managed to get your nose above the snow it was only to have it bitten off by the frost.

79

In such variable climate you might see people wearing almost anything—or nothing. Edward Talbot found it was the children who were in the latter category:

Numerous children may be seen in all the new settlements so destitute of clothing that if any modesty remained in their parents they would be prevented from appearing before strangers; and yet the moment you enter a Canadian cabin the naked inmates of it array themselves in the most conspicuous point of view, unweeting, it would seem, of the unpleasant feelings which such an exhibition must produce on the minds of strangers.

Women sometimes wore woollens because cotton dresses not infrequently caught fire while they prepared meals before

Green, *The Old Log House*

FAMILY OF JOHN MORRIS AND ELIZABETH PIERCE, HIS WIFE

This typically large pioneer family lived in Colborne Township,
County of Huron.

cpen fireplaces. The 'common people', says one writer, wore flannel shirts in summer to dry up the sweat, and in winter to keep out the cold. But Talbot observed that the women could rig themselves out in the most incongruous colours:

Perhaps no people in the world, secluded as they are from the society of strangers, are so much attached to gaudy apparel. . . . It is really laughable to witness the taste which they display in arranging the various articles that compose their dress. A black silk gown trimmed with pink or green ribbon, a pair of garter-blue worsted stockings, shoes that never knew the radiant powers of Day and Martin, muslin ruffs trimmed with azure or scarlet, a bonnet of the finest lutestring or the richest sarsnet,—these not infrequently compose their riding-dress.

The Playfair Papers

'LIBERTY HALL TABLE D'HOTE'

'There were doctors, barbers, lawyers, preachers, Scotch, English, Dutch,
four Spaniards, and two Russians; Old maids, young virgins, widows,
and French teachers; Some Irish duellists, some well-drilled
Prussians; A London tailor, twenty other stitchers;
Sharpers, brokers! . . .'

The Playfair Papers

'DRAWING-ROOM, LIBERTY HALL'

These satirical caricatures of American hotel life are from Hugo Playfair's
*The Playfair Papers: or Brother Jonathan, the Smartest Nation in all
Creation* (1841). Harriet Martineau could hardly believe her eyes when
she saw a girl playing (as here) a hotel pianoforte amid a *promiscuous*
company of *total strangers*.

But Susanna Moodie, in describing a friend, compliments Upper Canadian women upon their taste in dress and the general effect of their appearance:

Like most of the Canadian women, my friend was of small stature, slight and delicately formed, and dressed with the smartness and neatness so characteristic of the females of this continent, who, if they lack some of the accomplishments of English women, far surpass them in their taste in dress, their choice of colours, and the graceful and becoming manner in which they wear their clothes.

Dr. John Bigsby was similarly impressed by the women, but found the males very careless of appearances:

The settler is apt to fall into a dull and moping state. . . . There is no stimulus at hand preservative of the domestic proprieties. All are necessarily careless of dress in summer; while in winter a whole wardrobe of old clothes is called for at once. . . . The females, I am bound to say, bear a woodland life far better than the men; are cheerful, active, and tidy in their persons. I have been often very pleased with their healthy, satisfied, and smart appearance while mounting their Dearborn springwagon on Sundays to go to church.

In his *George Stanley, or Life in the Woods* John Geikie describes the clothing that might be brought forth for grand occasions:

During the winter a great ball was given across the river [St. Clair] in a large barn which had been cleared for the purpose, the price of tickets being fixed at a dollar, which included an abundant supper. It was intimated, however, that those who had no money might pay in 'dicker'—a Yankee word for barter; a bundle of shingles, a certain number of eggs, or so much weight of butter being held equivalent to the money and securing a ticket. . . . The girls were, of course, in the height of fashion as they understood it, some of them exposing themselves in ridiculously light clothing for the terrible season of the year, in the belief, no doubt, that it made them look the nicer.

Fashions in those days did not travel fast, and what was in its full glory on the river had been wellnigh forgotten where it took its rise. . . . The taste shown was often very praiseworthy, but sometimes, it must be admitted, a little out of the way. I have seen girls with checked or figured white muslin dresses wearing a black petticoat underneath to show off the beauties of the pattern; and I knew of one case where a young woman, who was engrossed in the awful business of buying her wedding dress, could get nothing to please her until she chanced to see, hanging up, a great white window curtain with birds and flowers all over it, which she instantly pronounced to be the very thing she wanted and took it home in triumph! There was one gentleman's coat on the river which might have formed a curiosity in a museum as a relic of days gone by.

The collar stood up round the ears in such a great roll that the shoulders and head seemed set on each other, and as to the tails, they crossed each other like a martin's wings somewhere about the knees. But it was in a good state of preservation, and for aught I know may be the holiday pride of its owner to this hour.

In Scottish settlements particularly one might see people dressed from head to foot in homespun. A contemporary picture shows a man wearing a long smock tied with cords at the wrists and waist. On his hands are woollen mittens pulled up over the ends of the sleeves, while the legs of his heavy trousers are tucked inside the tops of his long boots, which were commonly worn several times too large in order to allow for heavy socks; and even then the aid of a boot-jack was often required to take them off. On the head was a woollen cap, or sometimes a tam o' shanter. Thus covered, none of the skin was exposed except around the eyes and nose, for whiskers almost invariably covered the chin. Wide-brimmed straw hats became so common in summer that a farmer was seldom pictured without one.

Yet aristocratic settlers—if that is the best name for well-to-do people of good family with social pretensions—usually contrived to appear dressed to suit the occasion. John Langton and numerous others at a distance from the town attended 'bachelors' balls' in Peterborough in the eighteen-thirties, and most of them wore formal full-dress. Yet his sister Anne says in her journal that borrowing clothes when visiting was a common practice, and particularly when parties were given. Even wedding rings, she says, were borrowed on occasion, for none could be obtained in Peterborough, much less in the smaller settlements nearer home.

In the early 'seventies John Geikie attended a public meeting which, he said,

gave us an opportunity of seeing the population of a wide district in all the variety of winter costume. . . . The village was already thronged by numbers who had come from all parts, for it was a political meeting and all Canadians are politicians. Such costumes as some exhibited are surely to be seen nowhere else. One man, I noticed, had a suit made of drugget carpeting with a large flower on a bright green ground for pattern, one of the compartments of it reaching from his collar far down his back. Blanket coats of various colours, tied round the waist with a red sash, buffalo coats, fur caps of all sizes and shapes, moccasins or coarse Wellington's with the trowser legs tucked into them, mitts, gloves, and fur gauntlets, added variety to the picture.

Canadian Illustrated News

STEEPLE CHASE RACES, TORONTO HUNT CLUB, 1870
The more well-to-do displayed the latest fashions.

The women and their sleighs were much more colourful, of course.

The female beauty of some of the Canadians [wrote James Taylor, who was definitely susceptible] cannot be surpassed: their features are finely formed, and the expressions of their countenances quite fascinating. . . . When taking an airing in their sleigh-cutters . . . in their winter costume over the frozen snow the set-out is quite attractive. Sleigh-cutters are a simple but elegant carriage without wheels, embellished with buffalo skins which hang over the sides, lined with cloth of various dazzling colours, scolloped out vandyke shape, and squirrel skins attached to various parts of the robes; but those who wish to appear the most conspicuous have their dress and robes composed of American wolves' skins lined with scarlet and sky-blue or some other brilliant colours, which gives them quite an eccentric appearance.

In general it cannot be questioned that both food and clothing were better than the same people would have had in the

Old Country. Mary Jane Watson, who had been on relief in the quaint little village of Sedlescomb in the south of England, worked in America as a *help* (not a servant!), soon married 'a man in good circumstances',* and was rejoiced to find that she had good clothes; 'and I can dress as well as any lady in Sedlescomb. I can enjoy a silk and white frock, and crape frock and veil, and Morocco shoes, without a parish grumbling about it.' One of the Sussex settlers in Halton County wrote home that all the farmers he had seen were independent. 'I wish,' he said, 'that the poor people in England had the leavings of their tables that goes to the dogs and hogs; they live better than most of the farmers [*i.e.*, landlords] in England.' A Scot told Patrick Shirreff that the beef of Canada was so tough that teeth could not chew it; but however tough it was, 'in the Old Country he got beef only once a week, on Sunday; here he had it three times a day.'

But if the beef was plentiful but tough, most British travellers thought many Upper Canadians equally so, and not only in their rough clothing and appearance but in their lack of table manners, their rough-and-ready use of utensils and dishes, and their *Yankee lingo*. Isabella (Bird) Bishop, author of *The Englishwoman in America*, found that the *smart gals* could hold up their end with the best of the men when it came to the *Yankified* jargon of table conversation on a steamboat or at an inn. A young man accosts a couple of girls with

'Miss, it's feeding time, I guess; what will you eat?'
'You're very po-lite; what's the ticket?'
'Chicken and corn-fixings, and pork with onion-fixings.'
'Well, I'm hungry some; I'll have some pig and fixings'. . . .

And after eating, one of the girls observed:

'Well, you eat considerable; you're in full blast, I guess.'
'Guess I am; it's all-fired cold, and I have been an everlastin long time off my feed'. . . .
'You're trying to rile me some; you're piling it on a trifle too high.'
'Well, I did want to put up your dander. Do tell now, where was you raised?'
'In Kentucky.'
'I could have guessed that; whenever I sees a splenderiferous gal, a kinder gentle goer and high stepper, I says to myself, That gal's from old Kentuck, and no mistake.'

All of which, of course, was blamed upon democracy.

*Dr. William Dunlop observed relative to female servants that 'if you bring out anything tolerably young or good-looking' she would be married within two months.

CHAPTER VII

FARM IMPLEMENTS AND TOOLS

FROM the first Loyalist settlements to the eighteen-forties the farmer's implements were few and crude, hand-made and cumbersome. As we have pointed out in the chapter on the Loyalists, they petitioned for all sorts of implements and tools that could have been obtained, though with difficulty; but they were given little more than an axe and a hoe, their other needs being met by makeshifts of their own manufacture, supplemented by such supplies as they could obtain on occasional trips to Montreal, Prescott, and other depots.

Conducted emigrations to Canada, and especially those at state expense, were naturally much better supplied with the necessities of pioneering. The Lanark-on-the-Clyde Scottish emigration of 1820 from Glasgow and other districts, totalling some 1500 to 2000 people, is typical of many. Some of the members received considerable aid, many actually none at all, but a report of 'Implements for General Use of the Concessions'* lists the following as dispensed:

> 40 grindstones, 40 whipsaws, 40 cross-cut saws, 85 adzes
> 120 files of sorts, 2805 pounds nails
> 167 augers, felling axes, hand axes, pickaxes, hammers, kettles, frying-pans, bills, iron wedges, latches and catches, locks and keys, pitchforks, saw sets, handsaws, spades
> 569 blankets—one for each man and each woman, and one for every two children
> 334 files, gimlets, pails, hemp, 1503 harrow leets

Early settlers elsewhere and most of these supplies were entire strangers to one another, and it long remained true that most farmers had merely a few of the more necessary tools,

*This report is among the innumerable invaluable documents in the Public Archives of Canada. It is printed in the late Senator Andrew Haydon's *Pioneer Sketches in the District of Bathurst*, which ranks high among the more scholarly of our local histories.

with such makeshifts as they could contrive to supplement them. Crude wagons and sleighs were similarly made, as well as ploughs and harrows, and often they had no iron in their composition. 'Yankee' peddlers brought over the first scythes, and the earliest machines for lumbering and agricultural purposes came from the same quarter. Refinements of the axe and

Conservation Authorities, Ontario

STUMP-HAULING WAGON, HUMBER VALLEY
The solid wheels were usual in early times.

adze, like the mattock, which 'Ex-Settler' says he got in Dublin for 4s. 6d., and handspikes, peevees, etc., gradually came into common use. Of all his equipment 'Ex-Settler' found his 'light hoe', which was six or eight inches wide, not only fine for cultivating turnips and potatoes, but altogether 'the nicest thing for clearing land or gathering the rubbish off it I saw anywhere'.

In fact the proper felling of trees was always preceded by the clearing away of saplings and underbrush, and the bushwhack or bill-hook was in many districts indispensable, and a good *bushwhacker* an asset in any family which sought to extend their cleared land.

With an axe or a strong long-handled billhook, made to be used with both hands, [wrote Samuel Thompson in his *Reminiscences of a Canadian Pioneer*] you cut away for some distance round—a quarter or half an acre perhaps—all the small saplings and under-wood which would otherwise impede your operations upon the larger trees.

In 'a good hard-wood bush', that is, where the principal timber is maple, white oak, elm, white ash, hickory, and other of the harder species of timber—the 'underbrush' is very trifling indeed; and in an hour or two may be cleared off sufficiently to give the forest an agreeable park-like appearance—so much so that, as has been said of English Acts of Parliament, any skilful hand might drive a coach and six through.

Timothy Street, in 1819 one of the first settlers on the site of Streetsville, operated both sawmill and grist-mill on the River Credit. A clever mechanic, he had first to rig up his grist-mill without bolts, and, we are told,

the settlers, for a time, were very glad to get their grists in that state. The reader will understand that the river is a powerful stream; Mr. Street therefore prepared the two millstones in a summary way, without much chipping, and placed them together to work in con-tact upon the mill frame. He then put a power of water on—the smoke arose, the flint, fire, and stone then flew in a fearful and dan-gerous manner. They were, however, allowed to run at good speed, and at length became so far smoothed as to be fit for his use.

Most settlers became tool-makers, and some of them were most skilful and ingenious. In fact emigrants were urged to acquire some acquaintance with carpentry before crossing the Atlantic.

I was once amused [wrote Mrs. Traill] with hearing the remarks made by a very fine lady, the reluctant sharer of her husband's emigration, on seeing the son of a naval officer of some rank in the service busily employed in making an axe-handle out of a piece of rock-elm.

'I wonder that you allow George to degrade himself so,' she said, addressing the father. . . . 'I would see my boys dead before they would use an axe like common labourers. You will allow this is not a country for gentlemen or ladies to live in.'

'It is the country for gentlemen that will not work—and cannot live without—to starve in,' replied the captain bluntly; 'and for that reason I make my boys early accustom themselves to be usefully and actively employed.'

'My boys shall never work like common mechanics,' said the lady indignantly.

'Then, madam, they will be good for nothing as settlers; and it is a pity you dragged them across the Atlantic.'

Under date of May 4th and 5th, 1819, Joseph Abbott wrote in his diary: 'Wet days—made four rakes, and handled and

Anna Jameson

CAMPBELL'S INN, TALBOT ROAD, 1837

'A long pole stuck into the decayed stump of a tree in front of
the hut served for a sign.'—Anna Jameson.

ANDY MORROW'S BLACKSMITH SHOP, KIRBY

An attractive stone building on Highway 115 until recently torn down.

ground the new axes, one having been partially ground and a temporary handle in it before—cleared out and repaired the barn.' On December 20th he was making a one-horse sleigh, and in this case industry certainly had its reward, for on the 31st he wrote:

Went to the party in my new sleigh accompanied by her who after-wards became the affectionate sympathiser in all my sorrows and the happy participator in all my prosperity—had a glorious dance and a beautiful drive home by moonlight afterwards.*

The blacksmith, now a rarity, was for a century and more characteristic of every settlement, and most towns had a num-ber of blacksmith shops. Seventeen men were listed in Co-bourg in 1857 as blacksmiths, though some shops had no doubt more than one employee. Like the mill and the tavern, the blacksmith shop was indispensable in early Canadian com-munities. Not only were blacksmiths essential to shoe horses in pre-motor days, but they were the general handymen of the locality. Where door hinges, latches, and other iron parts were found on house and barn they could usually be traced to the blacksmith. Almost anything could be repaired in his shop, for he had a large bellows operated by a projecting arm to pump air beneath the fire on his forge, and it readily produced a white heat to render iron malleable.

Many a farm had a dinner-horn, like a fireman's trumpet, with which to call the men in to meals when they were work-ing in distant fields.** Samuel Thompson's old homestead had one which he describes as 'a bright tin tube . . . nearly four feet in length, requiring the lungs of that almost forgotten indi-vidual—an English mail coachguard.' A few were brought from Britain, others made by the blacksmith or improvised on the farm. The blacksmith, in fact, made many an excellent tool or farm implement, and the more ingenious smiths were inventors of early types of farm machinery.

*The Abbotts were the parents of Sir John J. C. Abbott, Prime Minister of Canada in 1891-2. Besides the three editions of *The Emigrant to North America,* Joseph Abbott also wrote much the same material in fictional form in *Philip Musgrave: or Memoirs of a Church of England Missionary in the North American Colonies* (London, 1846).

**People, especially children, were often lost in the woods. For an example, the loss of six-year-old Jane Eyre, see the author's *Cobourg, 1798-1948,* pp. 189-93. Some adults are said to have carried tin horns for possible use when going home through the woods at night after attending bees.

CHAPTER VIII

ECONOMIC CONDITIONS

PRIOR to the middle of the 19th century there were no large industrial enterprises in Upper Canada, but plenty of small industries were highly important in their own locality. Until 1849, in fact, the Navigation Acts restricted major industrial development. Most manufactured goods were imported, and the balance of trade was adverse because of their excess over exports.

Poor communication long restricted exports, of which the chief were furs, lumber, ashes, and agricultural products; but there was considerable trade in provisions within the province, and especially in winter when the roads were best. Pork, wheat, flour, and beef were the staple products, and wheat was as good as cash.

Currency was confused, for sterling ($5 to the £) was paid for imports from Britain, dollars to the United States, and both Halifax Currency ($4 to the £) and York Currency ($2.50 to the £) in Canada itself; while there were in addition all sorts of coins in circulation, as well as considerable counterfeit money. Local trade was usually carried on by barter or credit, with the merchant also the banker of the community. Most people spent as little as possible—in fact they received very little cash in the course of a year, and their sales-resistance was high.

When the old Dutch or Yankee settlers get cash [wrote 'Ex-Settler' in 1835] they literally bury it in half dollars; nothing will induce them to part with a six-pence; and this custom in a milder form has become general. Those who get money keep it.

New settlers were always advised to make an arrangement with a storekeeper, who would advance goods and take in payment produce of all kinds—but especially wheat—when their

FIVE-SHILLING NOTE, 1848

first crops were harvested; and this combination of credit and trade came to be known as *store pay*. Many a storekeeper was also land-agent and tavernkeeper, and could turn his wits to any profitable financial deal or speculation.

Public improvements are impossible without taxation, though in the pioneer period it was never high; yet people sometimes had to get cash to meet it by selling produce at considerable sacrifice, even half price. Otherwise cash usually did not pass in business deals, though it served as the standard. Merchants frequently advertised what they would accept in exchange, and doctors, teachers, and other professional men were often paid in produce. Labourers were commonly paid in kind, and their families preferred it, for it evaded much of the temptation to spend wages on strong drink. 'Ex-Settler' advised farmers who intended to employ labourers to 'sally forth' as soon as snow made such sallying feasible, and buy pork and flour for wage payments wherever they were available on the cheapest terms.

Early store prices for meat were from 3d. to 5d. per pound for fresh pork, beef, veal, or mutton, with venison at 3d. Turkeys and geese were commonly sold for from 2s. 6d. (half a dollar) to 5s., according to size, with smaller fowl 1s. 3d. a pair. Poultry were often kept in good condition by packing in snow during the winter months. Eggs sold at 6d. or 7d. a dozen and butter the same per pound.* Potatoes were commonly 1s. 8d. a bushel, and salt rather high in price at 7d. a pound or 5s. a bushel. Game was widely used, for it was prevalent almost

*If bought direct from the farmer eggs were often as low as 3d. a dozen, and turkeys 15d. each. In the Guelph region a traveller found flour at 14s. a barrel, or 3 farthings per pound. The period is the 1840's.

everywhere. Deer were frequently driven into lakes and rivers, where it was easy to drown them.

No doubt Edward Talbot's account of wagers in produce at a racetrack is more ludicrous than factual,* but barter was usual and to *dicker* over all purchases was almost a national pastime. John Thomson, near Lake Simcoe, wrote in his diary that he had exchanged a cow and two barrels of flour for a bull-calf plus 500 feet of lumber; and Thomas Need, at Bobcaygeon, took 3000 feet of lumber for his cow. Butter, eggs— even a bundle of shingles—might be taken as admission to a ball. A newspaper, the *Bathurst Courier*, offered to take a few cords of wood as subscription—'to keep our ink from freezing.' Heavily discounted 'notes of hand' (promissory notes) passed about, but were often of little or no value.

The cash brought over by immigrants was sometimes worth a 25 per cent premium, but the Bank of Upper Canada at York, observed 'Ex-Settler', paid what it pleased on English money, 'and they do not please to give the highest'—often only par.** The uncertainty and confusion in currency led to *shrewdness* and *taking advantage*, which was usually just plain cheating and dishonesty; and bad debts, uncertain values, and high prices were the general results.

Labourers received from 50 cents to a dollar or more a day, depending on the demand and the season.† Tradesmen had set rates, occasionally fixed by law, for various processes. The charge for threshing was one-tenth of the grain, for milling one-twelfth of the flour,‡ for sawing one-half of the lumber, for tanning one-half of the leather, with similar shares for carding, spinning, weaving, etc. Meat and other produce were commonly taken in payment by shoemaker, blacksmith, tailor, carpenter, mason, and candlemaker, credit accounts running until the harvest or slaughtering season.

Labourers on the construction of the Rideau Canal, a British Government project, were paid in American half-dollars brought in boxes from Montreal. Their employers the contrac-

---

*For the details see Volume II, p. 132.

**For a detailed account see the author's 'Pioneer Banking in Ontario: the Bank of Upper Canada, 1822-1866', *The Canadian Banker,* Winter 1948.

†Thomas Forster's Account Book (Toronto Public Library) notes that he was paid £1 11s. 6d. for cutting 25 cords of wood, or at the rate of about 1s. 3d. per cord.

‡It was formerly one-tenth, says a wisecrack of the day, but millers thought they should get more and fixed it at one-twelfth!

tors were paid in vouchers, usually long delayed; and many a contractor was ruined due to the slowness of this opening of the military chest. There, as elsewhere in Canada, French sous, merchants' tokens, English money, and numerous foreign pieces were in circulation, and there were all sorts of exchange and premium rates that were highly baffling to the uninitiated.

William Anderson of Dumfries Township, who came from Scotland under the direction of the Glasgow and Gorbals Emigration Society in 1842, experienced two most generous offers of credit that sound almost too good to be true:

I have not given myself any concern about land as yet [he wrote home], for I think one is better to learn the customs of the country first, as their mode of working is very different from home; but however, I have got the offer of a 100-acre lot from a gentleman in this place, with 40 acres cleared on it and a house and barn and the frame of a saw mill; it is situate in a fine place for timber. I told him I had no money for such an undertaking; he told me there was no use for money here—that a man must go ahead in this country without money. He said I was the only man for it, seeing I had a family of stout sons, and just to go and commence and he would credit me. There was likewise a millwright that offered to put the mill in order for me, and both of them was to take boards for their pay. The whole cost would be about 2200 dollars, but whether I may try it in the spring or not I do not know.

There is no evidence that such generous practices were usual in Upper Canada, though many a man of small capital made such rapid progress that he must have been pretty generally trusted as well as enterprising.

CHAPTER IX

DISEASES AND THEIR REMEDIES

CONSIDERING the primitive conditions of life, the state of medical knowledge and practice at the time, and the superstitions and old wives' tales that, in the absence of trained practitioners, people were forced to accept as medical advice, the wonder is that the death rate in pioneer Ontario was not far greater than it was. Many women, with no medical attention except such as midwives could give, died in childbirth, and there was a heavy infant mortality from fever, ague, smallpox, cholera, and diphtheria. But most people were too busy to have imaginary or psychological illnesses that plague our society today.*

The commonest complaints were malarial fever, rheumatism, and ague—the name for variations of what we call a cold or influenza. These were thought to arise from swamps, 'poisonous vapours', and 'the exhalations of decaying vegetable matter', for it was not then known that mosquitoes carried disease germs and were responsible for much more than vicious bites.

The *Fever and Ague* of Canada [wrote John Mactaggart, from experience] are different, I am told, from those of other countries: they generally come on with an attack of bilious fever, dreadful vomiting, pains in the back and loins, general debility, loss of appetite, so that one cannot even take tea—a thing that can be endured by the stomach in England when nothing else can be suffered. After being in this state for eight or ten days the yellow jaundice is likely to ensue, and then *fits* of trembling. . . . For two or three hours before they arrive we feel so cold that nothing will warm us—the greatest heat that can be applied is perfectly unfelt; the skin gets dry, and then the *shaking begins*. Our very bones ache, teeth chatter, and the ribs are sore, continuing thus in great agony for about an hour and a half; we then commonly have a vomit, the trembling

*Though there were 'ladies' in the towns, says Susanna Moodie, who affected 'delicacy' as fashionable, and preferred to be thought fragile rather than like 'coarse and healthy country girls'.

ends, and a profuse sweat ensues, which lasts two hours longer. This over, we find the malady has run one of its rounds and start out of bed in a feeble state, sometimes unable to stand and entirely dependent on our friends (if we have any) to lift us on to some seat or other.

Alternate fits of fever and shivering were sometimes called *the shakers* or *the chills*. 'A man out west,' we are told in Yankee colloquialism, 'was took so bad with the shakers that every tooth rattled so in his head that you could hear the noise at the far end of a 50-acre farm!' The obituary of Robert Fenton, Otonabee Township, in 1832, is typical of many:

Unfortunately his very first season proved wet and unhealthy, and the necessary exposure and fatigue operating upon a totally un- prepared constitution soon brought him to a bed of sickness, which his constant anxiety for a beloved wife and child, solely dependent upon his exertions, rendered ultimately fatal.

The remedies were various. Many were made in the home from such plants as spikenard, bloodroot, catnip, tansy, smart- weed, plantain, burdock, and mandrake; nor were these all, for snakeroot was sometimes used as a remedy for rattlesnake bites, following the Indian example; and ginseng, sarsaparilla, gold thread, elecampane, lobelia, spearmint, and mullein were put to one use or another. The berries, bark, and roots of the prickly ash were compounded into a remedy for rheumatic complaints. Brandy and other 'ardent spirits' were commonly used, and quinine was frequently prescribed. Calomel, 'ginger tea', and concoctions of pepper, nutmeg, and other ingredients were given as remedies, and they were no doubt of value; but there were many illiterate settlers who relied on charms and superstitions to an extent not far removed from the ignorance of the days of the Great Plague of 1665.

In the early eighteen-thirties, and again in the late 'forties, there were epidemics of cholera and 'ship fever' (typhus) en route to America, at the ports, and to a considerable extent in the settlements.* Between 400 and 500 people, mainly newly- arrived immigrants, died in Toronto in one month in 1834, when the population was about 6000. Doses of calomel relieved some victims of the disease, but holding 'doctors' drugs' to the nose—even wearing charms—were held by many to be most

---

*In 1828 'languid fever' was rife, and those who survived were often two months recovering from it. In 1846 the ague was epidemic, and John Langton noted that 'sometimes we had difficulty in finding men strong enough to carry the coffins up to the churchyard'.

Archives of Ontario

Capt. Thomas Burrowes

PICNIC AT SLOAT'S LAKE, TOWNSHIP OF LOUGHBOROUGH, 1830
The collection of Burrowes' paintings is the finest in the Ontario Archives.

efficacious in combatting what were considered by many people to be 'visitations of God's wrath'.

Many people took a mixture of opium and brandy in doses large enough—as the Reverend Isaac Fidler put it—to 'extinguish life in the most athletic constitution'. People were warned to avoid excesses of all kinds; not to eat fruit of any type, and especially water-melons; to avoid fatigue and 'irritation of the gastric nerve'; and to eat plenty of nutritious food. The extent of medical knowledge is apparent from the various ways in which it was suggested the plague spread. 'Street-going hogs' were blamed in some quarters, hides and skins in a warehouse were believed to have spread it to others, while wind and water were considered good conductors by those who did not hold the fixed belief that the disease passed from place to place 'under the surface of the ground'.

As qualified physicians and former ship's surgeons were few and far between, many settlers prescribed for their own ills or relied upon people in the neighbourhood. In 1856 Mrs. Edward Copleston, newly arrived in 'the Bush' near Lefroy, had 'all the symptoms of ague and intermittent fever'. The nearest doctor was twelve miles away, so

the landlord with much sympathy undertook my cure; and as I was too ill to turn restive I swallowed his prescribed nostrums. His 'R.R.R.', which interpreted signifies 'Radway's Ready Relief', was the vilest and most pungent decoction of the hottest capsicums it had ever been my lot to taste. Nevertheless I am bound to say this quack remedy, though severe, was not without its good results; such a glow and warmth as it diffused I shall not easily forget—it must have assisted in dispelling my chill; and thanks to this all-stimulating powerful agent I was enabled to pursue our journey on the Monday.

In many a settlement there was at least one woman with a reputation for healing the sick and acting as midwife. In 1894 died 'the family doctor of North Dummer', Mrs. Elizabeth Clague, and it was recorded in her obituary notice that 'many a person had been enabled to leave a bed of sickness through her untiring efforts'. Farther north, in Haliburton, Mrs. Thomas Mason, a week after her first baby was born, got Mrs. James Hewitt to doctor her husband, who had been badly injured while felling trees. One had rolled on him breaking his left leg at the thigh, crushing three ribs, and splitting his throat open, exposing the windpipe. She sewed up the throat with darning needle and thread, but the leg was not set, and though he lived to be over a century old, one leg remained two inches

Thomas Mason
(1829-1932)

Amy (Henderson) Mason
(1832-1903)

PROMINENT HALIBURTON PIONEERS

ELIZABETH AND JOHN CLAGUE

MEMORIES OF THE SEVEN SEAS

Mrs. Clague was 'the family doctor of North Dummer', her husband an old sailor who painted canvasses for the neighbours and flags and animals on pine boards. The romance of 'Miss McDonale' (third panel, above) was an episode at Breezes boarding-house, Stoney Lake. The remaining pine-board paintings are in the author's cottage on Stoney Lake and in the Mount Julian Hotel, where they were made in exchange for drinks.

shorter than the other. Later he broke the same leg below the knee, but 'the patriarch of Boskung', as he was often called, reset it himself while pulling off his stiff Wellington boot.*

It was usual, in fact, for untrained but by no means unskilled settlers to act in the capacity of doctors, both in ordinary circumstances and emergencies. Drugs were administered, and bleeding, blistering, and surgery were carried out according to the ideas of the day, and often with success; but accidents in 'the Bush' were numerous, and rough-and-ready remedies— even amputations—took the lives of many who would have survived under other conditions.**

There were, too, itinerant peddlers of drugs and alleged remedies, often quacks and humbugs and largely from the United States. Some, however, were healers and herbalists, skilful practitioners so far as their knowledge went, and in many instances performing a public service; and in the same category may be placed midwives, who undoubtedly saved many women's lives during confinement. In the chief settlements were usually more or less qualified doctors. In his *Sketches of Upper Canada* John Howison describes the visit of a doctor when he was present, and his account is as valuable for its accurate vernacular as for its representation of the medical knowledge of the day:

In this house there was a woman afflicted with acute rheumatism. She had tried the mineral oil without receiving any benefit from it, and consequently had been induced to put herself into the hands of one of the doctors of the settlement. This gentleman happened to make his daily visit when I was present, and entered the room carrying a pair of large saddlebags in which phials and gallipots were heard clattering against each other in a most formidable manner. He did not deign to take off his hat but advanced to his patient and shook hands, saying:

'How d'ye do, my good lady, how d'ye do?'

*Many a settler injured himself in clearing land. I like the comment of the indomitable William Singer who cut himself badly several times, his injuries including the cutting off of two toes: 'Mr. Silcog sewed them on again: they seem to be getting on very well considering the time. You must not think I dislike the country on account of my misfortunes, for if I was to cut my right leg off I should not think of returning to Corsley again, for I could do much better here with one leg than in Corsley with two.' His letter home from Southwold Township is quoted in William Hickey's *Hints on Emigration to Upper Canada* (1832), p. 84.

**T. H. Ware noted in his diary one complaint that was related to the Canadian snows: 'The glare of the snow very often produces opthalima, but this disease may in a great measure be prevented by wearing green or blue colored glasses.'

'Oh, doctor!' cried the patient, 'I was wishing to see you very bad. I don't calculate upon ever getting *smart* again.'

'Hoity, toity!' returned the doctor, 'You look a thundering sight better than you did yesterday.'

'Better!' exclaimed the sick woman. 'No, doctor, I am no better —I'm going to die in your hands.'

'My dear good lady,' cried the doctor, 'I'll bet a pint of spirits I'll *raise* you in five days and make you so *spry* that you'll dance upon this floor.'

'Oh!' said the woman, 'If I had but the *root* doctor that used to attend our family at Connecticut; he was a dreadful *skeelful* man.'

(Here they were interrupted by the entrance of her husband, who was a clumsy, credulous-looking person.)

'Good morning to you, doctor,' said he. 'What's the word?'

'Nothing new or strange, sir,' returned the doctor.

'Well now, doctor,' continued the husband, 'how do you find that there woman? No better, I conclude? I guess as how it would be as well to let you understand plainly that if you can't do her never no good I wouldn't wish to be run into no expenses—pretty low times, doctor, money's out of the question. Now, sir, can *you* raise that there woman?'

'Yes, my good sir,' cried the doctor confidently. 'Yes, I can. I offered to bet a pint with her this moment, and I'll make it a quart if you please, my dear friend.'

'But, doctor, are you up to the *natur* of her ailment?' inquired the husband.

'Oh, perfectly,' said the other. 'Nothing more simple: it arises entirely from obstruction and constitutional idiosyncrasy and is seated under the muscular fascia. Some casual excitement has increased the action of the absorbent vessels so much that they have drawn the blood from the different parts of the body and occasioned the pain and debility that is now present.'

'Well now, doctor,' cried the husband, 'I swear you talk like a lawyer, and I begin to have hopes that you'll be pretty considerably apt to raise my woman.'

The doctor now opened his saddlebags and having set forth many small parcels and dirty phials upon the table began to compound several *recipes* for his patient, who, when she saw him employed in this way, put out her head between the curtains of the bed and cried, 'Doctor, don't forget to leave something for the debilitation.'

When he had finished he packed up his laboratory and ordered that something he had left should be infused in a pint of whisky and that a tablespoonful of the fluid should be taken three times a-day. 'Will that raise me *slick*?' said the woman; 'I guess I had as well take it four times a-day!'

As the doctor was mounting his horse I heard the farmer say: 'Doctor, don't be afeard about your pay; I'll see you satisfied: money. you know, 's out of the question, but I've plenty of good buckwheat.'

Except in the spring, when roads were generally impassable and the ice in the lakes had not yet broken up, doctors undertook arduous journeys to relieve suffering, even to distant and isolated settlements. At least one doctor advertised free medical advice, including vaccination, to the poor of his community three days a week.* But others were just the reverse and took all the traffic would bear:

The English medical gentleman near us [wrote the Reverend Isaac Fidler] was often sent for. . . . His charge for an ordinary journey was a dollar a mile. He was making a rapid fortune and becoming one of the wealthiest gentlemen in the neighbourhood. . . . A medical gentleman who emigrated last spring . . . assured me he had fallen into practice which would realize for him eleven hundred pounds a year.**

The first medical man in Norfolk County was Dr. Troyer, and his log-cabin erected soon after 1790 about a mile and half east of Port Rowan appears to have been the first erected in that district by a white settler.

He was insanely superstitious [wrote E. A. Owen in 1898], being a hopeless and confirmed believer in witchcraft. This peculiar mental malady caused him a world of trouble and made him ridiculously notorious. To prompt the recital of some witch story, all that is necessary is to mention the name of Dr. Troyer in the presence of any old settler in the county. . . . He looked upon certain of his neighbours as witches, one of the most dreaded being the widow of Captain Edward McMichael. . . . He kept a number of horse-shoes over the door of his house, and at the foot of his bed a huge trap was bolted to the floor where it was set every night to catch witches. . . .

Strange as it may appear, Dr. Troyer believed all this, yet, aside from witchcraft he was considered a sane man. He is described as wearing a long white beard; and it is said he lived to be ninety-nine

*His announcement, characteristic of pioneer advertising, appeared in the York *Upper Canada Gazette* of January 14, 1830, as follows:

DOCTOR REES

Has taken Rooms in the Brick Buildings, corner of Market-Square, King-Street.—He will vaccinate and give advice gratis to the poor, on Mondays, Wednesdays, and Saturdays, between the hours of 10 and 1 o'clock. York, 8th January, 1830.
. . . .

The office of a professional man in that day might be no more than his bedroom over a store, 'or a corner of the small shop, crowded with stoves and hardware, barrels of pork, bolts of cloth, and kegs of beer and spirits', as was John A. Macdonald's in Napanee when the future Canadian prime minister was a young lawyer of 18. (Donald Creighton, *The Young Politician*, p. 25.)

**The first doctor was near Thornhill, the second on a farm near Niagara Falls. £1100 would represent from $30,000 to $40,000 in terms of modern purchasing power.

SAND POINT, McNAB TOWNSHIP, IN 1874
The first settlement in the County of Renfrew.

From a lithograph

LONDON IN 1848

years old, and that just before his death he shot a hawk, offhand, from the peak of the barn roof.*

Those who lived near Dr. Troyer took pleasure in scaring and teasing him about his aberration, but they themselves were only a degree or two above him in their belief in superstitions. Many early settlers, and particularly women, were dominated by them in all sorts of ways, and the doing of many kinds of work was regulated by old wives' tales and other foolish notions.

For instance [writes Owen] they were averse to giving their daughters in marriage on a Friday, or the commencing of a new undertaking of any kind on that day. They made soap when the moon was in a proper phase, and to plant 'cowcumber' seed when the moon wasn't 'right' was considered an act of gross ignorance on the part of anyone who desired a good supply of 'pickles'. The unfortunate babe that was so thoughtless as to 'cut its teeth' when the 'sign wasn't right' was expected to have a 'harder time' of it and cause its mother an extra amount of trouble. Roots, barks, and herbs must be gathered in the 'right of the moon', and if 'my ole man' killed the hogs in the 'wrong of the moon' the 'dickens' would be to pay in the 'fryin' of the fat'.**

By the end of the century, when Owen wrote, the progress of education and enlightenment in the more progressive districts had driven such superstitions 'back into the regions of darkness whence they came', but many otherwise intelligent people have allowed them to persist in their thinking to the present day.

The distressing reality of toothache was the chief fact of dentistry as far as the pioneers were concerned. But many of the ignorant, as well as others who should have known better, were then superstitious enough to believe that toothache was just one more manifestation of God's wrath or the Devil's malice. In an issue of the *Christian Guardian* in 1830 appeared an Irishman's letter describing a cure for the toothache suggested by a Roman Catholic and consisting of a small piece of paper which the afflicted was not to open lest its virtue disappear.

---

*The first doctor in Guelph, named Welsh, was also an eccentric. He built himself a log house with an aperture six feet from the ground in place of a door. It is said that he had only two patients, and both died.

**Similar belief in superstitions was rife in a later period in Haliburton and other isolated regions, as well as in witches, ghosts, haunted houses, hidden gold, and similar fantasies. See the current excellent series 'In Quest of Yesterday', by Nila Reynolds of West Guilford in the *Haliburton County Echo*. A copy of the series is in the Archives of Ontario.

MILL OF KINTAIL, NEAR ALMONTE

Former home and studio of Major Tait McKenzie, prominent sculptor
and physical educationist, this early mill is now preserved as a historical
museum in his memory by Major and Mrs. J. F. Leys.

Courtesy Nigel Drayton   Reginald Drayton

INDIAN ENCAMPMENT, PINE TREE POINT, RICE LAKE, 1873

Royal Ontario Museum   Charles Fothergill

SMITH'S CREEK (PORT HOPE) IN 1819

But the faith of this particular sufferer did not outlast the pain, and on opening the letter he read as follows:

> *In the name of the Holy Trinity. Amen!*
> *As Peter sat on a marble stone,*
> *Jesus came to him alone,*
> *Saying, Peter, what dost make thee quake?*
> *Lord and Master, it is the tooth-ache.*
> *Rise up, Peter; thou shalt be hailed,*
> *And your trouble shall be quailed;*
> *Not thou alone, but every one*
> *That carries this, for thy sake*
> *Shall ne'er be troubled with the tooth-ache. Amen.*

Dentists were very few, though occasionally one advertised in the press of towns like York, Kingston, and Cobourg, and at times travelled to lesser settlements for a day or two. Filling of teeth and the provision of plates were not for the poor, however, as we find a set of artificial teeth priced at £30, equal in modern purchasing power to from $800 to $1000. One settler observed in a letter home that he had just made an ivory tooth for a pretty girl in his neighbourhood, but it is one of exceedingly few references to anything like remedial dentistry.

Pliers or 'tooth-drawers' were used to pull teeth when the occasion demanded, and dentists and doctors* were not alone in extracting them, for many a farmer built up a local reputation as a tooth-puller. It is obvious, however, that the use of tooth-brushes and the care of teeth are comparatively recent developments, and the great mass of the pioneer population had no choice and merely let their teeth decay. Many contemporary writers pointed out that Canadian girls had a piquant beauty, but one or two said that most of them lost it—with their teeth—before they were thirty years of age. This generalization is obviously too sweeping, for from all accounts the females of Upper Canada, as John Howison observed, exercised a strong power of fascination over men, and 'a traveller runs more risk of being *charmed* by *their* eyes than by those of the rattlesnake'.

*By far the best description of pioneer diseases and remedies is found in William Perkins Bull's *From Medicine Man to Medical Man* (1934). For an account for medical services, 1792 to 1797, submitted to the Jarvis family by Dr. Robert Kerr of Niagara see William Colgate, 'John Kerr', in the *Journal* of the Canadian Medical Association, 1951, pp. 542-6.

CHAPTER X

TRAVEL AND COMMUNICATION

NOTHING better illustrates the vast difference between the period of pioneering and our own times than a comparison of means of travel and communication.* In 1810, for example, a traveller required twelve days to reach York from Detroit by water—the only practicable method—waited eleven days for a ship sailing to Kingston, almost made Kingston after four days, only to be driven to Oswego by a storm. After eleven days' further delay and various dangers and hazards he finally reached his destination, Montreal, forty-nine days after he had left Detroit. Today the journey takes about fourteen hours by rail and a little more than an hour by air.

In 1792, when William Berczy's settlers arrived at the mouth of the Rouge River, the only feasible means to proceed to their location on the 6th concession of Markham Township was by the use of small boats, and it took them four weeks to travel the twenty-two miles. Solomon Orser, in 1831, needed twelve days to travel from Kingston to Reach Township, north of Perry's Corners (Whitby). With him were two steers and a dog, and in his lonely outpost of settlement, four miles north of Prince Albert, he was often, it is said, beset by bears and wolves.

The most roundabout route sometimes proved the speediest and most practicable. Immigrants in 1831 to Adelaide Township near London did not travel the 125 miles overland from York via Hamilton and Brantford, but sailed by schooner across Lake Ontario, proceeded through the Welland Canal and Lake Erie to Kettle Creek (at the mouth of which is now Port Stanley), and thence continued overland to Adelaide.

*There are many chapters in the author's *The Great Migration, Early Life in Upper Canada,* and the five volumes of *Pioneer Inns and Taverns* describing travel, transportation, and communication in detail. A short outline only can be given here.

Paul Kane

WILLIAM WELLER
King of stageline proprietors.

Courtesy O'Keefe Brewing Company

Jack Martin

RACING AGAINST TIME
This spirited drawing depicts Weller's record Toronto-Montreal
trip of 35 hours 40 minutes.

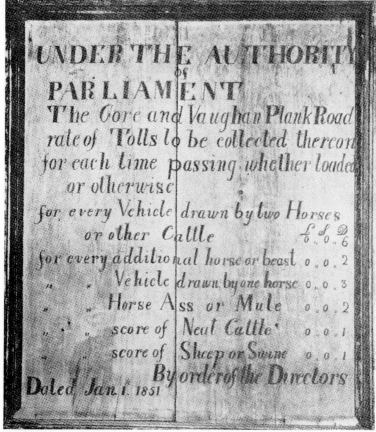

TOLLGATE SIGN, PEEL COUNTY, 1851

It hung at the junction of the 9th Line and the Indian Line.

LOG TROUGH

Still to be seen between Newcastle and Newtonville, this trough is of a type which long provided the washing facilities at rural taverns.

When the steamboat was introduced into Canada at Montreal in 1809 by John Molson, there followed, particularly in the 'twenties and 'thirties, similar vessels on the lakes and rivers of Upper Canada. Even backwoods lakes like Simcoe and Rice had their small steamboats, and it was not long before pleasure travelling in them became the first travel for enjoyment in Canada, excepting winter trips by carriole or sleigh which were always prominent. But early steamboats were an uncertain means of travel due to engine difficulties, and several disasters resulted from boilers blowing up.

Public Archives of Canada · A. Sherriff Scott

THE POSTMAN AT THE CHURCH DOOR

Journeys of hundreds of miles were possible overland in winter, for sleighs could go almost everywhere during a normal season. It was, in fact, highly important to have plenty of snow, for most of the trade of inland regions was carried on during the winter. Sleighs for such purposes were merely large wooden boxes on runners, but it was a characteristic and engaging sight to see them travelling through the country, their heavy loads hauled along at a good rate by horses with sleigh-bells attached to their harness. Many a traveller, however, got into serious difficulties when he lost his way in ten-foot snowdrifts, for it was not usual, even if possible, to follow the road closely.

At other seasons concession lines and lesser roads, perhaps

J. C. H. Forster

WALLACE ELLIS' GENERAL STORE, MOUNT PLEASANT

On August 3, 1876, Alexander Graham Bell received in this Ontario store a call from his uncle in Brantford. Isabella Ellis aided the inventor in 'the first great test' of the telephone.

Currier & Ives print

THE PROGRESS OF THE CENTURY

merely blazed trails amid stumps, had to be followed, and they were often impassable for wheeled vehicles of any type. Some early roads were first blazed by the co-operative efforts of settlers near them, and statute labour was the means by which others were opened and maintained, an uncertain and uneven method.* In some districts ox-sleds were all that could be used on bush roads, winter or summer. Curious makeshifts were sometimes seen, even in city streets.

I one day saw in the streets of Toronto [writes James Beaven] a very primitive vehicle indeed. It was a cart, with small wheels cut solid from the trunk of some large tree, with a hole through the centre for the axle. The bed of the cart was of small trees laid side by side; the sides and ends were of still smaller trees and stakes set upright at certain distances, and it was drawn by a yoke of oxen.

Important roads might be blocked by clergy reserves or other unoccupied grants. In newly-settled regions bridges were not built at first, fords being used instead; and elsewhere spring floods often washed out the bridges along a river's entire length. Five or six miles per day was all the progress that could be expected on the worst roads, and thirty or forty on the best. At times even the main highways were so bad that the mail had to be carried on horseback, but in general the stages were able to operate on these roads, though a 125-mile trip might take two or three days even under the best conditions.

Just before the coming of railways the plank road was extensively developed in the province, providing for a year or two a remarkably smooth surface. The heyday of this improvement in transport was the 'forties and 'fifties, and farmers living near by enjoyed an increased prosperity. Not only was their land's value enhanced but the new road was an equalizer of seasons, for travel upon it was no longer predominantly in winter. Enthusiasm was unbounded at first. Fair prices for farm produce were now readily available at the nearest market, and a farmer could carry—so he was told—three times his former load in half the time. The wear and tear on horses and wagons was now

---

*Before the inauguration of municipal councils following Lord Durham's *Report* (1839) there was a type of local self-government. On the first Monday in January the inhabitants of a township met in the Town Meeting and elected from among themselves a town clerk, two assessors, a collector, two townwards (church wardens), a poundkeeper, and as many pathmasters as they deemed necessary. The pathmasters called out the settlers and supervised their statute labour on roads and bridges, the amount of which depended upon the assessed value of their property. The Town Meeting could pass such laws and regulations for the locality as did not clash with legislative enactments.

Toronto Public Library   T. H. Ware

HODGE'S HOTEL, ORO, 1844

Courtesy Phyllis Denne

THE WHISTLE-WING, 1878
Popular steamboat on Rice Lake and the Trent.

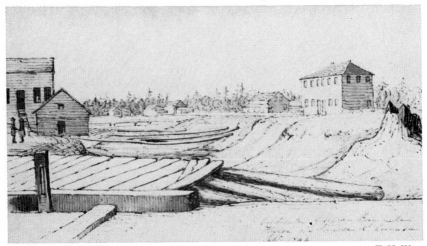

T. H. Ware

COLDWATER, GEORGIAN BAY, 1844

CHEMONG FLOATING BRIDGE, 1892
Erected in 1854, this famous bridge remained until recent years.

infinitesimal, horseshoes lasted twice as long—even cleaning and rubbing down the horse was no chore at all! Indeed the farmer could drive to town in wet weather when little can be done on the farm. But after a few Canadian frosts heaved the planks about, repairs were essential but neglected, replacement was costly, and the plank road retreated into historical perspective as a temporary expedient whose success failed to justify the high hopes of its projectors.

Notable journeys were sometimes made in summer as in winter, and without benefit of plank roads. One traveller describes how a pair of 'Indian ponies' from the vicinity of Brantford hauled him and a driver in a light wagon at the rate of 60 miles a day for ten days in succession, and 'at the end of the journey were all ready to set out on the same trip again'.

Communication by post was slow and expensive. At first only the chief settlements along the front had any postal service, and as late as 1824 some counties had but one office. Enterprising settlers sometimes made arrangements like those effected in Reach Township in 1827, under which letter-carrying commenced:

The system originated with Mr. Donald Cameron, a settler in Thorah, who proposed to the settlers who lived on the line that unless the Postmaster General objected to it, a person might carry letters between the front and the back townships and obtain adequate pay for his trouble. The idea was endorsed by the settlers, and the Postmaster General gave his consent. Kenneth Campbell commenced his travels, walking to and from the front once a fortnight,* and besides a fixed amount secured by subscription he received a small payment for the letters or papers which he bore to the settlers.

Long delays, lost mail, and high cost caused innumerable complaints in most districts, but not much improvement resulted while the service was under British control. In 1851 the Canadian Government took charge of postal services and issued the first stamps. While sailing-ships carried the Atlantic mail it usually took four months to send a letter and receive a reply

*Innumerable accounts of long walks and arduous boat trips are found in early records. In October 1862 Thomas Mason travelled from Boskung Lake, Stanhope Township, to Fenelon Falls for winter supplies, and returned with 900 pounds of flour. He covered 63 miles by water and made 18 portages— one above Minden being nearly three miles. Later he brought a heavy sideboard for his wife over the same route. He lived past his 103rd birthday. Watson Kirkconnell visited him in 1922 and wrote a good account of his reminiscences of an adventurous life in various parts of the world. See 'The Patriarch of Boskung', *Minden Echo*, July 21, 1922. Nila Reynolds' series currently in the *Haliburton County Echo* greatly expands our knowledge of the Masons and of the history of Haliburton in general.

HOTEL COVER, 1869

No other picture of this Toronto hotel is known to exist.

PIONEER POST OFFICE

The small building, which still stands, was Port Hope's original post office.

**GORE BAY MAIL STAGE AND THE OCEAN HOUSE
MANITOULIN ISLAND**

The trip to the mainland was thirty miles over the ice.

from Britain, but steam-and-sail ships had greatly reduced the time by 1840, and in 1853 the first Canadian ocean mail service was inaugurated. In the late 'forties the electric telegraph was in operation in the Canadas, and in the 'sixties the Atlantic cable; but not until 1908 was rural mail delivery commenced.

Perhaps there is no better expression of the contrast between old and new in travel conditions than these verses by Percy H. Punshon of Oshawa:

> *When I picture the cart that the Patriarchs used,*
> *That oxen drew patiently day after day,*
> *It is not surprising that Joseph refused*
> *To go for his brethren and bring them away.*
> *The wheels they were hewn from the trunk of a tree,*
> *The creeking I cannot describe with a pen,*
> *And, picturing this, you will readily see*
> *How thankful I am that I didn't live then.*
>
> *When I think of the coaches of days long ago*
> *The gentry made use of with joy and delight,*
> *That often were stuck in the mud and the snow,*
> *And held up by highwaymen night after night;*
> *When I think of their springless condition, to me*
> *A great satisfaction is mine once again,*
> *And, joining with me, you will readily see*
> *How thankful I am that I didn't live then.*
>
> *When I think of the motor-car silent and swift,*
> *In the dark sky of transport, so long overcast,*
> *I see in my vision a limitless rift*
> *That heralds the dawn of the best thing at last.*
> *There is comfort and speed in the automobile*
> *That none can deny and no one gainsay:*
> *Then I know that with me you will readily feel*
> *How thankful I am that I'm living today.*

CHAPTER XI

INNS AND TAVERNS

THE inn, almost as much as the mill, was the nucleus of settlement in Upper Canada. Public meetings and gatherings of every type—church and school, land boards, auction sales, menageries, circuses, concerts, dramatics—all these centred around the tavern. As many travellers pointed out, they were long the only places of assembly and entertainment.

Liquor-drinking to excess was undoubtedly the most widespread of pioneer vices. Travellers attributed it to cheap whiskey, unremitting toil, and a general lack of education to enjoy the higher things of life. The terms 'inn' and 'tavern' were largely synonymous in the pioneer period, but a 'house of entertainment' was technically an inn without a tavern license—that is, it was not supposed to dispense liquor. Besides inns and taverns there were grog-shops and small grocery stores which sold liquor—or gave it away.

The pail of whiskey with the tin attached [writes the Reverend F. G. Weir in *Scugog and Its Environs*] was to be found at the back of most stores, and the customer was free to help himself.* In the numerous grog-shops there was no lack of drink at a penny a glass or five cents a grunt, a grunt being as much as one could swallow in one breath. . . . Many a man drank himself off his farm in those days, and there were unprincipled barkeepers who found pleasure in seeing the debts of certain customers pile up, and in anticipating the day when they should be enriched by the possession of another good farm.

There was a Yankee 'lingo' relative to drinking, as elsewhere, and it astonished the more cultured visitors. 'Will you *liquor?*' or 'Will you have a *horn?*' meant 'Will you have a drink?' And if you did not understand it you received a rebuke like this:

*Pails or kegs of whiskey were often found in the homes of the day, and were as commonly used by the family and visitors as a pail of well water or a jug of milk were later.

Tremaine Map of Peel

EMERSON TAYLOR'S TAVERN, SPRINGFIELD, 1859
The Toronto-Hamilton Half-Way House, Dundas Street.

Courtesy Mrs. E. Wilkins,
a granddaughter

EMERSON TAYLOR

Prominent hotelkeeper, magistrate,
and businessman of Springfield-on-
the-Credit (now Erindale) who was
in the forefront of every broad-
minded and progressive activity.

OBITUARY CARD OF EMERSON TAYLOR

'Well now, if here ain't a caution it's a pity! Here's an English-man as don't know his own language!' Patrick Shirreff, in driving from Peterborough to Cobourg, remarked that two-thirds of the people he met were tipsy. 'This', he said, 'was a painful sight, which the heat of the weather did not soften or justify.'

John Howison found that the French taverns near the Detroit River and Lake St. Clair were best in winter, for they had a small stove in each room. But he visited La Vallée's on Lake St. Clair the day before the quarter sessions opened at Sand-wich, and the public room was crowded with people delayed by a heavy snowstorm. So offensive was the all-night 'drinking, talking, smoking, swearing, and spitting promiscuously' that his otherwise pleasant visit was spoiled. In the morning there was the 'shocking spectacle' of bottles, glasses, benches, and drunks all over the floor, so he advised his readers that

whoever wishes to attain a just conception of the enormity which the human character assumes when unchecked by restraint, un-refined by education, and unmodelled by dependence should spend an hour in the bar-room of some low tavern in Upper Canada when a party of common farmers are drinking together.

Taverns were many and poor rather than few and well-appointed, for hard travel conditions made frequent stops necessary. On the average there was one every six or seven miles, but often one a mile on the main highways and many more in the towns. In winter particularly, many farmers en route to market towns found whiskey warming and invigorating and got into the habit of patronising most of the drinking-places along their route; and the farmer's wife, meanwhile, was usually left in the cold holding the horses. Though hard drinking made the business lucrative, most British travellers found taverns 'low' and 'vulgar', 'dirty' and 'incommodious'. The typical tavern-keeper was an 'American', which might mean a man who haled from the United States, a citizen of Loyalist descent, or merely a Canadian by birth. In any event mine host was free-and-easy, inquisitive, and independent—all of which were obnoxious to the reticent British. It is not generally realized nowadays that democracy and all suggestions of political or social equality were repulsive and highly resented in Upper Canada by the ruling clique and 'superior' people generally, whether residents or visitors. Lieutenant E. T. Coke, the highly class-conscious author of *A Subaltern's Furlough* (1833), was scandalized when he had to sit at table in the Clifton Hotel, Niagara Falls, with two female servants. 'I felt my English blood almost boil in my veins', he wrote; for while assuming that he might experience such indignities in the United States, he 'never expected to have found the levelling system introduced into the British provinces to such an extent'.

But such opinions met with no acceptance from innkeepers, and as they had that ear for news and gossip usual under conditions of comparative isolation, they were still more unpopular with the reserved and class-conscious British. Perhaps the Reverend William Bell's experience at a 'paltry tavern' above Brockville indicates most effectively the type of thing that travellers found so objectionable:

On entering the house I found the landlady seated at table with three or four savage-looking fellows who appeared to be farm servants. They had no clothing on except woollen shirts and trowsers. On inquiring if I could be furnished with breakfast, the mistress replied with a very insolent tone and air, 'Yes, I guess so, if you will walk into the other room and wait till I have finished my own.' I had forgot the instructions I had received. Had I seated myself at table *sans cérémonie* with the good lady and her servants, all would have been well. The tavern-keepers in Canada are mostly from the United States, and they seldom fail to resent the least appearance of superiority shown by travellers. Had I known of another tavern on the road I would have proceeded: but as there was no other for many miles I concluded it was best to walk into the log cabin and rest myself till my saucy mistress had leisure to attend to me. After a delay of half an hour breakfast made its appearance, consisting of rye-bread, rancid butter, a stinking mutton chop, and tea sweetened with maple sugar. For this repast I was charged two shillings, which was sixpence more than the usual charge.

'An English Farmer', the author of *A Few Plain Directions for Persons Intending to Proceed as Settlers to His Majesty's Province of Upper Canada,* wrote similarly in 1820. The innkeepers of Upper Canada, he found, were too

independent in their principles to pay the least attention to the comfort or convenience of their guests. They do not behave even with common civility. An Englishman who expects to find that ready compliance with his wishes and wants to which he has been accustomed in England will be greatly disappointed. There are no *bells*, as there are no *servants*, at the inns in this country. The traveller finds himself solitary, unnoticed, and left to supply his own wants. If he is loud, or peremptory, or remonstrative he is treated in return with insolence or contempt. The chief aim of the host is to get the stranger's money; generosity and benevolence are not ingredients in his composition.

Bigsby, *The Shoe and Canoe*   John Bigsby

ANDREWS' TAVERN, ABOVE BROCKVILLE, 1850

Frame structures, or of logs in the backwoods, were the usual inns, and their 'shabbiness' and 'mean and disreputable' appearance are frequently commented upon by travellers. In the season of immigration it was often impossible to obtain a bed, much less a private room, and to sleep with others or on the floor was a matter of course. In a tavern at Bobcajewonunk (Bobcaygeon) during a house-raising in the vicinity, 'twenty-three human souls, including three married couples and two unmarried females, found sleeping room'. The dimensions of the building were twelve feet by twenty-two, so it was without doubt 'unusually full', as John Langton put it. The landlord of another backwoods tavern, on being asked for accommodation for some new arrivals including a woman, replied:

Very sorry, gentlemen, very sorry indeed, but the house is chuck full; haven't got a hole to put a cat in, couldn't give you a bed if you'd all lie in one and give me the weight of it in dollars. It's a bad fix, that's a fact; but you see just how it is; the beds are all taken—haven't got even half a one to offer you, for there are two or three in each; then there's this room, but the women and children who have no beds sleep here on the floor; then there's the bar-room, but a lot of choppers have got that and won't give it up to no man; and then there's the kitchen to be sure, but that's pretty full as it be with the men folks, and tho' it's considerable of a size, yet there ain't overly much room even there. But for all that it won't do for the

Public Archives of Canada

ROBINSON LYON'S EXCHANGE HOTEL, BYTOWN, 1846

In fancy I away have stepped
From where his school James Elder kept,
In that old house remembered well,
After, as Joseph Kirk's Hotel,
Ere it was haunted by a sound
Which shed such melody around,
Sweet almost as the songs of Zion,
From violin of Robinson Lyon,
Who drew such music from its strings—
Scotch reels, strathspeys, and highland flings
And Irish jigs in variation,
As made one feel that 'all creation'
Could scarcely match his wizard spell—
'Twas he that played the fiddle well!

—William Pittman Lett.

lady to camp out, that's a fact. I guess my old woman must turn out and do the best she can 'long with some of the other women, and the lady can have her bed and I'll sleep in the bar.

And the supper served in such out-of-the-way inns was typical backwoods fare,

not venison from the forest, gentle reader, nor wild fowl from the lake or from the woods—but of salt pork fried, hot potatoes, doughnuts made of strips of dough twisted into cork-screw forms

123

and fried in fat, and tea—concerning the native country of which very reasonable doubts might have been entertained.*

Some taverns in 'the Bush' had beds of boughs of trees 'with a netting of bark connecting the frame work'. Other furniture might be just as crude, or altogether missing. A chair and 'an apology for a washstand' were found in one by Catharine Traill, but equipment for washing or personal convenience was lacking as often as not. Fleas and other vermin were common enough, and it was thought best not to retire until very late and well tired out so that their attacks might be less noticed! The lack of servants in inns was a grave disability to many who found it hard or considered it degrading to wait upon themselves. It was often noticed that the female part of the innkeeper's family and employees kept out of sight, and in place of a cringing servility that was obviously desired by some travellers, there was 'offensive coldness'.

But Thomas Fowler found the accommodations and food very good along 'the front'. The meals at Carpenter's Inn, Cobourg, were especially pleasing:

In the course of a few days after I commenced boarding at Cobourg new potatoes, cucumbers, and cherries were presented at table every day. Breakfast was at half-past seven, dinner at one, and supper at seven in the evening. Breakfast consisted of tea, coffee, beefstakes, cold meat, potatoes, bread, butter, and eggs. At dinner, there was sometimes soup for a change, always a roast of either beef or mutton, sometimes fowls, always cold meat, and frequently ham besides. Some excellent vegetables usually gave us their presence, such as cabbage, cucumbers, potatoes, and peas, with either pies, tarts, or puddings to finish off with. There were spirits and wine at dinner every day, and each guest could help himself according to his desire. Supper consisted of tea, various kinds of cold meat, fruit pies or apple sauce, butter, generally four kinds of bread, and frequently currants or cherries in sweet sauce. This is considered the head inn, but the other two are allowed to be pretty much the same. The regular charge for board and lodging is twelve shillings and sixpence per week.

Conduct at meals usually insulted the English sense of decorum. In towns a horn or bell was the signal for rush and bustle, table manners were conspicuous by their absence, and ten or fifteen minutes was devoted almost exclusively to *feeding*. Such conversation as there was occurred in the bar afterwards,

*John Mactaggart, without whose *Three Years in Canada* (1829) we would be much the poorer, is the reporter of the sleeping and eating conditions of this tavern, which was in the Bytown (Ottawa) district.

Willis, *Canadian Scenery*   W. H. Bartlett

HOLT'S HOTEL, AYLMER, LOWER CANADA, 1840
'A superior description of inn, which surprised us in so wild
a country.'—Charles Daubeny, *Journal of a Tour.*

where the inevitable drink and cigar finished the business. The
food, as Fowler pointed out, was of considerable variety, especially in desserts and trimmings; but in 'the Bush' the tea might
be replaced by a drink compounded of hemlock, hickory, and
'nauseous vegetables'. A quarter dollar was the usual price for
a bed or any one of the three meals.

Rowdyism and brawling, apparently inevitable accompaniments of alcohol in excess, were characteristic of pioneer drinking-places. John Howison and many others blamed it all on
democracy and the spirit of equality. J. S. Buckingham, who
visited Upper Canada in the 'thirties, in referring to fights gives
an example of the mixing of liquor and justice which, though
presumably rare in its completeness, fits superbly into the veri-
ties of backwoods life:

In a back township [he says] a magistrate who kept a tavern sold
liquor to people till they got drunk and fought in his house. He then
issued a warrant, apprehended them, and tried them on the spot;
and besides fining them, made them treat each other to make up
the quarrel.*

Walter Johnstone's account of a court of justice he saw in
1820 in a tavern in Prince Edward Island might readily have

*John Mactaggart wrote in 1829: 'Law without justice prevails greatly all
over the country, and the villages swarm with lawyers. . . . They fill their
petty prisons with debtors, and scores are there incarcerated for sums not
exceeding a dollar.'

been duplicated in Upper Canada. Here is the description from his *Travels*:

I came to a small public-house, what they call a *tavern*. It was then the only house all the way between the settlements in question [i.e., Malpeque and Tryon]. Finding a great number of horses, with saddles and bridles, fastened to the fence at the road-side, and a great crowd of people about the house, I turned in, anxious to see what was going on. The house was small, consisting only of one apartment. . . .

When I had got near to the centre of the apartment I saw some drinking rum, others considerably affected with what they had drunk. On the opposite side there were three magistrates seated upon a plank, holding a court of law. The day being warm and the house crowded, some of them were sitting without their coat.

The magistrates being of nearly the same rank in life with those who were appearing before them, very little respect was paid to their authority or their orders. I observed one of the defenders, who was also without the coat, often clench his fist behind him, ready to give the prosecutor a blow when he could not carry his point with milder arguments; and every moment I looked for this method of overcoming his antagonist being resorted to. . . .

They had a number of more causes to decide, and after finding a careful hand to forward my letters to Malpeque I left this clamorous court of law. After I left the house I reflected upon the imprudence of holding a court of law where drinking rum was going on all the time; and one of the magistrates acknowledged to me afterwards that it was very improper to hold a court where there was no jail to commit offenders to, in order to overawe ignorant passionate people who thought their own will should in all cases be the law. He also told me this poor tavern-keeper had not a Bible in his house, and that they had to swear the people upon the book of common prayer.

The better inns had a ballroom upstairs—in fact it contributed greatly to prestige. The room might become a dormitory later in the night, particularly if some of the attendants at the frolic or carousal kept it up too late to go home until morning; and if so, boys and girls would not be thought immoral if they slept together on the floor. Light sleepers elsewhere in the house, meanwhile, were kept awake until sheer exhaustion relieved their misery for an hour or so.*

Members of the Sons of Temperance, and others of like mind, usually supported 'temperance hotels' which attempted, not

---

*We are not yet civilized in this respect, for the same nuisance is frequently found in our modern hotels, and especially in the largest and most expensive. An increasing number of people, it would seem, rent hotel rooms not for sleeping but for carousal and dissipation.

National Gallery of Canada   James Pattison Cockburn

BATH, 1830

ABNER CHERRY AND HIS INN

This picture appeared on the occasion of his receiving his 50th annual
licence for his tavern at the southeast corner of Dufferin Street and Steele's
Avenue. Early in the present century, when this picture was taken, the
locality was ten miles from Toronto.

Sigmund Samuel Canadiana Gallery   James Pattison Cockburn

JOSEPH KEELER'S TAVERN, CRAMAHE (COLBORNE)

'Mr. Keeler treated us kindly, free gratis.'—Phoebe Roberts' *Diary of a
Quaker Missionary Journey to Upper Canada* (1821).

too successfully, to carry on the business without the lucrative bar-room. Not only were they much quieter, but in frequenting them the traveller, as one put it, 'is sure of society of one stamp, so that the conversation he may enter into will be of a correct and very likely of an improving character'. Sometimes the landlord of the house even led in religious services.

In spite of the defects of the majority, many Upper Canadian inns were well-appointed, capably run, and served satisfactorily a great variety of purposes. Mrs. Aldgeo's Tavern, along the Thames River near the present Caradoc, was found by Patrick Shirreff comfortable and excellently managed by its Irish proprietor. Adam Fergusson stayed at Campbell's Tavern, Matilda Township, which he calls 'a snug, comfortable inn, . . . one of the best-kept taverns in Canada'. And there was Abner Cherry and his wife, for over half a century tavern licensees to the northwest of Toronto, who always closed their bar until the horses were fed and watered.

There were at one time sixty-three taverns to supply the needs of travellers on Yonge Street between Toronto and Barrie, and the Half-Way House, where horses were changed on the Toronto-Holland Landing stage route, was among the best known. Dr. Scadding mentions Finch's Inn, north of Willowdale, and Crew's, seven miles farther, as great hostelries 'of high repute about 1836'. Emerson Taylor's Tavern at Credit or Springfield (later Erindale) was similarly the excellent half-

John Ross Robertson Collection   C. H. J. Snider

FIVE-HORSE BOAT ON TORONTO BAY

way house on the Dundas Street route between Toronto and Hamilton.

Many farmers who came to Toronto with produce were familiar with taverns near St. Lawrence Market. One of the more intriguing of the capital's hotels was Michael O'Connor's 'Retreat on the Peninsula'.* The proprietor, a veteran of Sir John Moore's famous Spanish Dunkirk of the Napoleonic wars, inserted in the press of 1833 this neat announcement of his hotel and his horseboat to carry visitors to it, the *Sir John of the Peninsula*:

Michael O'Connor, formerly Steward of the Steam Packet *Canada*, begs leave respectfully to announce to the Inhabitants of York, and to strangers visiting the capital of Upper Canada, that he has opened a Hotel on the Peninsula, opposite the town; where he will be ready to accommodate Sportsmen, Parties of Pleasure, and individuals who may wish to inhale the Lake breeze, with every kind of refreshments. His Wines and Liquors are particularly selected and will be found equal, if not superior, to any in the country. He trusts that from long experience and strict attention to business to merit a share of public favour, and that the Retreat on the Peninsula will be patronized especially by those whose recollection of the Spanish Peninsula will ever be dear to their memory, as recorded in the pages of British History.

*Until a storm broke through at its eastern end in 1858 Toronto Island was a peninsula. For a detailed account of the inns and taverns of the province's capital the reader is referred to the author's *Toronto: from Trading-Post to Great City,* pp. 295-328, and to *Pioneer Inns and Taverns,* Volume 1.

CHAPTER XII

THE PIONEER WOMAN

CRUDENESS and monotony characterised women's life in the period of pioneering even more than the men's activities. The conventions of the times prevented women from participating in many outdoor sports and activities that from time to time were enjoyed by the men, and they were consequently much more closely confined to the house and farmyard. Outside of marriage and homemaking, domestic service and dressmaking were almost the only occupations open to women; and where —as in school-teaching in the towns—they entered into competition with men, they were (as they often are today) exploited by being paid a wage which was usually one-half that given to men for the same—if not, considering the age and needs of the children, better—work.

Yet if she were not overburdened—as most were—with a large brood of small children in a day when any type of 'family planning' was frowned upon,* the pioneer woman had variety within the limited compass of the farm. She could—speaking ideally—tend the garden, milk cows, care for poultry and bees, and manage the young of the stock. Sometimes she was a skilful horse-woman, an expert maker of maple sugar, soap, and candles, and skilled in the innumerable other domestic duties that characterised early farm life.

Market-day was often a highlight of her life, for it enabled a variation in scene, a little shopping, a sight of what was new and different in the nearest town. But preparations were often

*Women's organizations might benefit from a study of woman's position in other times, when male domination and very restricted activities were the rule. Particularly would they profit by a knowledge of the lives and struggles of those who were leaders in emancipation—Emily and Augusta Stowe in Ontario, and internationally, women like Emmeline and Sylvia Pankhurst, Frances Willard, Amelia Bloomer, Jane Addams, Millicent Fawcett, Mary Wollstonecraft, Margaret Sanger, and Marie Stopes.

long and arduous, and perhaps a start had to be made at two in the morning; and the vicious drinking habits of the time, combined with the numerous taverns where the husband's appetite could be gratified, might well render the wife abject and pitiful long before the close of the day.

John Ross Robertson Collection   C. H. J. Snider

OLD TORONTO MARKET AND WELL

In his *Narrative of a Voyage* (1846) James Taylor gives a lively account of the colourful Toronto market at Christmastime*:

The old market square is small and incommodious; females who attend this market to dispose of their butter, eggs, fowls, &c., as well as vendors of other commodities, are fully exposed to the inclemency of the weather. . . . I have frequently noticed the market so crowded that some people bringing produce from the country into the town for sale were obliged to dispose of it out of the market, thereby incurring a loss to themselves and depriving the city of that portion of its revenue.

Meat shambles here will not bear comparison with those in England. . . . Christmas, 1844, my attention was directed to the shambles, it being customary at this season, same as in England, for the butchers to ornament their meat with evergreens, flowers, &c. The show of fat meat, both beef and mutton, was equal to any I have seen in England on this occasion. The peculiar style in which the Canadians adorn their meat at Christmas appears to excite great attention from the numerous spectators who are drawn to the market through curiosity.

*There is a notable lack of reference to both Christmas and New Year's in pioneer records and contemporary travel books, for the commercialization of these days was still far off. Feasting and drinking, wherever they occurred, have gone almost unmentioned. An exception is the Abbott diary, December 25, 1819 (see Appendix A, Volume II, p. 311) where the dinner is described.

The carcasses of the cattle are also decorated with silken flowers arranged in a variety of ingenious devices, some of the dead sheep being ornamented with stag's horns and gilded heads, with part of their flesh tattooed in a very singular manner. The hogs are also dressed out in a similar style. Nor is the spirited competition confined to the butchers alone. The dealers in vegetables also exhibit their productions in Market-square, elevated on the summit of long poles. Those articles of their produce are exhibited a few days to please the eye, but are not allowed to be cut up for sale until the day before Christmas, when parties are permitted to purchase for the gratification of their appetites.

Taylor found, too, that farm women were largely independent when it came to markets and marketing, and were colourful, efficient, and shrewd as well:

Farmers' wives and daughters, of respectable appearance, frequently enter the market with their neat four-wheeler and pair, loaded with vegetables which they sometimes dispose of by giving friendly calls as they enter the city. Females generally attend to this branch of agricultural produce; indeed it would be considered a remarkable occurrence if a farmer was seen driving his team to market unaccompanied by a female companion, who, in all weathers, may be found at her post, delivering her commodities whilst her master is taking his potations of whiskey.

Females of tender years are in the habit of driving alone, from considerable distances, to the markets with various articles to dispose of, and dispatch their business with very becoming sedateness and punctuality; indeed, they manifest a shrewdness and sagacity for their years which is truly astonishing: the loveliest of their sex, who appear in splendid attire and profusely veiled, will descend from their market carriages on the road, and throw off the horse's reins at watering places, and occasionally pump water and perform all necessary avocations, then re-mount their carriage with great agility and drive off, pair in hand, with all the courage and skill of a whip of the first masculine celebrity. Canadian farmers, however rich, always bring up their daughters to perform all kinds of domestic employment. . . . Some of the elder female stagers are provided with a travelling whip of an enormous length, called a cow-hide, which when brandished over the heads of the cattle by the hands of a lady produces rather a striking effect.

The equipment of the earlier farm home was primitive, and space restricted. Everything was in evidence, for there were at first no pantries, cupboards, or kitchen cabinets. Bake-kettles, pot-hooks, and frying-pans—tongs, ladles, pounders, sausage machines, rolling-pins, and pewterware, with all sorts of fireplace equipment for cooking—these were scattered in profusion, and perhaps not too orderly in arrangement. Cooking over

Russell Taber

WASH-DAY

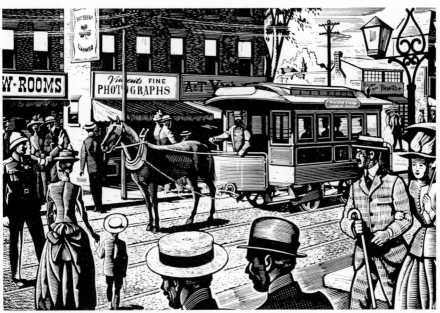

Russell Taber

THE STREET CAR

an open fireplace in a log house was an art in itself, while shanty baking was restricted to cakes made in bake-kettle and frying-pan. Among the more popular of later varieties were potato cakes, plum cakes, seed cakes, and loaf-cakes.

Cleanliness was not always an easy achievement. The broom was usually of cedar or hemlock branches tied tightly to a handle and trimmed off with an axe, but there were also brooms and brushes of finely splintered green hickory, blue beech, or birch, the unsplintered end serving as handle; and later the homemade corn broom came into use. Buckets and dash-churns of wood were common, and even a wooden clothes-wringer might be found; though the laundry—or at least the rinsing place—was often merely a deep quiet spot along the nearest creek. The white wash that was hung out to dry was not achieved without hard work. White things were boiled in a copper boiler, and rain water, soft soap, wooden tubs, hand wringer, and one's own arms did the rest. While the mother worked, her baby was probably sucking a bit of maple sugar tied up in a rag. Flat-irons heated on the stove provided the finishing touches to the wash.

Milking cows in cold weather in the miserable straw-stack shelters that were long considered sufficient was not a pleasant occupation; and the storing of milk and butter in cellar or root-house was neither sanitary nor otherwise satisfactory. Earthen crocks, wooden tubs and firkins, wooden trays with peg-holes to let off the milk, and clumsy wooden cheese-presses formed the equipment. The milk, still warm from the cows, was placed in these wooden containers and left to cool. Later, when milk cans were available, they were immersed in cold water from spring or well. When the cream had risen to the top the milk was drained from the bottom; and the process was a little more accurate through the presence of a narrow glass window, for when the cream line came in sight the tap could be turned off.

In many early settlements, not only in Loyalist days but much later, no mills were available near by to grind grain, so to avoid a long journey a crude method of softening whole grain was followed. First the wheat or corn was parboiled in weak lye, then dried before the fire; and when the heat burst the skin the grain was tied up in a bag and beaten until it was free of the bran and could be separated and sifted. Then it was boiled for hours until soft, and eaten as *mush* with milk. Heads of unripe grain were sometimes pulled off, crushed in the hand, and

GRIST MILL, OTTERVILLE
Built in 1845 by Edward Bullock, South Norwich.

eaten; and some pioneers even chewed corn to render it edible for their children.

Since so much depended upon one's own industry, there was an almost universal contempt for any settlers—whether men or women—whose wealth enabled them to avoid work. Toil and efficiency were respected, and most people were doggedly determined to become self-sufficient and independent. Yet, though they themselves had risen by their own efforts, it is characteristic that the pioneers worked and planned for a better opportunity for their children.

But isolation, especially through the long winter, was particularly hard for women to bear. Anna Jameson, prominent English feminist of her day, had one woman's loneliness explained to her by the husband:

'But,' said I, 'surely wherever you are is her *home*, and she ought to be happy where she sees you getting on better, enjoying more of comfort and independence than you could have hoped to obtain in the old country.'

'Well, yes,' said he hesitatingly, 'and I can't say but that my wife is a good woman; I've no particular fault to find with her; and it is very natural she should mope, for she has no friend or acquaintance, you see, and she doesn't take to the people and the ways here; and at home she had her mother and her sister to talk to; they lived with us, you see. Then I am out all day long looking after my business, and she feels quite lonely like, and she's a-crying when I come back—and I am sure I don't know what to do.'

And Mrs. Jameson goes on to say that she had not met one woman recently settled who considered herself happy: 'I *heard* on one, and doubtless there are others, but they are exceptions to the general rule.'* But if women survived the early years in 'the Bush' they usually came to love Canada with an enduring loyalty.

Toronto Public Library   T. H. Ware

CAPTAIN ST. JOHN'S RESIDENCE, ORILLIA, 1844

My love for the country [said Susanna Moodie in later life] has steadily increased from year to year, and my attachment to Canada is now so strong that I cannot imagine any inducement short of absolute necessity which could induce me to leave the country where, as wife and mother, some of the happiest years of my life have been spent.

As a means to combat monotony and melancholy Mrs. Traill suggested hobbies like the identification of Canadian wild flowers, of which she was so fond.** But both she and Anna

*Charles Daubeny describes in his *Journal of a Tour* (1843) a cultured Englishman's wilderness home in Oro Township where there was no visiting because of the lack of paths sufficiently trodden for a female to venture upon; and he visited another clearing near Lake Simcoe where, in three rooms, a half-pay officer, his insane wife, and ten children were living. Such people, said Daubeny, came to Canada in the hope of being 'important personages' instead of 'sinking to an inferior grade at home'; but much preferable for them would be to let the 'rough farmer or regular backwoodsman' clear the land, whereupon they might purchase it and have a much better chance of success. Women died from no other cause than loneliness and melancholy resulting from isolation and intense hardship. 'I am getting melancholy, and there is a melancholy peculiar to Canada', wrote John Mactaggart; and to counteract it, 'the Canadians have their boat-songs and their convivial meetings, . . . their *bells* upon horses to cheer along the caravan of sleighs'.

**Many men were equally impressed by the beauties of nature but had less time to gratify their tastes. There is no Ontario township named Trillium after our provincial emblem, but Richard Birdsall, first surveyor of Asphodel Township, Peterborough County, admired the profusion of trilliums and named the township Asphodel after the flower nearest in appearance in his English experience—the bog asphodel.

TRILLIUMS

At the author's home in Toronto.

Jameson were obviously thinking of the more well-to-do leisure-class women, and pre-supposing cultural interests that were unusual; while the mass of women, who lacked both their leisure and initial educational opportunities, were so busy that they had no time to mope and were usually much more content in Canada, where it certainly could be said that in general they were much better off than they could ever have hoped to be in Britain.

The local history of Ontario is full of heroic incidents, some of which are now almost legendary and not always free from exaggeration and amplification in re-telling. We know, however, that many a woman was the family doctor of outlying settlements. We are told that a Carleton County mother made several trips over a nine-mile bush path, helping her son carry six barrels of flour to their shanty in the woods. An Essex County woman managed the transport of supplies for her family for two years, often carrying a hundred pounds on her back and portaging her own boat. Another such achievement is credited to Mrs. David Darling of 'the Scotch Block' in Trafalgar Township, for in 1818 she rose nobly to the occasion.

First packing a tub of butter, she carried it forty miles through 'the Bush' to York, traded it for a heavy logging chain, and tramped back with it tired but happy, no longer handicapped by the lack of such an important essential for extending her clearing.*

Materialistic attitudes are understandable in the circumstances that obtained in Upper Canada, though some of them are rather curious. Sons and daughters were considered 'the riches of the Canadian colonist', not for their inherent worth but because of the farm work they could do or the wages they might earn. A widow, if 'smart and pretty' and on the right side of 35, was recommended as a fine wife for a settler, and especially if she had three or four children *ready-made*. Wives 'from home' were sometimes considered best by men newly-arrived from Britain, for they were alleged to work harder, the native (usually called *American*) women having become (they thought) somewhat pampered, and often refusing to work outside the house. Adam Fergusson came upon a fellow-Scot who said he needed a wife. 'But I'll have her frae Auld Scotland', said he, 'for these Yankee lasses are good for nought; they'll blaw the horn and tak a man frae the pleugh to fetch them a skeel o' water.'** Perhaps this opinion is on a par with another unfair generalization from too few instances—or from mere gossip—as a result of which one or two travellers wrote that Canadian women were often unchaste and immoral. As usual, nothing is said about the numerous men who were promiscuous —who were often, in accordance with the usual pattern, responsible by prior seduction for any such loose conduct among women.

Certainly there is no evidence that the population in general held any such views about the womenfolk. Insofar as female hopes for an improved status existed, they were but another aspect of the independence that was everywhere so prominent a characteristic of the New Land, but it is not a matter of any doubt that pioneer women were at least as hard-working as their men.

*Everyone likes to tell a good story, and it should not be assumed that they are all true. Many stories, both of Loyalist and later settlers, are just too lovely to be factual, for to exaggerate the sentimental and romantic in life is irresistible to many.

**It looks as if Fergusson were quoting Robert Stevenson, or vice versa (see Stevenson's letters, Appendix B, Volume II, p. 329). The story, in fact, sounds like a joke on the ladies, currently going the rounds.

FURNISHINGS OF THE PIONEER LOG HOUSE

Women were known to participate in logging with the men,* even to engage in the laborious potash-making without male aid. Anne Langton, in describing the settlers of Fenelon and Verulam townships in 1838, mentions Alexander Daniel and his wife, the latter being commended as 'a capital helpmate for a backwoodsman, for she can do the work of a man, as well as her domestic duties'.**

In old age men sometimes recalled how much their wives did to help around the farm, and especially where they could point a lesson at the expense of their own daughters or 'the young folks' in general of the succeeding age.

Yes [said a Windham pioneer], the old lady an' I have done our share of clearin' land. She was also born an' brought up on a Charlotteville farm, an' when she was a girl at home she used to pick up roots an' brush an' work in the 'foller'; an' after we settled up here in the woods she picked up chunks an' fired many a log-heap in these old front fields. She did all the milkin' too, mind ye, an' spun, an' wove, an' knit socks to sell to the storekeepers, which is more than girls do now-a-days I tell ye. . . . I guess the young folks in my day didn't lie 'wake nights crackin' their brains tryin' to study up labor savin' schemes like they do now-a-days.†

Many wives, in fact, not only carried on such multifarious tasks but as well earned cash in a variety of ways to supplement the family budget. The wife of a settler along the St. Clair kept a few Scottish boarders, and, as her husband said in a letter home, 'washes for nine or ten gentlemen in the neighbourhood, and bakes bread for nearly the same number, so that when she has constant employment she can earn a dollar per day'. Her husband worked for a settler named M'Crea, from whom he obtained a house free; and a friend having advanced him some money he speculated with it in purchasing 1200 acres of land near Toronto, sold five-sixths of it the same afternoon for £22 more than he had paid for all of it, repaid the loan, and went on his way rejoicing. Perhaps it is no wonder that he concluded his letter:

*In his *Reminiscences of a Canadian Pioneer*, pp. 57-8, Samuel Thompson describes a woman who was 'in her glory' at such work and at least equal to the men in logging, chopping, and burning. Unfortunately she is identified only as 'Mary —— from Galway', and apparently lived in Nottawasaga. She was a great walker as well, for she once tramped 17 miles to the nearest store for seed potatoes and carried 90 lbs. of them back home the same day.

**Among aristocratic settlers, however, she said that women were 'very dependent' and gave 'a great deal of trouble' because of their 'weakness'.

†The comment is quoted in E. A. Owen's *Long Point*, and 'now-a-days' was the eighteen-nineties.

ORANGE PARADE, HALIBURTON, 1880

Urge my brothers to come out if ever they wish to free themselves from bondage. This is the land of independence to the industrious —the soil that will repay the labourer for the sweat of his brow!*

In the early pioneer period particularly, many young women went out of the home to do domestic work, including spinning. Female workers often suffered discrimination and exploitation.** During the War of 1812 their wages were only some 4s. to 7s. weekly, those engaged in spinning sometimes receiving 1s. a week more than the servants and houseworkers, and sometimes 1s. less.

*Letters home are not necessarily the best of sources, however, for some exaggerated to emphasize their own prowess and success or to aid emigration propaganda, while others sought to get friends and relatives to come out, settle near by, and relieve some of the isolation—even to corroborate the old saying, 'Misery loves company'.

**The conventions, social controls, and religious superstitions, most of them shaped by men in their own interest or to bear out claims of superiority, are only being abandoned in our own times. The lines
Love and Duty walk hand in hand
But Wisdom walks alone
were intended to convey to women that their brainpower and abilities fell far short of partnership with men. That women needed 'churching after childbirth' and must wear hats in church had their origin in the belief in female inferiority, that sex is 'sin', and other interested male hypotheses which form no part of a rational religion in a democratic society. In the United States, President Kennedy has set up a commission to 'demolish prejudices and outmoded customs which act as barriers to the full partnership of women in our democracy'.

Male workers were commonly in a much better position, for men received a great deal more for unskilled work, and as much as 5s. a day in harvest time; and in addition domestic service was often looked down upon, while the work of agricultural labourers was not.

There were other peculiar attitudes of mind then as now. A traveller in the vicinity of Fenelon Falls considered the Jordans 'worldly-minded' because the daughters of that house were habitually up before daylight, cleaning the house, making the fire, and preparing breakfast. But Anne Langton wrote: 'Jordan's worldly-mindedness will, however, get him on well. He has a large, active, and industrious family, and is the most thriving amongst the neighbours.'

There was, moreover, a healthy distrust among most old-timers for 'new-fangled' things—whether agricultural, mechanical, or cultural; and they were zealously on guard lest the social snobbery of Britain raise its ugly head against workers in Canada.

The fact of a girl going out to work [wrote Canniff Haight with too much assurance but with obvious feeling] did not affect her position. On the contrary it was rather in her favour, and showed that she had some ambition about her. The girls in those days were quite as much at home in the kitchen as in the drawing-room or boudoir. They could do better execution over a wash-tub than a spinet. They could handle a rolling-pin with more satisfaction than a sketch-book; and if necessity required, could go out in the field and handle a fork and rake with practical results. They were educated in the country school-house—with their brothers—and not at a city boarding school. They had not so much as dreamed of fashion-books, or heard of fashionable milliners. Their accomplishments were picked up at home, not abroad. And with all these drawbacks they were pure, modest, affectionate. They made good wives; and that they were the best and most thoughtful mothers that ever watched over the well-being of their children many remember full well.

Innumerable mothers, indeed, earned this eulogy many times over. Instances are not rare of widows left with ten to fifteen children—or of women deserted by their husbands—who conquered adversity and raised their large families in exemplary fashion, carrying on, meanwhile, with their children's help, the heavy and multifarious activities of farm life. The best memorial to the sacrifices of pioneer women is the influence they exerted in moulding the characters of their descendants.

CHAPTER XIII

AMUSEMENT AND SOCIAL LIFE

THE pioneer settler had hardly arrived in the New Land before he was introduced to the bee, a type of community co-operation that aided in raising his log-house, logging his land, and harvesting his crops, all of it accomplished with that zest and relish that only people who are much alone and isolated can evince. As time passed and conditions became less arduous the women met in sewing bees, pumpkin-slicing, and apple-paring; and still later there were house-warmings, singing-school, and spelling bees, as well as *sparkin'* bees and numerous others at which no work was done. Sparking and courting deserve a lengthier account.

When a marrying-man pays a visit to a neighbour where there is a marriageable daughter [says the author of *Journal of a Wanderer*], if the young lady feels disposed to encourage his addresses she detains him after the usual hour at which the family retire to rest, for the parents leave the daughter to manage the affair in her own way. Thus the happy couple are left to themselves. They can sit chatting and making love all night; and under these peculiar circumstances such consequences often follow as render it almost imperative that he should marry her. The laws in the United States are very severe in all cases of refractory gallants—heavy damages, long imprisonment, or *marriage* are the alternatives. This is what is called 'sparking' in America; and is somewhat similar to the mode of courtship which exists among the Indians.

At first characterised by hard drinking and often by brutality and other coarseness, there was a gradual improvement in conduct at bees and other gatherings* as bush farms became cleared and the contact of religion and education relieved the hardship and isolation of first settlement. The bee was no less a bee, but the conviviality, the eating, and the amusement that accom-

*For a detailed account of this predominant element in pioneer life see the author's *Early Life in Upper Canada*, pp. 273-294.

Courtesy B. K. Van Buren

SINGING AROUND THE PIANO

panied all such events tended to become less crude, though opportunities for kissin', courtin', and sparkin' continued to be found—if not made unavoidable by the type of game popular on such occasions.

Those who drank to excess were often the butt of crude jokes, and occasionally their escapades were recorded in equally crude songs, as, for example:

THE LOAFER AND THE PIG

I went down to New Brunswick some friends for to see,
I met a fair damsel and went on a spree;
The whiskey was strong and it went to my head,
So I went out the door to lie down in the shed.

Along came an old sow and lay down by my side,
And I dreamed I was sleeping with a handsome young bride;
I turned to embrace her but her breath was too strong,
So I turned back over and left her alone.

When the Ostler came by and saw us lie there,
He said 'twas a shame to disturb such a pair,
So he called all the women both little and big,
To see the damned loafer asleep with a pig.

I jumped to my feet and made haste for to run,
But the women clapped hands for they thought it was fun.
Good luck to old bottle, though you made me feel shame!
Good luck to old whiskey, I'll drink it again!*

Dancing was enjoyed by the majority, yet there were many families who shunned it as irreligious and an instrument of the Devil. Methodists particularly opposed it, and sometimes Roman Catholic priests prohibited their parishioners from engaging in it. Whether it was held in the barn or the ballroom of a tavern the fun waxed fast and furious, even the aching muscles of the more elderly yielding to the scraping of the fiddle and the monotonous tones of the caller-off. There was always at least one expert in *calling the tune,* and each had his own version, which he droned in a sort of free verse to the accompaniment of fiddle, jew's-harp, zither, paper-covered comb, or of poker and tongs, the jangling of tins and kettles, or some other noisemaker:

> *Ladies in the centre,*
> > *Gents take a walk,*
> *Do-si-do and pass her by,*
> > *Don't be shy.*
> *Balance to the next and all swing out,*
> *Gents hook on, ladies bounce back,*
> *You get a shovel and I'll get a hoe,*
> *Join your hands and circle half.*
> > *Partners swing*
> *Right and left back to the same old thing.*
> *Around the hall, gents, take your own little doll*
> *For a promenade;*
> *Stand her by and swing to the next,*
> *Then bring her back with a half galopade.*

Reels and jigs continued until morn, when the heavy work of backwoodsman and bush farmer started anew.

At rural gatherings in the more remote districts savage wrestling and fighting between individuals, or even rival groups, sometimes ended in disgraceful eye-gouging and other mutilation. Seeing a half-breed with but one eye prompted Sir George Head to describe the process:

The American practice of 'gouging' may not be generally known; it is particularly simple, and very particularly cruel. The combatant

*These verses, obtained by Mrs. Lila Reynolds from the descendant of a Cavan Blazer who had settled in Stanhope Township, are perhaps as bawdy as we could publish with acceptance, but others much bawdier were current in early bar-rooms. Stories of drunken men embracing pigs go back at least to the 14th century and Geoffrey Chaucer.

first twists his antagonist's hair firmly round his fingers, and having done so takes advantage of the strong purchase thus afforded, and then—pokes out his eye with his thumb.

In the remote bush country, indeed, amusement and social life in general were commonly crude and savage. John Mactaggart, surveyor in the wilderness for the Rideau Canal, found little that was pleasing in activities 'where all abominations (instead of being detested) are admired'.

The amusements are few [he wrote], and of the rudest kind. Sometimes they will have *balls*: on notices being placarded up and down the woods the settlers—young and old, male and female—flock to the place of *rendezvous*; dancing, drinking, smoking, &c., are kept up for several days; much obscene conduct is beheld, and vulgarity of the lowest and most brutal kind.

Writing of the first quarter of the 19th century Robert Gourlay says that 'the vulgar practice of pugilism', once prevalent, was declining. Describing it as 'a relic of the savage state', he noted that personal quarrelsomeness and vengeance was 'a departure from the first principle of civilization', and was giving way before the rule of law and justice; but while it lasted it sometimes involved whole townships in animosities. Contests became less brutal and more sporting as settlement proceeded, for races, feats of strength, and ploughing matches gradually supplanted them. Football, cricket, lacrosse, baseball, and other group games gradually developed, and winter sports in their season. Civilization had superseded an age of violence.

Many settlers took an increasing pleasure in the fine hunting and fishing that the country offered. Two- or three-day contests between teams, designed to rid a settlement of bears, squirrels, crows, and other depredators, were in some districts not infrequent, and while the men and boys were engaged in the hunt the womenfolk provided the meals. When the score was totalled the losers paid for a banquet and *hoe-down* at the largest tavern. Regattas and canoe races are not solely a modern diversion, for they were at least equally enjoyed in pioneer days by those who lived near lake and river.

Yet it has been said by travellers that the old settlers—the real pioneers—were seldom seen to smile. The isolation which characterised pioneering made the frontiersman serious and even morose, for labour and hardship were usually intense and unremitting. Often the newcomer's heart sank when he first

CURLING, HIGH PARK
Painted about a century ago by an unknown artist.

WINTER PASTIME

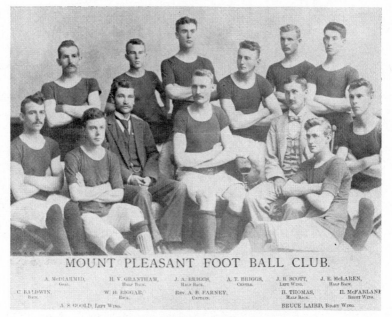

MOUNT PLEASANT FOOT BALL CLUB.

A. McDIARMID,   H. V. GRANTHAM,   J. A. BRIGGS,   A. T. BRIGGS,   J. R. SCOTT,   J. E. McLAREN,
    Goal.   Half Back.   Half Back.   Centre.   Left Wing.   Half Back.

C. BALDWIN,   W. H. BIGGAR,   Rev. A. B. FARNEY,   H. THOMAS,   H. McFARLANE
    Back.   Back.   Captain.   Half Back.   Right Wing.

        A. S. GOOLD, Left Wing.   BRUCE LAIRD, Right Wing.

Organized sports became increasingly prominent
as conditions of life improved.

entered the depths of the dull and cheerless forest, and some,
especially women, never recovered from the difficulties with
which they were surrounded in their isolation.

Smoking was common among all classes, and old women
sometimes smoked clay pipes. For many people drunkenness
was an escape, for whiskey was cheap and there were innumerable outlets—distilleries, stores, inns, taverns, and 'low
dram-shops'. It is not too much to say that in many parts of
Upper Canada drunkenness, immorality,* crime, profanity, and
general depravity were sufficiently common to be characteristic;
nor were bees, auction sales, and elections their only occasion,
for excessive drinking was found at weddings and even funerals.

Numerous travellers considered Upper Canada less refined
than Lower Canada and the United States. Patrick Shirreff, in
fact, said that 'the coarse manners of the people, and their
habits of intemperance, were so prominent that I heard more
oaths and witnessed more drunk people the first few days I was

*Cock-fighting has been generally illegal in America from early times, partly
to prevent bad effects on the morals of spectators. Writing in 1934 and particularly about the County of Peel, William Perkins Bull stated that secret mains
continued to be held, though less frequently than a century ago; see *From
Rattlesnake Hunt to Hockey*, pp. 107-123.

Courtesy Hamilton Public Library

EXCURSION OF THE HAMILTON ASSOCIATION, ABOUT 1880

At first not included, women were suddenly permitted to join such activities
as the study of plant and rock formations. Universities opened their doors
to women in the same decade.

Courtesy Dr. Clara Benson

'LOVESICK MAIDENS, WE'—TABLEAU AT PORT HOPE IN THE 1880's

Gilbert and Sullivan comic operas and the D'Oyly Carte Opera Company
were from their inception very popular in Canada.

Courtesy Mrs. George Irwin

BARN-RAISING, MANITOULIN ISLAND

in Canada than I had met with during my previous wanderings in the States,' though he attributed much of the bad conduct to newly-arrived British immigrants. Considering Upper Canada 'the germ of a numerously inhabited and wealthy state', he yet considered it in the eighteen-thirties 'a wretched, an immoral, and a misgoverned country'. But those who have had no experience of the hard, cruel, and drab life of the pioneer backwoodsman are unqualified either to criticise harshly or to assume any superior virtues.

A book might be written on the sordid side of pioneering. No doubt there were in Ontario, in various stages of its history, communities and villages with a reputation like fictitious Cromaboo, which is described as

the most blackguard village in Canada, and is settled by the lowest class of Irish, Highland Scotch, and Dutch. It consists of seven taverns, six churches, and about one hundred shabby frame houses built on little gravelly mounds. Fights are frequent, drunkenness flourishes, vice abounds; more tobacco is smoked there than in any village of the same size in the Dominion; swearing is so common that it passes unnoticed, and there is an illegitimate child in nearly every house—in some two, in others three, in one six—and the people think it no sin. Yet, even in this Sodom, there was at the time of which I write, a Lot.

150

Town Hall

In 1864, Otterville Town Hall was built by the Sons of Temperance. The Dramatic Club, with the help of the town, moved it from near where the Baptist Church now stands to the present site, put an addition at the back and bricked it up.

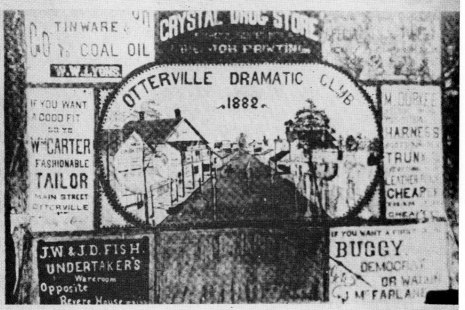

1882—Hall Curtain

In 1882 a drop curtain was painted by Tom Dearle depicting the Main Street of Otterville.

AN EARLY COMMUNITY HALL

It is suggested in the novel from which this is quoted that the wild conduct related rather to the eighteen-sixties than to the earlier, pioneer period, for the hero makes this comment with respect to one of the more vicious escapades, blamed upon Yankee 'pedlars and showmen and the like' who had come to the province in increasing numbers after the middle of the century:

Why, I've heard my mother say, when she was young a woman might sleep with the doors and windows open and be safe, or walk in the dead o' night for miles and never a hand raised but to help her on her way, nor a heart wish her evil, nor a tongue say worse nor 'God be wid you'—that's as it should be.*

Winter was the great season for visiting, for then only was travel easy and pleasant. People thought nothing of a hundred-mile journey by sleigh, especially when the severe work of clearing land was no longer a pressing duty; and it was, as well, the season for marketing produce and obtaining supplies. Among winter sports curling was early introduced from Scotland, and skating and carrioling—as sleighing was sometimes called in the towns—were popular.

Christenings, weddings, and funerals were occasions for gathering in crowds and feasting; while *shivarees*, at first only held when a second marriage occurred very soon after the death of a former partner, when there was a notable disparity in the ages of newly-weds, or when a group of neighbours had been slighted by not being invited to a wedding, shortly became the usual accompaniment of marriage and were often riotous affairs. Here is one writer's description of the noisemakers:

Two corn baskets full of cowbells tied to saplings; a score and a half of frying-pans beat with mush sticks; two-and-thirty Dutch oven and skillet-lids clashed as symbals; fifty-seven small barrels drummed with fists and corn-cobs; one hundred and ninety-five quills prepared and blown as clarionets; forty-three tin whistles and baby-trumpets, blown till they all cracked; two small and one large

*See James Thomas Jones [pseudonym for Mary Leslie]: *The Cromaboo Mail Carrier. A Canadian Love Story.* (Guelph, 1878.) Because of libel suits and other repercussions the book was speedily withdrawn (or, it is said, ordered burned by the courts), but there are copies in the Toronto Public Library and the Library of Congress, Washington. Natives of the district state that 'Cromaboo' was the village of Erin, and that everyone knew who were meant by the fictitious characters. Included was a reflection on the Masonic Lodge, 'their symbols, their compasses, death's heads, and other rubbish', which no doubt increased the resentment. Mary Leslie intended to write another book, but the reception given the first, which is mild by modern standards, ended her authorship.

military drums with six fifes, blown on D *in alt.* or *thereabouts*—add imitations of scalp and war cries, and inhuman yells, screams, shrieks, and hisses of the most eminent vocalists!*

Life in the towns, to which many neighbouring settlers resorted for social life, was naturally more organized and refined than in rural regions. Market-day was always a good reason for a visit to the nearest town, but circuses and other shows, elections,** militia-parade days, and the inauguration of steamships and railways attracted many a countryman to the larger settlements, though a prominent tavern in his own locality might be the stopping-place of travelling menageries and of dramatic companies, usually American, with melodramas and farces prominent in their repertoire.† The tavernkeeper furnished accommodation for all sorts of activities, and it was only natural that he stood to profit from the eating and drinking that followed.

An outlet for musical talent, at first about the mid-nineteenth century in towns and later in rural regions, was the local band. Everyone likes a parade, and bands were in demand at Orange walks, firemen's activities, meetings of lodges and the National Societies, fairs, and all sorts of activities. Many a man was so

*While 'chereverreeing', as it was early spelled, was considered to have originated among the French of Lower Canada, there was a similar proceeding in parts of England when a marriage or sexual practice outraged the community.

**Elections were as crude as other aspects of life. Robert Davis, author of *The Canadian Farmer's Travels in the United States of America* (1837), found Americans comparatively civilized. In Upper Canada, he said: 'The Orange mob is worse every election, so that it is impossible for any honest peaceable reformer to give his vote to a member of Parliament without the fear or realization of having his head broken. . . . If you had been in London at the last election you would have seen a set of government tools called Orange men running up and down the streets crying five pounds for a liberal; and if a man said a word contrary to their opinion he was knocked down. Many were knocked down in this way and others threatened; and all this in the presence of Magistrates, Church of England Ministers, and Judges, who made use of no means to prevent such outrages.' See also the author's *Toronto: from Trading-Post to Great City,* pp. 329-40, for detailed accounts of 'bloody riots' at elections. Assault and battery actions were more frequent in the courts than any others, and pioneer pathmasters were not infrequently threatened or attacked as they sought to enforce the regulations as to road-work. In Simcoe County, among others, the Family Compact gave numerous landgrant patents just before elections. They were in return for votes, and performance was easy to check as votes were recorded orally, not by ballot. Sometimes more new patents were issued than the total number of settlers in a township. For the Ottawa region see *The Carleton Election, or the Tale of a Bytown Ram. An Epic Poem in Ten Cantos (1832).* Its substance is summarized in two of its lines:

> *And there were sundry cuffings, such as press*
> *The wind from out men's guts, and leave black eyes.*

†The reader is referred to the author's *Early Life in Upper Canada,* where there are several long chapters on town and country life.

attached to his band or other local activity that he found it difficult to remain in the locality when it broke up.*

Among the later pioneers of the last half of the nineteenth century, and in the earlier settlements where the second and third generations had succeeded those who had cleared the land, farm life included variations from that of earlier times. G. H. Green, in recalling his youth in Huron County, gives a lively description of manners and customs which were no doubt prevalent elsewhere in the province. At bees and similar gatherings, he says, *wrastles*, fights, and feats of strength were still common. There was always at least one exhibitionist or *smart Alec* who offered to 'lick any damn man in the township' or perform feats of strength and daring with or without the encouragement of bets. These might include silly stunts like eating a handful of pismires or frozen ants from a maple stump—washed down with whiskey of course. Many a man gloried in his strength and vigour. There was in Colborne Township James Sallows, who 'could chop wood in the bush all day, come home and do his chores, take his flail and thresh grain until 12 o'clock, and get up fresh as a daisy next morning'. One day, thinking he was playing a joke on his wife, this ebullient specimen ate twelve yeast cakes and had to drink a gallon of water 'to get the risings off his stomach'. Another such exhibitionist sucked 3½ dozen raw eggs at a sitting, and offered to 'add 'em up to five dozen if his incredulous crony would continue to pay for them; and still another could eat a gallon of batter in pancakes at one meal.

Other feats were more sensible. David Bogie chopped and split eight cords of beech and maple in one day, and on another occasion cradled seven acres of grain. Others could load logs on wagons single-handed, lift horse-power threshers so that a wagon could be backed under, or carry 700-pound anchors (for there were many sailors in the district) under such encouragement from the captain as 'I will buy the drinks for all the sailors between Hell and Kincardine if my sailor, Big Bob, cannot lift and carry the anchor of the *Jeannie* across the deck.**

Then there was John Buchanan, who carried eleven bushels

---

*James Beebe of Cobourg told the writer many years ago that he removed to Toronto when the local Fire Brigade came to an end; and Eric Whaley left Orangeville for Toronto when the band was discontinued.

**Similar feats of strength for the earlier period are described in Owen's *Long Point*, pp. 25-6.

Courtesy Orangeville Public Library   Owen Staples

NORTHWEST REBELLION PARADE, ORANGEVILLE, 1885

Eric Whaley, who is leading the band, left town when it was discontinued.

Canadian Illustrated News

O'DONOVAN ROSSA RIOT, ST. LAWRENCE HALL, TORONTO, 1878

This woodcut was made from a photograph, and from sketches
on the spot by Mrs. Florence Rogers.

of wheat (660 lbs.) across the barn floor, and said he could have made it four bushels more if the onlookers could have fastened it on his shoulders; Andrew Green, who shouldered a barrel of whiskey (500 lbs.) along the 1½-mile cowpath from Goderich harbour to a tavern at Garbraid; and John Morris, whose feat was to carry a No. 4 plough, 100 lbs. of flour, and a parcel of groceries from Goderich to Morris settlement, 5½ miles distant. Characteristically strong and of the *no foolin'* type that got along best as bartenders was 'Big Anthony' Allen, Dunlop tavernkeeper. With his 6-foot-6 height and his 300 lbs. he was obviously not a man to argue with:

He could take two ordinary everyday men by the coat collar [says Green in his *The Old Log School and Huron Old Boys in Pioneer Days*], and crack their heads and heels together. Now the wild bad boys from Goderich town never came along to clean out Anthony's tavern. One of the pastimes of the bad boys from town was to swoop down on country taverns and take possession of the bar when they got liquored up. If you came drunk to big Anthony's tavern you would get no more liquor and out you would go—peaceably too, or Anthony's big foot would follow you out.

Local events sometimes prompted a type of primitive versifying. Mrs. John Harrison of Carnarvon remembers her father, who was a sailor before he settled in Stanhope Township, singing this ballad:

It's of some lads of Stanhope an evil eye they've got,
They jumped into their boats one night and went and robbed poor
    Trot.

They broke into the house and they run up the window blind,
But the worst of it was, my boys, they left their tracks behind.

There was a fresh tub of butter which they did take away,
We were going to sell it at Minden when we could go by sleigh.

Lots of our groceries they did take, oh didn't they think it fine!
Yet they may still regret the night they run up the window blind.

When you go a-thieving, go on your bended knees,
And pray God to forgive you for stealing of the peas.

And when you eat of the preserve jar I hope it won't digest;
Instead of going a-thieving go to bed and take your rest.

So now I've told you of the truth you can't say I'm a liar,
It often pictures in my mind the school when set on fire.

And if this thing should ever come out there'd be nothing left behind.
You'll have reason to regret the night you run up the window blind.

Green, *The Old Log School*   Courtesy Neil F. Morrison

'BIG ANTHONY' ALLEN   WENDEL WIGLE

Tavernkeeper of the *no foolin'* type.   As a hunter of wild turkeys.

Courtesy Dr. W. C. Givens

LITTLE YORK VILLAGE, DANFORTH AT DAWES ROAD, 1900

Congested traffic did not originate with the motor car.

Public Archives of Canada   Susanna Moodie

MARMORA IRON WORKS

Public Archives of Canada   Susanna Moodie

MARMORA IRON WORKS

These sketches were probably made during the early years of
the Moodies' residence in Belleville.

The first log school at Boskung was actually burned by settlers
without children, who resented taxes for education.

In social life with the fair sex the young farmers often
needed a push to overcome gawkiness and embarrassment, but
were in no respect slow when a start had been made. Sparkin',
takin' a shine to a girl, or shinin' up to her soon became a

major sport in many a locality. At bees and barn-dances *conversation lozenges* often proved efficacious as ammunition for calf love-making. Heart-shaped candies with messages such as 'Oh how I pine for you!' and 'Will you be my sweetheart?' were bandied about, and if the girl did not throw it back in your face you were well on your way. Perhaps 'Can I see you home?' drew the reply 'You are the boy of my heart!', and your temperature not only rose but your single status was greatly endangered in the ensuing buggy-ride. And if these encouraging innovations were not available in earlier times, the pioneers seem to have had equally effectual means of overcoming timidity and perpetuating the race.

Birthday parties, often arranged as a surprise, were popular occasions of getting together. Among poorer settlers in 'the Bush' the visitors often brought their own refreshment—perhaps no more than tea, which was served in cups or mugs, no saucers being available. In some localities men kept their hats on at such events, and the presents were usually articles of produce—a chicken, some vegetables, or a little jam or preserves; for even if other articles were available in the general store no one had spare cash to spend. These were the days when the commercialization of such religious festivals as Christmas and Easter had hardly commenced, nor were there any Mother's Days, Father's Days, or Easter Bunnies to whip up business via maudlin sentimentality; but if there had been strident advertising of this or any other type few settlers would have been financially able to respond; and strong sales-resistance became a habit among farmers which persisted far beyond the period of their financial stringency.

But there was almost always dancing and liquor. The vicious drinking habits and accompanying excesses were worst in the early stages of bush settlement, gradually improving with the rise of education, temperance societies, and religious life. In the 'sixties, we are told with respect to Minden in Haliburton County,

the arrival of a barrel of whiskey at the hotel was an event which was marked by a general meeting of the entire settlement, the meeting sometimes lasting several days and refreshing itself at intervals with a violin and cotillions. There was a dance at Buck's Hotel, Minden, which commenced on New Year's Eve, 1864, and lasted, with slight intermissions, for four days and five nights. The population in those days was greatly addicted to dancing, and the festive meetings at Buck's were numerous. The same social characteristics still prevail, but the temperance sentiment is now [1884] sufficiently developed to have caused a diminution in the number and duration of the dance meetings.

Yet even in this county, still very close to first settlement, there was in the early 'eighties in Haliburton village a successful Amateur Dramatic Company under the public-spirited Mr. Crosthwaite's direction, repeating the course of events half a century earlier in such towns as Cobourg and Peterborough nearer 'the front'.

Social life, then, was vicious or highly civilized, varying with the 'all kinds of people' that it takes to make a community; but its general tone gradually improved as the first crudities became more a memory than a reality. To balance our emphasis upon the foolish and frivolous—at times depraved —sections of the community, we conclude with an account of social life among the Mennonites, serious and sober-minded people who have always been highly regarded from the time of earliest settlement in Upper Canada.

The characteristics and long persistence of folk customs in Ontario form a field of historical research where much of great value remains to be done. One of the best pieces of work is that by Blodwen Davies on a Mennonite barn-raising in Waterloo County in September-October 1960. The 'Old Order' Mennonites do not believe in carrying fire insurance, but it is traditional among them to aid one another mutually when exceptional difficulties are experienced. They have 'disaster committees' for the purpose, and their work is often reinforced by public-spirited non-Mennonites in the district.

The replacing of a burned barn near Elmira occupied ten days, with forty to fifty men working every day and their women providing meals. Everything from clearing away the debris and building cement foundations to putting the finishing touches on the roof was part of the project; and as squared logs and other necessary materials are no longer available new, they were hauled from a distance largely by horsepower, two pioneer barns being taken down for the purpose. But little direction seemed to be needed and few orders were given, for everyone seemed to know from experience just where he fitted into the project.

The girls and women were as well organized as the men, with every detail of food—hams, sausages, and smoked meat in great quantities, and everything else needful—and even

Photograph by Blodwen Davies

MEALTIME INTERVAL

baby-sitting on a wholesale scale not forgotten. Their costume is notably severe, and all who had been baptized into the community wore sheer white prayer-coverings tied under the chin with narrow black ribbons.

This useful type of community gathering takes the place of parties among the Mennonites, and there was on this occasion a festive air over all, with an obvious liveliness and happiness everywhere. As many as 300 were served in three sittings of a meal, with the women eating last. With the exception of a nominal fee to the master-carpenter, all the labour was voluntary and unpaid.

The folklore of the pioneer, so long ignored in most of Canada, [concludes Blodwen Davies after pointing out that a jet plane flying overhead during the raising formed a most effective contrast] will some day be recognized as a rich heritage of human values, courage, ingenuity, neighborliness, and a love of freedom genuine enough to be paid for in physical effort, and in faith, hope, and charity.*

*Miss Davies' valuable record, with notes and fifty-three photographs of the sequence of events, is in the Archives of Ontario.

CHAPTER XIV

PIONEER SOCIETIES

AT first social organizations were necessarily centred in the towns, but it was not unusual for farmers settled in the surrounding district to be members and attend the meetings. Societies were consequently important in breaking down class distinctions, both in the towns themselves and between urban and rural residents. These organizations fall into a number of classes, though they tended to overlap. Many were religious, philanthropic, or reformative, others educational and tending to self-improvement, and a third group primarily social.

The first group served as an outlet for benevolent feelings, for the extension of religious fellowship or a helping hand to those less favoured, for the expression of the belief that there is a common humanity and equality, however hard it was for 'gentlemen' to follow such precepts in a day of aristocratic government and social exclusiveness. The names of some of these organizations, examples of which were found in various towns and smaller settlements, will sufficiently indicate their purpose. There was the British and Foreign Bible Society, with numerous branches, and several lesser organizations such as the societies for Promoting Christian Knowledge, Propagating the Gospel, and Civilizing the Indians. A number of tract and missionary societies had similar objects.

Human sympathy found expression in relieving the sad condition in which many immigrants arrived, and quite substantial sums were raised in many towns—and especially lake ports—for the purpose. Perhaps the famous precept, 'There, but for the Grace of God, goes John Bunyan,' had as few real believers then as now, but there were undoubtedly some among the members of the Society for Relief of Strangers in Distress, the Female Benevolent Society, and others for aiding orphans, 'Poor Women in Confinement,' and similar unfortunate or underprivileged groups. In the eighteen-fifties there was an Anti-Slavery Association in Toronto, and soirées were held in St. Lawrence Hall in aid of the hundreds of negro refugees from the United States.

Temperance and Total Abstinence societies, and other organizations like the association at Perth for the Suppression of Vice and Immorality, might be taken as in varying degrees both benevolent and educational, public-spirited and self-improving. But then, as now, there were financial interests which profited hugely upon human frailties, and they sought to obstruct such societies and even to laugh them off. Hotel and liquor interests in a few instances went so far as to form 'intemperance societies', usually ostensibly based upon the 'sacred right of personal liberty'.

The hard drinking in taverns, and at bees, elections, and other pioneer gatherings, was responsible for the growth of Temperance Societies, which originated in the United States. The 'old pledge' societies differentiated between spirituous liquors and beer and wine, permitting use of the latter; while the 'new pledge' group were total abstainers except for medicinal purposes. Total Abstinence Societies were also common, mak-

Courtesy B. K. Van Buren

MAPLE LEAF BAND, NEWTONVILLE, 1885

163

ing no compromise whatever with 'the enemy'.* In some instances societies had members of each type, with part of the meetings' proceedings devoted to avowed changes by members from one to the other. By the late eighteen-thirties almost all societies were 'new pledge', but it took a good many years to unite all under a provincial body, with consequent power to influence government and effect temperance legislation.

On the cultural side were numerous debating, literary, and drama clubs, at first almost all in towns and villages. Among the earliest was a society for the encouragement of literature and science formed in 1832 in York by Archdeacon Strachan, who donated a lot on which to erect a clubhouse. Each member was to give an address on some aspect of literature, philosophy, or science. Rural inhabitants sometimes met in spelling bees or singing-schools, generally under the direction of schoolmaster or clergyman. Cobourg and Peterborough had amateur dramatic productions as early as the eighteen-thirties, and there was a debating society in early Perth.

The development of the Mechanics' Institute in the field of adult education followed its introduction early in the 19th century in Britain to provide opportunities for educational improvement among clerks and tradesmen, who were commonly grouped under the name 'mechanics'. Lectures and demonstrations were provided, often well beyond their hearers' ability to comprehend, and there were sometimes scientific and art exhibits and usually a library enabling the borrowing of books. In many instances the local Mechanics' Institute eventually became the foundation of a town's first Public Library. The administration of these organizations was comparable to that of the present Young Men's Christian Association (which is in many respects similar), consisting largely of men prominent in business and industrial life. Somewhat more professional in nature, despite its name, was the York Artists and Amateurs Association, which was holding meetings in the capital in 1834. In 1857 was established the Hamilton Association, whose members were especially interested in nature and science;

---

*It is not hard to visualize these Temperance crusaders marching along to the tune of songs like 'The Water King' or 'The Cold Water Army':

> *We love the clear Cold Water Springs*
> *Supplied by gentle showers:*
> *We feel the strength cold water brings—*
> *The Victory is Ours!*

For a longer account of Temperance Societies and temperance hotels see the author's *Pioneer Inns and Taverns*. Volume I, pp. 50-66.

and in the 'eighties women became prominent in its activities.

In one of a series of Tax Collectors' Rolls of North Monaghan Township* is an account of a meeting of a society formed

Courtesy Hazel Anderson

MADOC I.O.O.F. BAND AT BANCROFT
In front of the old Bancroft Hotel.

about 1866 in a rural district, with the object of intellectual improvement.** It is quoted in its entirety:

North Monaghan Intellectual Improvement Society
The Rev. Mr. Allen of Millbrook delivered the Inaugural Lecture on Wednesday evening the 16th inst. Subject—'The Battle of Life', when on the motion of Mr Sproule seconded by Mr Bennett, George Young Esqr was called to the Chair. The Chairman said that he found himself very unexpectedly occupying his present position. It was not however without very much pleasure that he found that the Rev Mr Allen was present to give the first lecture of the season & from the well known ability which he possessed he felt quite certain that not one present would be disappointed. Without detaining them further he would at once call on the Rev Mr Allen, who was received with loud and prolonged applause.

*Given to the author by B. K. Van Buren, dealer in old books, Highway 28 near Bewdley, they are now in the Public Archives of Canada, Ottawa.

**It should be remembered that Charles Dickens was alive and reading his works to British audiences, that Browning, Tennyson, and Arnold were at their greatest, that Wordsworth, Coleridge, Lamb, Hazlitt, Ruskin, and Washington Irving were not long dead. Many a settler of intellect had at least some of their books and was familiar with the progress of cultural life, even if he had but little time or opportunity to share in it amid the difficulties of pioneering.

Mr Allen commenced by stating that the year just ended had been noted for great contests both in the senate and in the field—indeed few more eventful ones had passed away.

It was not however his intention to attempt to depict the bloody battle fields where such frightful carnage had taken place* but rather in accordance with the subject he had chosen, confine himself to his theme—The Battle of Life—a subject fraught with deep interest to every human being—as all had to engage therein.

In a clever and forcible manner and abounding in deep research with well chosen illustrations Mr Allen brought the subject before the meeting, pointing out the difficulties—sometimes apparently insuperable—which many endured. These tended to strengthen and develop resources otherwise unknown. In the Battle of Life we can not over estimate the power of perseverance which history both sacred & profane amply testifies.

We should not engage in this battle for mere human aggrandizement nor for earthly possessions or temporal power—if so we will be disappointed. Higher aims than these sh^d influence us, and then if successfully fought, the conquest, how much greater than any temporal reward.

In a most impressive manner and well becoming his sacred avocation, he tendered his advice respecting the subject under consideration and concluded in the language of Holy Writ by hoping that all present would run the race.

Mr W. A. Morrow moved a vote of thanks to the learned lecturer for the able, interesting & instructive address he had delivered which was seconded by Mr Wood and carried amidst much applause.

The evening terminated by singing the Doxology.

More predominantly social, but including some benevolence to members and their families, were lodges of which the Masonic was earliest developed. In towns and villages the volunteer Fire Brigade was at least as much social as useful to the community, for there were social evenings, inter-town festivals, and even international conventions. The Firemen's Ball was the event of the season for many citizens, and the Fire Brigade, with colourful uniforms, was prominent in all holiday celebrations, receptions to notabilities, torchlight processions, and similar events so popular in the period. The Orange Lodge was another prominent social organization, but its pronounced sectarian bias frequently led to disgraceful riots on its own parade days or those of Roman Catholic religious groups. The Celtic Society crossed religious lines and was 'Constitutional', patriotic, and Conservative, in opposition to radicals of all sorts.

*The reference is, of course, to the American Civil War, 1860-65.

Canadian Illustrated News

INTERNATIONAL FIREMEN'S CONVENTION, COBOURG, 1871

Of special interest in the pioneer period, when so many had so recently torn themselves from their homeland, were the National Societies of St. Andrew, St. George, St. Patrick, and, occasionally, St. David. The feeling of nationality was then strong, and fond memories of other days were treasured; and as no predominant national feeling had yet developed, the loyalty tended to be to Scotland, England, Ireland, and Wales. St. George's Society was particularly prominent about the time of the anniversary of Shakespeare's birth, St. David's on March 1st, St. Patrick's on the 17th of March, and St. Andrew's on two occasions—November 30th (St. Andrew's Day)* and Burns' birthday on January 25th. 'Grand Dinners', innumerable toasts, and much drinking and conviviality usually characterised these occasions, but there were also processions to church—sometimes of all societies to the church of one patron saint—and festivals, balls, and social evenings. It was customary for farmers to belong to these societies in the town nearest.

Among the clannish Scots** were not a few versifiers in

*In the latter part of the century societies began to be formed as well for localized parts of Scotland. In 1962, for example, the Orkney and Shetland Society of Toronto celebrated its 75th anniversary.

**Typical of Scottish settlements was 'the Scotch line' in Sunnidale and Nottawasaga townships, almost all of whose Scots were from the isles of Arran and Islay off Argyllshire. Many of them spoke no English when they arrived, but their enterprise, industry, and thrift resulted in almost invariable success in Canada.

Courtesy Kenneth W. Johnson

EARLY ORANGE PARADE, ALMONTE

the tradition of Burns, Hogg, and Tannahill. Alexander Mc-Lachlan, if not quite in Burns' class as a bard, was yet much superior to many another local 'poet'. He wrote a song for a great Scottish Gathering at the old Crystal Palace, Toronto, September 14, 1859, and three of the verses follow:

Arthur Cox

ALEXANDER McLACHLAN AND HIS FARM, ORANGEVILLE, 1887

Pioneer Societies

My heart leaps up wi' joy to see
  Sae mony Scotchmen here;
Sae I maun sing about the laun,
  The laun we lo'e sae dear;
We a' hae climbed her heathy hills,
  And pu'd the gowden broom,
And wandered through her bonnie glens
  Wi' gowans a' in bloom.

  .   .   .   .

Oh when I left the mountains a',
  That was a waefu' scene;
I didna greet, but oh I drew
  The bonnet owre my e'en;
Benlomond seemed to hide his head
  Afar within the blue,
And Leven, with her hundred isles,
  Was murmuring adieu.

  .   .   .   .

And brither Scots owre a' the earth
  Will stretch a haun to save—
They're no the chiels wad sit and see
  Their mother made a slave;
The spirit of the convenant
  Wi' every Scot remains,
The blood o' Wallace and o' Bruce
  *Is leaping in our veins.**

At least one town—Cobourg—had in the eighteen-fifties an association called Native Sons, consisting of men born in Canada. This was an early evidence of national feeling in opposition to the sectional. The survivals of the National Societies in our day are in the nature of a 'high festival of once a year', for since Confederation the memories of the Old Land have receded and a distinctly Canadian national feeling has increasingly replaced earlier loyalties. There is the fact, too, that many people other than Scots revere Robbie Burns, while Shakespeare is now recognized as an international heritage, not just English.

*A number of versifiers and poetasters, much less inspired than McLachlan, were bards of local St. Andrew's Societies; for the defects of even the least qualified 'poets' were lost in the enthusiasm as the Scottish worthies, burns and braes, and bonnie lassies were toasted in conviviality that often lasted into the wee sma' hours.

CHAPTER XV

EDUCATION AND CULTURAL LIFE

IN general the pioneer period was one of comparative illiteracy for the greater part of the population, and particularly in the more isolated settlements. While no statistics are available, it is certain that a greater percentage of Loyalist settlers could read and write than of later emigrants from Britain, for elementary education was considerably more advanced in New York State, from which most of them came.*

The Grammar School Act of 1807, the first educational legislation in Ontario, put the cart before the horse and made some provision for what was intended to be secondary education before any had been made for elementary. It provided for a Grammar School in each of the eight large districts into which the province was divided, but many years passed before most of them had a school. In 1829 eleven Grammar Schools were in operation, but of the total of 280 pupils 61 were learning nothing more advanced than to read and write. The Common School Act of 1816 gave some state aid to such districts as erected an elementary school, had a minimum of twenty pupils, and arranged to pay through fees part of a teacher's salary; but the aid from the provincial government was negligible when divided among all the projected schools in a district.

To understand the peculiar educational legislation of the early pioneer period one must recognize that the government was both aristocratic and despotic. It is no accident that secondary education was provided before elementary—in fact every effort was made to provide higher education still earlier, though mainly to train Church of England clergy. In the ruling clique

*In 1828 the Legislative Assembly of Lower Canada sent a petition to England against union with Upper Canada. Of 87,000 petitioners some 76,000 signed by a mark, but illiteracy was much greater among the French Canadians than in Upper Canada. Writing in 1833 the Reverend Isaac Fidler said that the illiterate in Upper Canada were largely 'poor emigrants from Europe'.

there was no thought of democracy other than hatred for it, and education was designed to be—not from childhood up for all children—but from the upper grades downward and for the well-to-do and 'better' classes only. The prevailing philosophy was that those who could afford the fees might be educated, but that from the point of view of a stable class system the 'lower

Henry W. Peterson

DISTRICT OF WELLINGTON GRAMMAR SCHOOL, 1845

orders' could best be kept in their place if left relatively uneducated. Only with this knowledge are we able to appreciate the long struggle, under Egerton Ryerson's leadership, for a free, universal, and compulsory educational system.*

The earliest schools in the province were due largely to Scottish and Loyalist influences. At Cataraqui (Kingston) the Reverend John Stuart (1740-1811) opened the first school in 1785, specializing in the teaching of classics. This initial educational venture was followed by a school at Port Rowan in 1789, one at Niagara in 1792, one at Ancaster in 1796, and William Cooper's small school at York, 1798; and a few years later there were schools at Cornwall, Sandwich, and St. Catharines. Upper Canada College, 'the Canadian Eton', was founded by Lieutenant-Governor Sir John Colborne in 1829 with the magnificent endowment of 66,000 acres of Crown lands; but this private school was never in any sense a part of the province's educational system.

In the second quarter of the century schools of various types, private and public, became more common in Upper Canada.

*See the author's *In the Cause of Education* (1960)—the Centennial history of the Ontario Educational Association—for a summary of the development of schools in Ontario and a synopsis of a century of addresses on changes and developments in education, 1860-1960.

Sometimes clergymen established 'select' schools to eke out meagre stipends, but in general the teachers were old soldiers and other unqualified persons who had been unable to adjust themselves to civil life. A considerable proportion were of American origin and gave a pronounced slant to their instruction. Teachers were commonly paid less than labourers, often stayed but a few weeks in a locality, frequently taught but little other than respect for harsh discipline, and were seldom respected in the community. The trustees, some of whom were illiterate, usually chose the cheapest applicant, and he commonly 'boarded round' as part of his remuneration; while his wife might serve as dressmaker, servant, or accept any other employment that offered. It must not be supposed, however, that there were not conscientious and effective teachers, in spite of the adverse conditions. In 1830, when the population was some 200,000, the 400 elementary schools in the province had about 10,000 pupils.

The general run of settlers, though there were notable exceptions, were indifferent to both education and religion. They opposed compulsory schools largely for economic reasons, because children were considered an asset to be realized upon by early employment in workshop or on the farm;* but difficulties of access to schools, poor buildings and equipment, and inefficient teaching were contributory to the general dislike of education. The first school in Stanhope Township, in the eighteen-sixties, was burned down by settlers who opposed it because of the taxes levied to support it.

The early teacher's meagre salary was usually met by a payment per pupil of from twenty-five to seventy-five cents a month, very seldom in cash. Female teachers were very few, but we learn of one in the Rideau district who was paid in grain at the end of the year, and had to have it hauled to Kingston before she received any cash. Other teachers had difficulty collecting anything whatever for their services. Only when the obligations were met by public taxation did conditions improve, and even then the salaries were commonly disgracefully small.

Doan's Schoolhouse, situated on the River Lynn almost

*In stating that 'children are the best *stock* a farmer can possess', Dr. William Dunlop of the Canada Company said that the labour of a child of 7 was considered worth his maintenance and education, while a boy of 12 or 14 would be paid $3 to $4 a month and bed, board, and washing, which was more than a skilful ploughman would receive in Britain. In Upper Canada, consequently, the phrase 'a poor man with a large family' was a contradiction of terms.

midway between Simcoe and Port Dover, affords an excellent example of what a log school of the period 1825-1850 was like:

The School-House was of Logs [says a newspaper description quoted in Dr. J. G. Hodgins' *Schools and Colleges of Ontario*], about 18 feet by 23, with a huge Fireplace and Chimney occupying the end of the Room opposite the Door; on the side walls auger holes had been made and long pins inserted, on which were placed boards as Desks. The Seats were slabs from the Sawmill, with holes bored in them and pins inserted for legs, and on these facing the walls the scholars were seated, especially those who had school books; inside of these, and nearer to the centre of the Room, were a second row of Benches (similar to the first, only with shorter legs) for use of the small scholars. These Seats were just as they came from the sawmill in their rough state, and certainly possessed one merit—that the erect splinters served a useful purpose in preventing the smaller pupils from sliding off the seats.

Of 6800 elementary schools in the province a century later (1950) there were still 31 of logs, but in 1850 most of the 3000 common schools were of either log or frame construction.

Books and equipment were as defective as school buildings and teachers. The Bible and one or two American spelling texts or geographies might be in the hands of the teacher. Perhaps the pupils had slates, possibly the old horn-book method was in use,* perhaps the children merely copied the alphabet, numbers, and simple words from the Bible. Blackboards, globes, maps, and pictures were not found in the early schools,** and if ink was available it was usually buried in a hole under the floor to evade the frosts of winter. A pail of water with a dipper might be located near the teacher's desk. The log buildings were both cold and smoky, the teacher was janitor and woodchopper as well—the parents providing a quarter of a cord of wood per pupil—and "no lickin', no larnin'" was a generally-accepted principle of instruction. If the school had a stove it probably

*The horn-book was a paper containing the alphabet, numbers, and the Lord's Prayer, mounted on a wooden tablet with a handle and protected by a thin plate of horn.

**And in more recent times they have been but deficiently supplied in many schools. The late W. J. Dunlop, Minister of Education, 1951-1959, was dead against the 'fads and frills' of education, having been a rural teacher himself. He had heard as well many a story of what had been accomplished in 'the little red schoolhouse' with third-class teachers, a six-inch globe, and five dollars' worth of other equipment. And there were instances, it is true, where teachers exerted immense influence towards the good life and scholarly distinction in many fields—and were rewarded, along with occasional reminders of their good works, by a miserly annual salary, or in earlier periods by fees, instability, and low status without prestige.

fell down more than once a winter due to the large pieces of cordwood used for fuel.

Travellers from Britain were usually not kind in their comments about the educational and cultural standards that characterised Upper Canada. 'Boys of seven or eight years old are put to work in Canada and are kept at it during the remainder of their lives', wrote Edward Talbot, who was in the country for some years in the early 'twenties. The same man said he saw only two men with books during his five years in the province, and one of them was merely seeking a cure for a disease in a medical book; but in one week, he added, he heard more profanity than in twenty years in Ireland. Other writers give a fairer picture as to books. John Howison saw an innkeeper's wife reading Maria Edgeworth's *Tales of Fashionable Life,* and visited a home where he found 'Mackenzie's Novels, Thomson's Seasons, Cowper's Poems, Persian Tales, and several works of a similar description, and likewise a Love Dictionary'. Henry Taylor, selling a book of his own writing in the 'forties, received this reply from 'an intelligent farmer':

Yes, sir, I will buy your work if you will sell it cheap, for I believe it is a good one; and I will tell you why I buy it; it is because my opinion is, considering the present state of society and the world, that nothing will save it but the general distribution of good books among the rising generation, and I certainly believe, if in any country it is wise in a parent to encourage in his sons a turn for the knowledge that good books will give him, it is in Canada, where youth not restrained by love of useful knowledge are in danger of seeking amusements from injurious sources.

Anna Jameson, writing in 1837, was as critical as Talbot:

There is no march of intellect here! [she said]. I passed in these journeys some school-houses built by the wayside: of these several were shut up for want of schoolmasters; and who that could earn a subsistence in any other way would be a schoolmaster in the wilds of Upper Canada? Ill fed, ill clothed, ill paid or not paid at all— boarded at the houses of different farmers in turn—I found indeed some few men, poor creatures! always either Scotch or Americans and totally unfit for the office they had undertaken. Of female teachers I found none whatever except in the towns.

The results were what might be expected—ignorance and viciousness. She describes a prosperous family whose 'advantages are all outward: for any inward change was retrogression, not advancement'. Though there were no poor-laws, titled aristocracy, or poor-rates 'to grind the souls and substance of the

'THE MARCH OF INTELLECT'
The Superintendent of Schools for Middlesex County made this sketch in December 1845.

A MEETING OF SCHOOL TRUSTEES

Courtesy G. H. Needler   Anna Jameson

ANNA JAMESON *EN ROUTE* TO NIAGARA

people between them', as she puts it, yet there were everywhere 'the gross vices, the profligacy, the stupidity, and basely vulgar habits of a great part of the people':

In one log-hut in the very heart of the wilderness, where I might well have expected primitive manners and simplicity, I found vulgar finery, vanity, affectation under the most absurd and disgusting forms, combined with a want of the commonest physical comforts of life and the total absence of even elementary knowledge. In another I have seen drunkenness, profligacy, stolid indifference to all religion; and in another the most senseless fanaticism.*

The female teachers in the towns were almost always the conductors of private schools for girls, of which 'a select school for young ladies' in York in 1822 illustrates the type. Extras like French, drawing, painting on velvet, music, dancing, and flower- and card-work were provided. The charges were substantial, and it was stipulated in addition that every 'lady' was to provide 'a table- and tea-spoon, knife and fork, sheets and towels, and to pay for her own washing'. Mrs. and the Misses Dunn, Cobourg, charged £40 per annum in 1848 for boarders at their school, which was testified as respectable by the Lord

*But the Reverend Isaac Fidler, writing a few years earlier, observed that the Canadians were making 'astonishing improvements' in education. 'Their schools have multiplied abundantly within the last two or three years', he said.

Courtesy George M. Douglas

HAND-MADE DESKS IN LOG SCHOOL, DUMMER TOWNSHIP

Courtesy Adelaide (Batten) McGiffin

LOG SCHOOL, DUMMER TOWNSHIP

Erected in the 1830's as the home of Richard Batten and demolished
about 1910. Note the size of the logs used in its construction.

Courtesy Bertha M. C. Shaw

FIRST SCHOOL, PORCUPINE CAMP

Bishop and other members of the Church; while Miss Macnally of Toronto offered in addition to the regular subjects German, Italian, Dancing, and 'Pianoforte and Thorough Bass', each subject being paid for separately. If a pupil took everything offered the fee would be a substantial £22 10s. per quarter, and parents were advised that each young lady had 'to provide her own bedding and blankets, two counterpanes, two toilets, six towels, two pair of sheets, and a silver fork and spoon'.* It should not be assumed that many farmers' daughters attended such schools, but Mrs. Aldgeo, a widow who kept tavern near the present Caradoc, told Patrick Shirreff that she sent her daughter to a boarding-school in London.

As far as the regular schools were concerned, not much could be expected for the little that people were willing to pay for education. A strong blue-beech switch or something still heavier kept the boys and girls in order, for the teachers had often to be rough and tough to match the pupils. Many of them, in fact, were taught no manners whatever at home, and they were extremely precocious in everything that would have been better avoided. Great hulks of young men bigger than the teacher were

*The details of these and other educational announcements may be found in the appendix to the Reverend W. S. Darling's *Sketches of Canadian Life* (London, 1849).

Courtesy Protestant Home for Incurables

MRS. FORSTER'S SCHOOL FOR YOUNG LADIES, TORONTO, 1860

SCHOOL MERIT CARDS

Introduced by Egerton Ryerson in the 1860's.

sometimes sent to school in off seasons, and they not infrequently bullied and otherwise maltreated the smaller boys and the girls, so that the teacher had no easy assignment to keep order and teach anything; and at times his tenure of office was abruptly terminated when he was hurled through door or window.*

The pioneer rural teacher's dilemma, as it still is—pending the completion of consolidation—was to get each and all of the smallest children, as well as their elders ranged around the walls, to work at something within their capabilities. Quill pens were used in writing, and the other subjects might be reading, spelling, geography, and arithmetic, but seldom anything else. Certainly there were no frills in those days, and no one expected much of even the rudiments so they were not disappointed. Few pupils remained longer than from nine to fifteen months, during which time they learned to read and write haltingly and to do a few sums. Old teachers, it is revealing to learn, were seldom referred to as retired or superannuated, but merely as 'worn out'—as they most assuredly were.

At first Saturdays were teaching days, and there was only a two-week holiday in summer; in fact farm pupils usually attended only intermittently, and in seasons when work was not pressing. Before 1847 there were no regular school-sections, but merely a school wherever there were numerous children and a community of interested parents. Where women taught they were commonly paid much less than men—frequently only half the man's wage.

Egerton Ryerson's philosophy of education comprehended the entire youth of the land and their enforced attendance at free schools. The machinery of education, he believed, should be in the people's hands, and provincial aid was merely to assist and stimulate local effort the cost of which was to be defrayed by property taxes. The Bible and moral precepts were to be a part of the instruction, but nothing of a sectarian nature was to be permitted. Inspection to ensure reasonable uniformity and efficiency was provided, and in general it may be said that the Ontario system incorporated the best features current among other nations. The school laws of the more advanced states of the American union, the property tax of New England, the Normal and Model schools of Germany, and an adaptation of

---

*In some districts it was the custom to attempt to treat a new teacher this way on his first day; and if he successfully resisted the initiation he might find the going easier, especially if he accepted an early opportunity to 'lick' the biggest boy in the school.

Courtesy Gordon Walmsley   Capt. J. P. Downes

MAIN STREET, PICTON, 1847

Archives of Ontario

BAILIEBORO, 1834

At the left is Joseph Graham's Tavern, which was the original name of the settlement.

Courtesy Caroline Brown   Charles Davy Brown

HAYSVILLE AFTER A FLOOD

The artist, who lived near Haysville, was a pupil of Sir Edwin
Henry Landseer, noted English artist.

Irish textbooks acceptable to both Protestants and Roman Catholics—these were the ingredients from which the Ontario system was formed; and every effort was made to keep education out of politics and to base promotions entirely on merit. But Ryerson's opponents were many and persistent, attacking him on one hand as exemplifying Prussian despotism, and on the other as communistic.

In the late eighteen-forties the first legislation aiming at taxation to provide schools began the movement towards the abolition of fees; but while the aim was soon achieved for public schools, not until 1921 were all high schools free. The School Act of 1850 might be called the Magna Charta of the Ontario public school system, for fees were allowed but not compulsory, and school boards were made independent of municipal councils in the all-important matter of finance. Finally the Act of 1871 provided the initial legislation towards compulsory education, for by its terms all children from 7 to 12 were compelled to attend school at least fifty days a year. In the period 1841 to 1871 the population had increased from 456,000 to 1,620,000, but the common-school registration had soared from 80,000 to 446,000.

Yet by far the greater number of all pupils continued to attend in a desultory and highly irregular manner, and public opinion was not sufficiently advanced to enable educationists to do much about it. In Toronto, for example, there was not nearly enough accommodation for those who came voluntarily, without forcing those to come whose parents were opposed or showed no interest one way or the other. Many teachers had well over 100 on the roll, and classes of 90 in attendance in one room were not exceptional.

In a lecture on school attendance delivered to the Ontario Teachers' Association in 1873 David Fotheringham exposed an 'ominous and humiliating state of affairs' in the schools. Official statistics for 1871 were produced to show that 27 per cent of all children between the ages of 5 and 21 did not attend school at all, while 22 per cent more were in attendance less than fifty days, and another 20 per cent less than 100 days. The speaker deduced, consequently, that hardly one in ten of all children was a satisfactory product from school, and that only three in every hundred received any type of secondary or college education. But more stringent regulation of school attendance would be but a partial solution, for the facilities and instruction were defective.

Most of the instruction given in Ontario [concluded Mr. Fotheringham] is unattractive, vague, inaccurate, and valueless. It is a shame, a disgrace, the way in which children are huddled, tortured, and smothered in most of our schools even yet—dirt on the floors and walls, dust on the desks, dust on the sills, on the maps, on windows —outhouses exposed often, and often unfit to use, playground unsuitable, often muddy, uneven, exposed—no shade trees, no playshed—nothing but dreary, tiresome days, theirs at school. . . . Filth, disorder, rudeness should not be associated with the idea of the day-home of children. Schoolhouses should be as comfortable and cheerful as homes. Children should have the means of social and intellectual enjoyment provided as religiously as the birch has been in the past.

It is apparent that over-sentimentalized tales of 'the little red schoolhouse' have comparatively little relation to the truth with respect to the school system as a whole, but the basis for a broad advance and a gradual transformation had been well and truly laid. At every step for a generation Ryerson had been opposed by Bishop Strachan and the main high-church body of the Church of England, who aimed to keep education sectarian not public, sectional not universal, the privilege of the few not the right of all. The fight was fierce, but the victory complete. President J. H. Smith of the Ontario Teacher' Association, who lived through the controversy, stated the choices clearly, and the implications of the result of the battle, in his presidential address in 1888:

The ruling principle of government in this Province being more democratic than aristocratic in its tendencies, it follows as a natural sequence that the proper education of the masses is a matter of prime necessity. The reign of the common people has steadily advanced in influence, until now freedom, education, and religious equality are the inalienable rights of all. There was a struggle, long and at times very bitter, before these blessings were secured to us, and nowhere are the effects of this struggle to be seen more clearly than in our educational history. The leading actors in this drama have passed away, but they have bequeathed to us an educational system of which it may be truly said that it is a monument more durable than brass or marble, and more noble than the conquest of nations or the destruction of armies.

Roman Catholic separate schools in Ontario date from 1841, but it is not generally known that there is as well legislative provision for both Protestant and Coloured separate schools. While negro refugees from American slavery came in considerable number to Essex County, and were accepted as citizens, their children were not welcomed in the common schools.* In 1875 the maximum of three Coloured separate schools was reached, but the last of these, that at Chatham, came to an end in 1891, a laudable example of the growth of tolerance in the province.

Libraries, newspapers, and books were the chief other educational agencies. The first library, opened in 1800 in Niagara, included many books on farming. There were early private circulating libraries in York, Kingston, Cobourg, and one or two other of the chief towns, but the Mechanics' Institute provided the first town libraries that were in any sense public, and eventually, in the eighteen-eighties, they formed the nucleus of public libraries. In the townships, too, there were in a few districts enough rural people with intellectual interests to lead in establishing an Intellectual Improvement Society, as in North Monaghan, or, much more frequently, circulating libraries. Scottish settlers, who showed the greatest interest in education, were similarly advanced in their love of books, and townships where they were prominent, like Lanark, Ramsay, and Dalhousie, had public libraries as early as 1818-21. That in Dalhousie, wrote Dr. William Dunlop, was 'the best library in the province'. Old records still preserved in Ramsay show that the library there had 114 'readers'. As Presbyterian clergymen were prominent in establishing these libraries, religious books predominated, many of them dull and heavy reading; but they served at least to teach spelling and increase vocabulary, and many a pioneer was proud of the large words he could use (or misuse) as a result of self-education. Kingston had a circulating library in the eighteen-twenties, with a curious system of barter whereby people might obtain children's books and 'useful tracts' in exchange for clean rags which, in turn, were sold to papermakers. In various districts the more educated settlers loaned books to one another and circulated English newspapers to which a few subscribed; but Dr. Dunlop considered that it would be a long and tedious process to make Upper Canada the country of either the wealthy or the aesthetic.

*In general, however, there was no social ostracism of negroes in any sense comparable to that found in almost all parts of the United States prior to the Civil War, and which still obtains in the South. In the mid-fifties, for example, 25 negro children were in common schools in Hamilton, one was at Normal School in Toronto, and several attending lectures at the University. It is apparent, however, that the small number of negroes, rather than any substantial variation in human characteristics of the whites of the two countries, was responsible for Canadian tolerance.

Though the necessaries and most of the luxuries of life are cheaply and easily procured [he said], yet the elegancies of life, refined or literary society, public amusements, first-rate libraries, collections of the fine arts, and many things that are accounted almost as necessaries of life by the higher ranks, belong of necessity to a state of society much more advanced than the Canadas, or perhaps even the American continent, can as yet pretend to.

Though their circulation was in general limited to educated people, newspapers* were probably more an educational force than they are today. In general they were strictly divided according to party allegiance or political principles. In style they were much more literary than many published today, and in part this arose from the higher average intellectual status of their readers, for they had a small but select circulation. English news many weeks old occupied a prominent place, while local events were less frequently reported except where something notable had occurred in the community. Much of the material was copied from other newspapers, Canadian or foreign. Advertisements were usually stereotyped announcements which often remained unchanged for years. Poetry and short novels, as well as many of the articles on foreign events, seem to have appealed to the educated subscribers of the time, but they would be quite out of place in the average newspaper today. Subscriptions were often accepted in produce, and the fact that many neglected to pay them at all led to frequent failures and changes of ownership.

In the later pioneer period several literary magazines were produced in Canada, an evidence not only of the commencement of a native literature but of the beginnings of a distinctly Canadian feeling. The *Literary Garland* was published in Montreal, with a considerable number of Upper Canadian subscribers and contributors. A few years later, at the middle of the century, Susanna Moodie and her husband produced the *Victoria Magazine* in Belleville. The Moodies and Mrs. Traill provided much of the material, but Rhoda Anne Page, Cobourg poetess, was among other contributors. These magazines, an indication that the rigours of pioneering were being alleviated, allowing the leisure which is needed for the pursuit of cultural interests whether as writers or readers, were prominent in setting literary standards just as the province was entering the post-pioneer period.

*The first in the province was the *Upper Canada Gazette, or American Oracle,* published in Niagara 1793-98, and then in York.

ANNE LANGTON   SUSANNA MOODIE
A self portrait.   From a miniature.

Two of the more cultured pioneer women.

While many parts of Upper Canada had one or more writers of ability, no other district even approaches the Cobourg-Peterborough region in the number of highly cultured settlers and the quality of their literary productions. This is due partly to the leadership of 'the literary Stricklands'*, but in large measure as well to the inherent qualities of a very considerable number of others equally gifted.

Numerous Scots, influenced by the Immortal Memory, became versifiers of varying skill without seriously imperilling Burns' preëminence. Many of them were bards of the local St. Andrew's Society. Whether in imitation of the Bard's earthiness in writing odes to a Mouse and to a Louse, or merely a reflection of pioneering, these early Canadian writers** produced verses on

---

*Mrs. Susanna Moodie, Mrs. Catharine Traill, and their brother Samuel, author of *Twenty-Seven Years in Canada West*. The 'gallant colonel', as his sister Agnes in England loved to call him, wrote in most respects a good account of his and other settlers' experiences, but Agnes, who edited the book in England, is no doubt largely responsible for a considerable amount of affectation, sentimentality, and effusiveness. The Stricklands, like many another family, brought to the New Land an irritating pretentiousness that did not enhance their popularity; though the sisters, at least, mellowed a great deal under pioneer conditions, as may be readily seen from a comparison of their later with their earlier writing.

**There were, of course, many others much better qualified as poets: notably Archibald Lampman, Bliss Carman, Charles G. D. Roberts, Isabel Ecclestone Mackay, Wilfred Campbell, Pauline Johnson.

ALEXANDER McLACHLAN

WILLIAM TELFORD

JOHN STEELE

JOHN MORTIMER

CANADIAN SCOTS INSPIRED BY ROBBIE BURNS

very homely subjects, and in the process have added not a little
to the gaiety of nations. William Telford of Smith Township
wrote a series on Potato Bugs, of which these are the last two:

> *Each year when the vile bugs come round*
> *To feast on my potatoes,*
> *I let them taste the Paris green,*
> *I give it to them* gratis.
>
> *They eat it, sicken, and they die;*
> *Death stops them in their mission:*
> *'Tis just what every bug deserves*
> *That eats without permission.*

John Steele, a rugged, bearded Scot, was fond of his *parritch*,
and wrote five verses on Oatmeal to which he believed all Scots
owed their greatness:

> *Look round and tell me where's the lan'*
> *That flourishes sae weel,*
> *As where they daily fill their mouth*
> *With Scotia's fragrant meal.*

John Mortimer of Elora liked farm animals, as well as enjoying the friendship of wild things. If Robbie Burns could write
about a Mouse—

> *Wee, sleekit, cowrin, tim'rous beastie—*

why shouldn't *he* write

A Tribute to the Toads

> *The Spring has reached our northern clime,*
> *Crows in the air abound;*
> *The snow is melting, and the time*
> *For toads will soon be round.*
>
> *I'm glad the spring will turn them out—*
> *I love so much to see*
> *Those sober creatures hop about*
> *Upon the grassy lea.*
>
> *Around our door they watch for flies,*
> *In coats of wrinkled brown;*
> *They sit and wink their bulging eyes,*
> *Their throats move up and down.*
>
> *They are so lowly in their ways,*
> *With warts all dotted o'er;*
> *I'll write these lines to sound their praise*
> *Though I should write no more!*

Education and Cultural Life

> *Oh! may their sober faces long*
> *Be in our gardens seen!*
> *And may they still be hale and strong*
> *While fields and grubs are green!*

As for democratic feeling, Alexander McLachlan believed that his new home, Canada, was the very place to give it practical application. In his 'Young Canada, or Jack's as Good as his Master' he follows closely Burns' sentiments in 'A Man's a Man for a' That'. He describes a Canada

> *Where none are slaves that lordly knaves*
> *May idle all the year;*
> *For rank and caste are of the past—*
> *They'll never flourish here!*
> *And Jew or Turk, if he'll but work,*
> *Need never fear disaster:*
> *He reaps the crop he sowed in hope,*
> *For Jack's as good's his master.*

CHAPTER XVI

RELIGIOUS LIFE

THE introduction of the Christian religion into Canada was through the energy and fervour of French Roman Catholic priests, many of whom became martyrs to their faith. Among the earliest priests in Upper Canada in the British period was the Reverend Edmund Burke, who was ministering to settlers as early as 1786. In 1794, at the request of Lieutenant-Governor Simcoe, he was sent as missionary to the Indians in the River Raisin district, near Detroit, then a part of the province. When Jay's Treaty came into effect in 1796 he crossed to Sandwich.

Appointed Vicar-General of Missions, he spent some years travelling from settlement to settlement in Upper Canada. In 1798 he appears to have stayed at Abner Miles' Inn at York, having come on horseback from the La Tranche (Thames) River. It was recorded in the inn's register that for 2s. 6d. he was supplied with a bed, 'three quarts of corn for the horse', and 'a half pint of wine and breakfast for the rider', after which he proceeded on his journey, ministering to the members of his faith wherever he found them. Dr. William Dunlop, a Presbyterian who had travelled widely in Upper Canada, considered Roman Catholic priests 'a moral and zealous clergy, . . . more strict in their attention to their parochial duties than any body of clergy I ever met in any part of the world, and not a bit more intolerant than their clerical brethren of any other sect'.

There was no general enthusiasm for religion among early settlers, as there would no doubt have been if large groups had left Britain, as in earlier times, because of religious persecution. There was, in fact, more commonly indifference,* and in most

*Perhaps this comment about themselves by early inhabitants of Norwich Township represents the average: 'The inhabitants consist of the Society of Friends, some Methodists, a few Baptists, and some, as to profession *Nothingarians,* but, generally speaking, encouragers of good moral, sober, and industrious habits.'

backwoods districts Sunday was like every other day, with work and business carried on openly. At best Sunday was a holiday and an occasion for visiting.

It is certainly desirable to have a pious neighbour remind them of the weekly return of the Sabbath [says a Presbyterian, John Mc-Donald, with reference to the more worldly settlers], for some have forgot its recurrence for they come in with their waggons full and transact all their business on the Lord's Day.

. . . .

We greatly felt, after we came into the Bush, [wrote 'An Emigrant Lady'] the want of all religious ordinances; but we soon arranged a general meeting of all the members of the family on a Sunday at your sister's, when your brother-in-law read the Church of England service and all joined in singing the chants and hymns.

But she gave credit to 'the Scotch Presbyterians' for an example of Sunday observance, for when invitations to a raising bee were issued on that day the Presbyterians were 'offended' and only three people turned up at the bee. The locality referred to was in Muskoka, 18 miles from Bracebridge, which was in process of first settlement in the late 'sixties and early 'seventies.

In earlier times particularly, occasional visits by travelling missionaries formed the only contact with religion. While many earnest people looked upon these as golden opportunities and seized them eagerly, others accepted them in characteristic pioneer fashion as merely a chance to meet people and relieve the feeling of isolation, greeting the preacher as a novelty but not being permanently impressed. But many of our pioneers loved to sing with all their might,* whether quite in harmony or not; and Scripture readings, exhortations, and prayers interspersed with numerous hearty 'Amens!' and 'Hallelujahs!' from the benches characterised many services.

When Methodist camp-meetings were held, whether in 'the Bush' or along 'the front', they were the scene of great emotional excitement, and at times of hysteria, immorality, and other excesses. In fact many of that sect were known as 'shouting Methodists', and their revivals were characterised by noise and confusion. But no other religious group quite equalled the Methodists in their zealous missionary and educational work

---

*The obituary notice of Mrs. Martha (White) Watts of Warsaw, Dummer Township, notes that the members of the White family were all fond of music, and several of them were precentors—leaders in singing for choir and congregation. After a hard day's work, we are told, it was no hardship to walk long distances 'to take instruction from the late Mr. Nathan Choate who was so generous in providing a room, heat, and light and gave free music education to all who were interested, for 20 years.'

among the Indians, and the camp-meeting often provided the initial approach. Peter Jones, halfbreed son of the noted early land surveyor, Augustus Jones, and his Indian wife, was among many converted at a meeting at Ancaster in 1823. As Dr. William Canniff put it, camp-meetings were 'peculiarly calculated to impress the Indians with solemn thoughts'; for they

Royal Ontario Museum   Charles Fothergill

LOG HOUSES, RICE LAKE, 1819
The Widow Harris' Trading-Post, near Hiawatha Indian village.

were children of the forest, which seemed to them the true place for worship. So while unscrupulous traders were cheating and debauching the Indians with whiskey, the Methodists were undoing some of the mischief. The red glare of the fires in the forest, the excitement of the crowd swayed by the exhorters, the baptisms and conversions as they thundered out 'O for a thousand tongues to sing my great Redeemer's praise!'—these picturesque elements in the camp-meeting were almost universally recognized in the pioneer period as not only attractive but highly valuable; and for many, as for the Reverend Joseph Hilts, there was on this earth no place 'more like heaven than a good live camp-meeting'.*

*Patrick Shirreff's *Tour through North America* (1835) was considered by John Langton, himself one of the best of settlers, to be 'the fairest and most practical' of all travel books he had seen. Shirreff gives perhaps the best and most unbiassed account of a camp-meeting, pp. 184-8. Captain Basil Hall and his wife saw one in progress in a 'silvan cathedral' between Oshawa and Bowmanville, and were favourably impressed by the proceedings, which, they considered, 'must, upon the whole, do good'. (*Travels in America in 1827 and 1828,* Volume I, pp. 274-9). Many observers considered emotional religion an alternative to whiskey sprees as relaxation from toil and isolation.

E. C. Bigley

CHURCH OF ENGLAND, FENELON FALLS, ERECTED 1835-36
The land was donated by James Wallis.

JOSEPH SCRIVEN'S HOME, PORT HOPE
The author of the hymn *What a Friend We Have in Jesus!*

But discrimination was early characteristic of religious life in Upper Canada, and Methodists and other important sects were long forbidden by law to own land for chapels (the word 'church' was at first monopolized by the Church of England), or for parsonages and cemeteries;* nor could their clergy solemnize marriage. Petty persecution by magistrates and social ostracism by Episcopalians combined to embitter personal feelings.** The Loyalists, and American settlers generally, were prominent in the battle against despotism and for equal rights to religious, political, and educational freedom, for they had experienced more of these liberties than had most immigrants from the British Isles.

There were, on the other hand, choice spirits who rose above the pettiness of religious dogmatism. Nicholas Sparks, one of the founders of Ottawa, gave sites for several churches. William Dixon of Peterborough, reared an Anglican, allowed Methodists to hold services on his premises and liberally contributed to the building of their church. Peter Pearce and his wife, of Norwood, opened their home to various municipal and religious meetings, as well as entertaining without charge a continual stream of travellers before a tavern was opened in the village. Jesse Ketchum was similarly generous to various denominations in early York (Toronto), and the list of such people could be extended widely throughout Upper Canada.

As in the United States, from which, as now, came most of the province's social customs and manners, the growth of religion was the development of innumerable sects, a few of them characterized by more enthusiasm than sense. Another result of diversity was that few sects were adequately supported. At first church services were held in homes, and when a log building was erected as a school it frequently was used for church serv-

---

*There are numerous unpleasant stories of religious discrimination in burials. At first cemeteries were largely Church of England, and if 'dissenters' were allowed to be buried therein they were at times discriminated against in the use of facilities. Emerson Taylor, prominent citizen of Springfield-on-the-Credit (now Erindale), inaugurated the village's Union Cemetery when he bought a piece of land adjoining the Church of England Cemetery to accommodate the body of a man of questionable character who had been refused burial with the 'respectable'. (See 'Old Times in Ontario', *Toronto Daily Star*, December 20, 1958).

**All the bitterness was not between the Church of England and 'dissenters', however, for the dissenting sects often cordially hated each other, and reviled one another vehemently. Abject and public confession of sin was frequently insisted upon for 'backsliders', and for members of other sects seeking re-admission after their 'sin' of joining another sect, even when it had resulted merely through a wife's taking her husband's religion on marriage.

ices as well, sometimes by more than one religious body. One in Muskoka in 1871 was used by Church of England, Wesleyan, and Presbyterian adherents.

The first churches were erected by co-operative effort. When an Anglican church was built at Fenelon Falls in the eighteen-thirties the moneyed 'gentlemen' gave cash while 'the labouring classes' contributed tradesmen's work on the structure; but a more common pioneer procedure was for all to share in the construction at a raising bee, and sometimes a well-to-do settler or a friend in the Old Country donated the land or most of the cash needed for the project. Not infrequently religious groups

Photograph by the Author

OLD METHODIST CHURCH NEAR RENFREW, 1846

settled together in one district, and numerous townships could be named whose earliest settlers were predominantly Roman Catholic, Methodist, Mennonite, Quaker, Baptist, Anglican, or Presbyterian.

The chief denominations today were also most important in the pioneer period, with the exception that the Methodist church (which was itself formed by a union of the Bible Christian Church and several sects of Methodists*) became a component part of the United Church of Canada in 1925. The

*The chief of these were 'American', who were often accused of mixing politics with religion and of being republican in sympathy, and 'Wesleyan' which a Presbyterian, Dr. William Dunlop, described as 'much less numerous but infinitely more respectable'.

Presbyterian Church was early disrupted by division,* and in some districts, we are told, politics had as much to do with their membership as dogma. At times a knowledge of Gaelic was a *sine qua non* of appointment to a charge.

The Church of England habit of describing all non-Anglicans as 'dissenters' was brought by them to the New Land, where, however, that church was never 'established', though occupying a privileged position because of control from England and the consequent predominance of members of the denomination in high places. The Clergy Reserves, long almost exclusively for their benefit and designed to supply religion to Church of England adherents 'without charge', not only hindered the development of the province but militated against the best interests of the church itself, as one of its most public-spirited laymen—John Langton—pointed out; for some of its clergy were more inclined to expect a good 'living' provided for them, as in Britain, than to enter upon the arduous work of developing and extending their parish, which was necessary for their own success as well as to secure the respect and support of the settlers in 'the Bush', who found that *they* had to work hard for a living.

Yet there were a number of Anglican missionaries who pushed into outlying regions like Manitoulin Island, carrying the gospel to Indian and settler alike. A clergyman's stipend, though not always collected in full, usually consisted of a fixed allowance plus a grant from England. But the Reverend Vincentius Mayerhoffer,** who ministered to three charges in Markham and Vaughan townships, had his stipend reduced by £30 annually to allow a retiring allowance to his superannuated predecessor.† For the first year, consequently, he received a net salary of £20, and thereafter £50; and though his parishioners promised to make up the deficit they failed to

---

*The two main sects were the Established Church of Scotland and the seceders—the Presbytery of Upper Canada—who were largely with Ulster or American connections.

**This colourful character came to Upper Canada in 1829 as Church of England missionary to German settlers, and preached in both German and English each Sunday. He had had hair-raising adventures as a soldier and priest during the Napoleonic Wars and 'exposed' the Roman Catholic Church in *Twelve Years a Roman Catholic Priest* (1861). He was equally sure of himself during the Rebellion excitement, for we are told that 'the Orange Boys . . . came in a body to Markham and gave three cheers for "old Tory Mayerhoffer",' threatening to hang all rebels on the nearest tree.

†In general it may be said that clergymen of all denominations, in the absence of adequate salaries and superannuation allowances, lived an old age of poverty relieved only by 'purses' and other charitable presentations by their parishioners and friends.

do so. At Thornhill the Reverend Isaac Fidler received £100, but it was paid by the Bishop of Quebec who hoped to be reimbursed by the parishioners. Later there was a large income from the Reserves or 'Glebe Lands'. The controversy over Clergy Reserves embittered political and religious life for half a century.

The desire to be pompous and socially exclusive has not disappeared through the force of democracy, but it was much more widespread in parts of early Upper Canada. The early St. James' Church at York (Toronto), with all the orthodox gradations of pulpit, reading-desk, and clerk's pew, had as well reserved pews for the lieutenant-governor, chief justice, members of parliament, and officers of the garrison (sometimes escorted to service by a military band), and when the local gentry were seated in their places, there was (as more than one observer noticed) no place for the poor.* The church, in fact—as the Reverend Henry Scadding points out in *Toronto of Old*—resembled a courtroom. The more distinguished, of course, came in carriages, like Sir Edward Poore, a Grafton aristocrat who attended the Church of England in Cobourg. His carriage was equipped with footmen at front and rear, who, upon reaching St. Peter's, led Sir Edward and his entourage to the reserved pew, unlatched its gate, closed it again, and returned to the carriage to await the end of the service. It was quite a pageant.

In the absence of other schools, and to supplement their meagre stipends, Presbyterian and Church of England clergymen sometimes taught school as well. The Reverend Isaac Fidler came across one Anglican clergyman who, 'destitute of interest or patronage', was forced to remain 'a mere teacher'; in fact the consequence was that he emigrated to the United States, was similarly disappointed at conditions there, and returned to England. The Methodist ministers, who were almost continually travelling, could not teach, nor were they usually as qualified for teaching;**but three or four religious services a day, often in

*Mrs. Mary Lambert Smale, wife of an English clergyman, felt constrained to do something about it and gave £5000 in 1845 for the building of a Church of England for the poorer people of Toronto. Holy Trinity Church was erected as a result of her beneficence.

**The Reverend Isaac Fidler, Church of England, graded Roman Catholic priests 'second to Episcopal Clergymen alone' in the matter of sound learning; and he placed the Methodists, 'withal most inveterate against the established Church', at the bottom of the educational ladder. A glance at the numerous diaries of their early clergy shows that in language and method the Methodists were emotional and evangelical, not formal or intellectual; but they left a great legacy, the *Christian Guardian*—Upper Canada's most influential newspaper—and provided Egerton Ryerson, the founder of our educational system. There are several sects which, even today, prefer a minimum of education, considering that their beliefs and way of life are best accepted by the uneducated.

widely separated districts, were not too much for their energy and enthusiasm; and in many districts Methodists met several times a week in 'class-meetings' and 'love-feasts'.

All denominations emphasized Sunday Schools, and all persuasions might attend one school where the population was sparse. In addition to homes and schools, it was not unusual for clergy of all denominations to preach in barns, court houses, mills, taverns, and sometimes in the woods. Travelling clergymen and missionaries were seldom well paid, but as they lived without charge at homes along their route they needed but little cash. Difficulties of travel at other seasons made winter best for religious services, though adequate heating of any type of building was a problem. Emphasis upon Bible-reading and revivals often led to the use of Bible names for children, and others like Bethel, Salem, Jordan, and Zion for settlements.*

Baptist clergymen provided some townships with their first religious contacts. In Reach Township, for example, we find that a Baptist preacher, Elder Marsh, was the first to bring religion to the district; and that he was soon afterwards followed by Elder Scott, an agent of the American Missionary Society who did much to improve conditions among the Scugog Indians. Prominent in helping him in the work was a youth, Aaron Hurd, who though only fifteen years old taught Indian children in a log schoolhouse erected for the purpose on the northern side of the farm of his father, Abner Hurd.

In his *Retrospect of Thirty-Six Years' Residence in Canada West,* the Reverend John Carruthers, a Presbyterian, describes religious services he conducted as he made a missionary journey in 1833:

Zorra Township:
Walked through the forest three miles for public worship and entered a large log building, without windows, door, or fire. . . . I was struck with the number of persons closely seated together on boards and benches to the number of nearly two hundred, with their Bibles in their hands. We commenced by singing the 122nd Psalm and I delivered a lecture from a portion of the Book of Acts. Closed this interesting service by singing the 61st Scriptural Paraphrase.

Vittoria Township:
There was a goodly number of Baptists here, and I was invited to preach on the Sabbath in their Church, which I did, and had a very respectable audience of about 100 persons. . . . I was invited to deliver a lecture at Mr. Van Norman's Furnace, where a number of workmen were employed.

*See pp. 246-7 for other examples.

Eva Brook Donly Historical Museum · · · · · · · · · · · · W. E. Cantelon

BUILDING THE FIRST BAPTIST CHURCH, SIMCOE

Courtesy Orrie Vail

FIRST BAPTIST CHURCH, TOBERMORY

Innisfil, Essa, and Adjala Townships:

Rode into the township of Innisfil and kept an appointment there. This was the first Presbyterian service which the settlers here had enjoyed on the Lord's day. Next day travelled west to the township of Adjala. This township was chiefly settled by Roman Catholics. They have built a church and are to be visited by the priest once a month. There is a story told of the early settlers of Essa, cornering Adjala, that they would not allow a Catholic to settle among them.

Courtesy of the Artist   Edith Macklin

THE OLD KIRK, COBOURG

Boarded up its windows,
Taken off its tower,
Naught but graves around it—
Graves without a flower.
—Carrie Munson Hoople.

Methodist ministers were particularly noted for their energy in supplying the religious needs of large circuits. In 1827 the Reverend Egerton Ryerson, subsequently the founder of Ontario's system of education, served the Cobourg circuit, travelling on foot or horseback from 200 to 300 miles a month between Bowmanville and the River Trent and northward to Rice Lake and Seymour and Murray townships.

I require a man [wrote the Reverend H. Wilkinson to Ryerson ten years later] for a mission which lies about 200 miles from Bytown [Ottawa] up the Grand River, and which will be difficult of access in the winter. A suitable person could make his way northward with some of the rude lumbermen. . . . He would need to go on foot, and paddle a canoe or row a boat, as the case might be, and thus reach his appointments in the best way he can.

The Reverend Jabez Culver, the first ordained preacher in Norfolk County, rode about the country, says E. A. Owen, in a rude cart consisting of a home-made wooden axle-tree, to which was attached a pair of shafts and the two front wheels of a 'Jersey'

PRESBYTERIAN CHURCH, BEAVERTON, ERECTED 1840

linch-pin lumber waggon. A rope seat was arranged over the axletree, and a bell was attached to the horse, so that while that animal was picking his own living during the hours of religious service, it might be easily found when the time came for jogging along to the next 'appointment'.

There were certain customs at church services that surprised clergymen and travellers who were not used to backwoods life. One of these was that men usually sat on one side and women on the other. People not infrequently walked in and out during the service. Men often wore their work clothes, and if the room was overheated they thought nothing of taking off their coats, Women did not wear hats,* and on occasion might be seen suckling children during the service—'certainly a very odd appearance', as a Presbyterian clergyman put it.

*The introduction of the current custom of wearing hats is apparently a survival similar to 'the churching of women after childbirth', which originated in a belief that sex is sinful and childbirth consequently impure and a part of human depravity. That the human race perpetuates itself in sin and that children are born sinful ('the old Adam' in the christening service) seem to many not only incredible but a reflection upon intelligence, and a large number of church members consider all such beliefs archaic. See also p. 114 fn.

In general it may be said that, as illiteracy was prevalent, emotional rather than intellectual religion was most popular, but sermons were appreciated, even lengthy ones, provided they were not read. In the more evangelical churches loud singing and praying characterised meetings, a habit which some observers took to be a safety valve—a sort of letting off steam; but in many instances it no doubt represented depth of religious feeling or experience*. 'Other-worldliness'—that things would be better 'in the sweet by and by' (as the old hymn put it)—was a persistent belief and provided an escape from the present. The hymns sung in most churches have a sad and melancholy tone, reflecting the age in which they were written, when they were designed for emotional release and mental deliverance from the hardship, sorrow, illness, and death with which people were surrounded, both in the Old Land and the New.

Among the best settlers in various parts of the province were the peaceful Mennonites from Pennsylvania. The Society of Friends, or Quakers, were also more numerous and widespread in Upper Canada than is generally assumed. Their missionaries were sometimes sent into Canada from the United States, and the diary is extant of Phoebe Roberts, one of a party of four— the others were Jemima Burson, Jacob Albertson, and Cyrus Betts—who made a laborious tour of Upper Canada in 1821, calling upon many hundreds of members of the sect and holding meetings at numerous points along the main roads and in the rear concessions. These zealous Friends attended some forty-five meetings during their 2200-mile journey of great difficulty. Sober and industrious people, the members of this sect played no small part in the advance of religion amid the rigours and privations of pioneer life. Opposed to war and fighting of any kind, they were excused from militia duty upon payment of an annual tax. No religious bodies have made less compromise with the world in pursuing the tenets of their faith than the Friends and Mennonites.**

*There was, says E. A. Owen, only one kind of *meetin'* in the pioneer period —a *religious meetin'*—and many a man or woman experienced conversion there. One old settler in the Long Point region put it this way: 'True conversion is just like poppin' out of a tar barrel into the blazin' light of the noonday's sun!' Owen, historian of the district, tells of one man who had been pretty wild in his youth that upon his conversion he was so happy that he felt constrained to walk 500 miles to tell a friend in a distant settlement.

**For the Roberts diary, edited by Leslie R. Gray, see *Ontario History,* Volume XLII (1950), No. 1. There is at least one Mennonite church where the Old-Order horse-and-buggy people come to one service, while the New-Order who drive cars have a later service of their own. For the history of the Friends see A. G. Dorland, *A History of the Society of Friends (Quakers) in Canada* (1927).

SHARON TEMPLE

Probably the most distinctive of early Ontario church buildings.

Conservation Authorities, Ontario

INTERIOR OF MENNONITE CHURCH, EDGELEY, 1949

A local offshoot of the Society was 'King David' Willson's 'Children of Peace', at Hope (now Sharon) in north York County.* From time to time they entered York in a procession of wagons, the female 'disciples' dressed in white. An idea of their leader's opinions may be gauged from the subject of one of his addresses in the capital—'Public Affairs: their Total Depravity'. While considered eccentric in their day, they were at least as important as other religious groups in leavening the vicious and profane of the period of pioneering.**

Innumerable children went unbaptized in Upper Canada, though some parents who showed no other interest in religion were known to rush sick children to clergymen for baptism in case they died, and some of the clergy refused on theological grounds to do anything about it. Such unintelligent, narrow-minded ministers of the Gospel obviously did more to lessen religious faith than to increase its force.† Most adults were

*Sharon Temple has fortunately been preserved as a historical museum under the control of the York Pioneer and Historical Society.
**Contemporary descriptions of the activities of this colourful sect may be found in the author's *Pioneer Life in the County of York*, Chapter X. As it was considered a working-class movement it was distasteful to the socially exclusive. An interesting description of the Temple service is given by Mazo de la Roche in her autobiography *Ringing the Changes*, pp. 7-9, and it is the more valuable because one of her great-grandfathers was prominent among the Children of Peace.
†There were others who affected people's peace of mind by declaring that sickness, and particularly epidemics, were 'visitations of God's wrath'. (See Chapter IX, above, and Vol. II, pp. 51-2.)

similarly unbaptized, and perhaps we need not evince the same surprise the clergy of the day did when they found that few people were interested enough to call at a clergyman's home for prayer-books, tracts, or catechisms—even if free. Indeed, it is said that many church members would not make the effort or take the time (the pioneers always hated to *lose time!*) to send for the pastor when death was near in the family.

To understand the relation between religious belief and ideological philosophy in the pioneer period one must recognize that the undemocratic ruling clique—the 'Family Compact'—was exclusively Church of England and hated democracy as fervidly as it is the fashion to hate communism today.* In that period it was very definitely the classes against the masses. More than one fervent Churchman, like Thomas Magrath, in lamenting the spirit of independence and equality that was becoming characteristic of the New Land, suggested that one of the best arguments for the sending out from England of more Church of England clergy was that they would always be found in opposition to those democratic principles that received their chief impetus from the unorthodox dissenters.

But the general development of freedom and free-thinking led some people into highly fanatical religious sects, among which were the Millerites of the eighteen-forties who persuaded themselves that the world was about to end in a blaze of fire; and in some instances they burned their rail fences or sold their farms in preparation.** Other religious reformers were more sensible, merely taking exception to liturgy, ceremony, and language, however sanctified by tradition, custom, and authority. Many who had been Episcopalian in Britain joined other churches in Canada, either from choice or because of the fewness of Anglican clergy.†

*Sir Francis Head, great-great-grandson of Sir Francis Bond Head, Lieutenant-Governor of Upper Canada at the time of the Rebellion of 1837, has recently expressed his feelings on the matter in almost exactly the same terms. 'I believe old Sir F. B. Head gets a slightly better press nowadays in Canada than he used to do. In his day, of course, democracy was as dirty a word as communism is today, and one must realize that when judging his action.' (See 'Just in Passing' by Jo Carson, Toronto *Globe and Mail*, March 31, 1962.)

**It is recorded that Sarah Terwilligar made herself wings to fly to heaven and jumped from her bedroom window.

†The bishop's 1849 announcement on the state of the Church gave the total clergy as 130, of whom 32 were in towns, 5 among the Indians, and 93 in rural parts. He stated that 241 townships in course of settlement were practically destitute of religious instruction from the Church of England. In 1855 there were 1559 churches in the province, with 952,000 adherents; of these 226 were Church of England, 135 Roman Catholic, 148 Presbyterian, and 471 Methodist. As people do today, many—probably at least one-third of the total—claimed membership in churches which had no record of their connection.

The simplicity of the services of 'dissenters', even though the sermons were commonly more lengthy, attracted many who objected to the frequent change of posture in the more orthodox Church of England service. The liturgy was too long and fatiguing, they said, the Lord's Prayer too often repeated, and some of the many other prayers might well be omitted.* The place and the time seemed to be appropriate for a reconsideration of religious faith and practice, and in the New Land a large number who had never given the matter much thought in the Old suddenly discovered that parts of the marriage service were objectionable—especially the preamble—and some references even indelicate. Sometimes unmarried girls were known to prefer to live with the men of their choice, without marriage,** rather than say 'obey' or 'With my body I thee worship'—worship was due to God alone, they said, and the expression was in questionable taste as well. Women, of course, had no part in the writing of the prayerbook, which reflects male attitudes of an earlier age.

Burials and funerals, to which hundreds of settlers would come on the shortest notice, are usually associated with church and religion, but it was not always so in the pioneer period. Many settlers were buried on their own land, frequently without benefit of clergy and with no mark to designate their final rest-

---

*To Colonel Thomas Talbot, we are told, and no doubt to others from the Army or Navy, the Church of England service was merely a disciplinary survival to which he had become accustomed; and during his last twenty years he made no pretence of religious observance, which, indeed, had had no effect upon his dissipated habits or the rough treatment with which he granted—or refused to grant—land to those who sought to settle on his vast domain along Lake Erie. When he died the same scant respect was shown to his funeral and to his memory.

**Shakespeare says, 'There is nothing either good or bad but thinking makes it so'. Many a prominent early fur-trader 'married' one or more Indian women, and it is now quite fashionable in Montreal, where some of their descendants reside, to look back with pride to these 'illegitimate' ancestors. A curious example of the same kind is described in an account of an early scheme of settlement on St. Joseph Island. Prominent in it was a Welshman and Peninsular War veteran, Major William Rains, who obtained what is called 'a Church separation' from his wife and brought out to Canada with him two beautiful young Welsh sisters, Frances and Eliza Doubleday, and a young son that Frances had already borne to him. But the sisters were devoted to one another, and both in love with him, so Rains lived 'in sin' with both on St. Joseph Island, providing, says a granddaughter, 'a separate domicile for each'. The two families of women and children grew up harmoniously side by side, we are told, and took the name of Rains. 'The ladies seldom went anywhere, being content with their children and books. . . . They were keen, clever, and witty women, and endowed with more than ordinary beauty'. But it was probably fortunate, in the circumstances, that the planned settlement of the island did not materialize under Rains' direction. ('An Early Settlement on St. Joseph Island', *Ontario History*, Volume LIII, No. 4.)

Photograph by George M. Douglas, 1943

BURIAL PLACE OF CAPT. G. A. HILL, HIS WIFE AND DAUGHTER

Captain Hill was a veteran of Waterloo, first Warden of the district,
author, educationist, and clerk of the Township of Dummer.

ing-place. But J. B. Brown found it 'touchingly interesting' to see in the early eighteen-forties

a solitary grave-slab (of wood, not *stone*), meekly rising from the lowly grave-mound near an old established looking settler's homestead, its simple lettered story upon the white painted board telling of one or more breaches in the family since it came there; and further onward, again, in a quiet hollow nook by a clear running stream, you come upon a neatly-fenced square plot,* waving with long grass, and the plain and humble monuments, all new-like and of late date, and but, as yet, thinly sprinkled over it.

Courtesy George M. Douglas

ROGERS GRAVES, YOUNG'S POINT

The first white burial in old Charlotteville of which we have any account, traditional or otherwise, [wrote E. A. Owen] occurred in the year 1794 on the hill overlooking Turkey Point. The body buried was that of Frederick Mabee, the old pioneer head of the Mabee family. . . .

He was buried in a walnut log coffin. This rude casket was made as the old rain-troughs were made, and was provided with a tight-fitting slab which served as a lid. In after years when the remains were disinterred for the purpose of removal, the log coffin was apparently as sound as when first buried.

Because of the prevalence of suffering and the frequent deaths, even popular songs of the period took on a doleful, not

*John Mactaggart found cemeteries just the opposite, and said that he would hate to die in Canada: 'The churchyards are always placed on the most barren, sterile, rocky spots that can be selected, seldom or never fenced in but left to the mercy of the pigs and geese, the former to grub, the latter to gabble.'

to say morbid, tone. Here is one very similar in content and plaintiveness to the modern song *Where Have All the Flowers Gone?*, with its verses completing the cycle from flowers to young girls to young men to soldiers to graveyards and to flowers again:

> *Where! where will be the birds that sing,*
> *A hundred years to come?*
> *The flowers that now in beauty spring,*
> *A hundred years to come?*
> *The rosy lips, the lofty brow,*
> *The heart that beats so gaily now?*
> *Oh where will be love's beaming eye,*
> *Joy's pleasant smile and sorrow's sigh*
> *A hundred years to come?*
>
> *We all within our graves shall sleep*
> *A hundred years to come;*
> *No living soul for us will weep*
> *A hundred years to come;*
> *But other men our lands will till,*
> *And others then our streets will fill,*
> *While other birds will sing as gay,*
> *And bright the sun shine as to-day,*
> *A hundred years to come.**

In times of cholera and other epidemics many speedy and unceremonious burials occurred. One man in the Township of Ops, eight miles from a neighbour, had a burial which we may hope was unique. The father died soon after a heavy winter set in, and the young wife and two small children were unable to make contact with the outside world. Finding she could not even dig a grave in the frozen earth, she laboriously moved the woodpile, found the soil under it barely frozen, and dug her husband's grave. Wolves howled not far off, so she piled the wood back on the grave for protection.

Among deeply-rooted superstitions that long persisted in some localities were the *arvill* of the north of England and the *wake* of Ireland. Feasting, fighting, and drinking were often more prominent than any respect shown the dead—in fact, the corpse was occasionally given liquor as well!** For many an old

---

*Many, perhaps most, of the poems of Rhoda Anne Page were obsessed with suffering and death. See her *Wild Notes from the Back Woods* (1850) and the author's 'Canadian Literary Pioneers', Toronto Public Library. But Canadian folk-songs did not extend to pioneer farm life: see *Canada's Story in Song* by Edith Fowke, Alan Mills, and Helmut Blume.

**See M. A. Garland and J. J. Talman, 'Pioneer Drinking Habits, and the Rise of the Temperance Agitation in Upper Canada' (Ontario Historical Society, *Paper and Records*, Volume XXVII, p. 345).

BUTLER BURYING-GROUND NEAR NIAGARA

settler a 'burying' was a highlight among his few social gatherings, but the Irish wake was accompanied as well by extravagant demonstrations of grief* by those who could wail and shriek. John M. Synge, dramatist and authority on Irish peasant life, wrote that the *keen* was not so much to represent personal sorrow as

the whole passionate rage that lurks somewhere in every native of the island. In this cry of pain the inner consciousness of the people seems to lay itself bare for an instant and to reveal the mood of beings who feel their isolation in the face of a universe that wars on them with winds and seas. They are usually silent, but in the face of death all outward show of indifference or patience is forgotten; and they shriek with pitiable despair before the horror of the fate to which they all are doomed.

In towns and villages the crudities which often characterised religious services in 'the Bush' were either much less prominent or had long since disappeared. Church buildings of more advanced types were constructed in these larger settlements much earlier than elsewhere, and their clergy were usually established for years in the locality, though often ministering as well to neighbouring communities. Funerals were more regular, and cemeteries supplanted burial-places on farms.**

*Fortunately—but only in recent years—we have abandoned 'the widow's weeds', the wearing of deep black for a long period, sometimes six months.

**Something irrecoverable has been lost with the coming of the motor car, for the long processions of carriages and buggies that followed the dead to their graves demonstrated the dignified respect of the community in a very special way.

Courtesy Mrs. George Downey

STAGE AND HEARSE AT NELSON'S, UNDERTAKERS, TIVERTON

John and Flora Bannerman, early settlers in the Queen's Bush and grand-parents of Prime Minister Diefenbaker, are buried in Tiverton Cemetery.

The conflict of personal conduct and religion arose in some pioneer sects and churches, and not in others. Many an Englishman has been known to say that his private life is his own business and no concern of his church, but some sects expelled

FUNERAL OF BISHOP STRACHAN, TORONTO, 1867

members for bad conduct. Private confession of 'sins' in one denomination and public confession in another were insisted upon, while in others the subject was mentioned but indirectly, indefinitely, and very discreetly—or not at all. And many people wondered—in that day as in our own—whether good works and morality were not heavily overborne in almost all sects by superstition, dogma, and liturgy on the one hand and hysterical emotionalism on the other.

The author has a typed copy of the Records of the Beamsville Baptist Church from October 16, 1807, to August 7, 1859. The settlement was early called Clinton, and later named Beamsville after Jacob Beam, one of the founders of this church. The business meetings of the church were devoted largely to reports of investigations into the conduct of members, the qualifications and baptism of new candidates, the exclusion or excommunication of those whose conduct offended the church, and financial arrangements. Apart from their faith, the object of members was good conduct and an avoidance of anger, swearing, cheating, frivolity, adultery, tavern-haunting, bad company, intemperance, and whatever else appeared to them to be in the category of sin. Valuable lists of members appear in the record from time to time, with any changes of status noted.

It was the same in early times with respect to the use of spirituous liquors. The Methodists* were strongly opposed to their use, but there was no general condemnation until Temperance and Total Abstinence Societies paved the way, and even then sects were not a unit. In some churches, in fact, the connection between religion and whiskey was not infrequently close in the pioneer period, for distilleries were found everywhere. The farmer brought in his loads of grain, often receiving a share of the whiskey in part payment. The profit was good even at 17 cents a gallon, and it is known that many distillers were generous churchmen. One of them, Jacob Beam (originally *Boehm*), gave strong financial backing to at least ten Baptist churches in the Niagara district, and no one took exception to the origin of the support. The 'tainted money' attitude coincided with the subsequent development of Temperance Societies.

*'Port Hope . . . is full of enterprise and spirit, but so full of whiskey and sin that it bears the name of "Sodom". My text was, "Some have not the knowledge of God: I speak it to your shame". The wedge is now entered, and if we can manage to get a congregation, Sodom may yet be redeemed.' (*The Life and Times of the Rev. Anson Green, D. D.*). Port Hope was early noted for distilleries, but probably not more so than many another village.

The use of musical instruments at church services came gradually, and only after bitter opposition. Nothing—other than the scandalous feeling of exclusiveness that still prevents Christian sects from taking communion together—exemplifies more strongly the emotional basis of religion than the attitude towards church music.

The matter was not of great importance in Roman Catholic and Church of England congregations, for both followed closely the forms and liturgy of centuries. But the non-conformists took varying views, and at times became quite hysterical on the subject.

The violin, the common instrument of the day, was used for dancing, and the Methodists and occasionally other sects transferred their hatred for dancing to the instrument which accompanied it, which categorically became the Devil's own; and having outlawed the only available musical instrument, they were without any.

The more strict of Scottish Presbyterians vented their hatred upon the organ when it began to be available. In more than one district it was outlawed as 'the Deil's kest o' whustles', and only a tuning-fork was permitted to set the tone for congregational singing.

The Friends, Mennonites, and other sects provided religious life with or without music, according to their principles. David Willson's Children of Peace are of special interest, for they comprised seceded Quakers who were fond of music. Their Temple at Sharon was erected in 1825, but even earlier they had a very effective choir; and their band was one of the earliest in the province, and reputed to be the best. Colourful marches and parades by 'King David' and his followers added a good deal to the liveliness of the times.*

Elsewhere music added not a little to religious life. The diary of Joseph Abbott describes the life of 'Father' Tenny, to whom almost everyone in the district was indebted, and for a variety of reasons:

December 19th, Sunday.—Six double and nine single sleighs at church. Old Mr. Tenny broke the finest string of his bass viol, which

---

*A more detailed account may be found in the author's *Pioneer Life in the County of York*. The Salvation Army, which emphasizes music and marching, began its work in Canada in 1882, amid attacks and opposition from mobs of people including 'religionists' of other sects. Several efforts were made to burn their first place of meeting—the 'mother barracks' in Toronto. See the author's 'Old Times in Ontario', *Toronto Daily Star*, June 17, 1961.

created a good deal of confusion among the singers, enough to engross the whole conversation in the settlement during the following week. He was quite an original character, I mean this Mr. Tenny; he was by trade a carpenter, and a clever and ingenious one; an enthusiast in psalmody, he led the singing in the church, made himself this his own bass viol, played upon it and sung to it, taught the whole settlement all they knew of sacred music, built all the houses and barns in it—plastered the houses—cut the stones for the fire places, and built them—made all the furniture—in short he was the father of the settlement in every point of view, besides that which entitled him to this distinctive appellation, being the oldest man in it.

Haliburton village was similarly indebted to an Englishman, Dr. Peake; for prior to the presentation of an organ by Judge Haliburton (author of *Sam Slick*) he led the choir with an accordeon mounted on a frame and run with a treadle. His repertoire comprised but two tunes—'The Evening Hymn' and 'March of the Men of Harlech'—but we are told that both were utilized in as effective a manner as possible and to the satisfaction of all.

The celebration of festivals in the pioneer period was confused by controversy and jealousy between religious sects. December 25th is only one of several days which early Christians celebrated as the birthday of Christ, which is unknown. Some sects disliked Christmas because of its partially pagan pre-Christian origin, others because they considered it predominantly a Church of England or Roman Catholic festival.* Puritan immigrants who came to Canada from the New England States tended to replace Christmas by the celebration of Thanksgiving Day; and Scots, following the custom in Scotland, to ignore Christmas and celebrate New Year's Day, with 'first-footing' on New Year's Eve.

The typically English Christmas was brought to Canada by early settlers, both from the Old Land and the United States. Feasting and religious observance characterised the day, but many were too poor to make much of it. Turkeys were available but not common. The Langtons note that the ingredients for a plum pudding were hard to come by and a crude substitute had to be used; and a poorer settler recorded that a scrawny chicken

---

*Emotional thinking in religion, as in the spheres of war and politics, makes intelligent discussion impossible. The man of closed mind who considers his religion the only true one and believes those who differ from him are mere bigots has fallen into one of the most dishonest habits of thought. It requires no thinking to be intolerant.

Canadian Illustrated News

SANTA CLAUS IN 1862

Santa Claus, evergreens, and various other current accompaniments of the Christmas season have their origins in pre-Christian antiquity, but much else has been added in modern times. Santa Claus a century ago approached homes by a ladder, not via reindeer and sleigh through the air. He was a sober citizen with neither red costume, snowy-white beard, nor jovial laugh (or cackle), which probably originated in a Sunday School or a department store. The toys and stockings pass current, but the pipe strikes a foreign note. Christmas, if celebrated at all, was a family day in Upper Canada, associated with feasting, church-going, visiting, and winter sports. In many instances toys and dolls for the children were hand-made at home.

was with difficulty saved for the occasion. Mary (Gapper) O'Brien wrote in her diary: 'Our Presbeterian [*sic*] population gives us little sympathy in the associations of Christmas', but she observed that the Scots had no objection to partaking of a good dinner. John Thomson, settled in the same region (near Lake Simcoe) noted in his diary on December 25, 1833, merely: 'Christmas, all people idle & feasting'. It was frequently a time for visiting friends at a distance.

If Christmas was to many merely a holiday, the Children of Peace at Sharon more than made up for such perfunctory observance by their elaborate service. At 5 a.m. they assembled in the meeting-house, which was distinct from the Temple. After the service, breakfast was provided, and a second ceremony commenced at 11 a.m. Following this the whole congregation were led by their band to the Temple, where they offered their Christmas contributions, and another meal was then served to all in the meeting-house.

As the years passed, the day tended to lose much of its theological significance. Even eighty years ago commentators on the social scene like Goldwin Smith said that Christmas was becoming another family day like a Sunday or other holiday. The popularity of Charles Dickens' works, and notably *The Christmas Carol* (1843), tended to make the English Christmas more widespread.* The first Christmas cards, for many years usually merely flower pictures, were sent in England in 1843, while Christmas trees, a German custom, were more widely used after Queen Victoria married Prince Albert in 1840. Religion, including Christianity, has never lacked elements of commercialization within its practice, and they have often been offensively prominent, but the modern popularized, sentimentalized, and highly commercialized Christmas is obviously quite modern and very American.

Considering all the difficulties, it is apparent that the clergy of the pioneer period, whether Roman Catholic priests, regular Protestant ministers, the quiet and unostentatious Mennonites and Sons of Peace, or itinerant preachers and missionaries,** are to be credited with providing, within their limitations, Christian enlightenment and spiritual consolation† amid conditions often materialistic, crude, and primitive.

*'*Twas the Night before Christmas*, written by C. C. Moore for his grandchildren in 1822, had a gradual but ever-increasing influence on the popular image of Santa Claus, at first a sober-sides in dark, even drab, clothing.

**See the author's *The Valley of the Trent*, Section IX, for journals of one Methodist and three Church of England clergymen, descriptive of their experiences as circuit-riders and itinerant missionaries.

†Other religions were unimportant in the period of pioneering. The Jewish religion was formally introduced into Canada in Montreal in 1777, but the first Jewish synagogue in Ontario appears to have been Holy Blossom, opened in Toronto in 1849. The Unitarian Society, which early attracted intellectuals of the calibre of Emerson and Thoreau in the New England states, was introduced to Canada in Montreal in 1842. Toronto, described by Florence B. Steiner as 'particularly inhospitable' to freedom of thought and 'rational tendencies in religion'—a statement for which there is ample justification historically—had its first Unitarian congregation in 1845. (See her pamphlet, *One Hundred Years of Service, 1845-1945*.)

CHAPTER XVII

CHARACTERISTICS OF THE SETTLERS

WANTED IN THIS VILLAGE
FOR THE YEAR 1831

More industry and less idleness;
More economy and less extravagance;
More honest men than rogues;
More money than credit;
More shirts than ruffles;
More morality than grog-shops;
More mechanics than dandies;
More stocking-yarn than street-yarn;
More stability than excitability;
More laborers than loungers;
More justice and less law.

—*The Genesee Farmer*, Rochester, January 29, 1831.

WHAT were the people like who had long been settled, as well as those who were emigrating from Europe and the United States in ever-increasing numbers to continue the settlement and accelerate the progress of this part of Canada? The era of pioneering was one of real enterprise, and there is no question but that initiative and hard work were necessary to ensure success. People who would succeed in these circumstances, however servile and downtrodden they had seemed in the Old Land, speedily became independent in the New, with a great dislike for all restraint. But though some of them would boast that they were 'self-made men' who owed very little to school, church, or other agency beyond their own efforts, yet it is characteristic that they strove hard to provide something better for their children.

In 1791 there were about 10,000 inhabitants in Upper Canada, as it was then named by the terms of the Canada Act.

They were largely of American origin, but some were French.* When the War of 1812 opened the population had increased to some 70,000, of whom at least three-fifths were of American origin and many of them Loyalists or their descendants. The War of 1812, and the Napoleonic wars of which it was a part, were no sooner over than emigration to America began to be something more than the casual and occasional removal of British citizens to the New Land. Retired officers and men who had fought against the Americans were offered special terms if they would take up land in Canada. Most formalities and all fees were omitted, and they had merely to apply in order to obtain grants according to their rank, from 100 acres for privates to 1200 for lieutenant-colonels. Almost three-quarters of the personnel of some regiments accepted this opportunity of settling in Canada, and several 'military settlements' were set apart, with a senior officer in charge of each.

Among the most important were the settlements near Perth and Richmond, in the Bathurst District, where disbanded soldiers were allowed rations for themselves and families for one year, as well as 'implements of husbandry and tools'. Several of these regiments were not British at all, but a sort of Foreign Legion of Germans, Poles, Belgians, Italians, and other nationalities who had been taken prisoners in the campaigns against Napoleon and pressed into the service of Britain.

Travellers' accounts of America were frequently encouraging and flattering, and the consequence was that many people in Britain turned their eyes in that direction when economic conditions became depressed after the war. Taxes were heavier, half-pay retirement a hardship, and many a 'gentleman' found himself unable to keep the rank in society to which he had been pleased to become accustomed, preferring to emigrate rather than submit to the mortification consequent upon a change of life for the worse among those who had been his equals.**

*Notably along the River Detroit. The Scots of Glengarry have in recent times increasingly married French girls from over the Quebec border, and we now find the Macdonells and many another old Scottish family speaking French. John Mactaggart, who saw them along the Ottawa River, considered the French Canadians to be 'by far the most respectable people in the country for what is worthy of human nature, . . . and live in comparative happiness'. The influence of Indians on settlement and settlers was not great, though notable in the days of exploration. But the noted poet Emily Pauline Johnson (1862-1913) was a daughter of Chief George Johnson of the Six Nations and Emily Howells of Bristol, England.

**For an outline of the British system of commission purchase and half-pay retirement see the introduction to Appendix C, Volume II, p. 342.

And there were many poverty-stricken unemployed—people who had been accepted as useful citizens as long as they were needed in wartime factories, on the field of Waterloo, or in the fleet at the battles of the Nile and Trafalgar; but when these emergencies were past they suddenly became 'superfluous' and 'redundant' population, to be 'shovelled out' as paupers* to relieve the British taxpayer.

But at the other end of the financial scale were capitalists, some of them well fattened by war contracts. Quite a number of these well-to-do people settled near Cobourg before 1820, and in succeeding years their wealth aided in opening up trade by road and railway with the 'Back Lakes' region. One of them brought with him from Britain no less than £50,000, an amount that placed him in the millionaire class of his day. Yet professional men usually found it hard to obtain a start in Upper Canada—if, indeed, they were not entirely excluded, as in the legal profession. So great was the nepotism of the 'Family Compact' ruling clique that, as the Reverend Isaac Fidler put it, 'I would recommend no professional gentleman to emigrate to Canada without letters of introduction to the governor'.

By 1820 the population of the province was 110,000, and ten years later it had increased to 200,000. Some thirty or forty thousand more, largely British, arrived each year of the next decade, making the population well over half a million. The course of settlement followed the shores of the St. Lawrence and lakes Ontario and Erie, with a continual pushing back of the frontier into the rear townships, and especially along lake and river. Through the efforts of the Canada Company, whatever its defects, the 'Huron Tract' between Galt and Goderich was somewhat earlier settled than it would otherwise have been, and the same applies to the Rideau Scottish and military settlements and the conducted emigrations of Irish to Peterborough and Victoria counties and along the Mississippi River in Lanark.

In general it may be said that the Loyalists were no more

---

*Thomas D'Arcy McGee (1825-1868), an Irish revolutionary before he came to Canada, hit the mark accurately in his 'Song of the Surplus'. One verse of the poem follows:

> The oak-trees wave around the hall,
>   The dock and thistle own the lea,
> The hunter has his air-tight stall,
>   But there's no place for such as me;
> The rabbit burrows in the hill,
>   The fox is scarce begrudged his den,
> The cattle crop the pasture still,
>   But our masters have 'no room for men'.

loyal than other groups; many of them, in fact, were as republican as their fellows who remained in the United States. For many years it was a grave sin in official eyes to be democratic, so that it is impossible to judge pioneer political philosophy by modern standards. When Kingston was selected as the site of Queen's University many people thought and some publicly stated that a place farther north would be preferable, at a distance from 'the contamination of democracy' across the border.

Settlers of American origin, whether Loyalists, late-Loyalists, or mere land-seekers, got along most readily at the beginning because they were used to pioneering and American farming methods. 'Americans go in swarms into Canada', wrote the Reverend Isaac Fidler in 1833, 'preferring its richness yet hating its government.' But the more aristrocratic and cultured of the British, whether settlers or travellers, found them objectionable because of their American slang and their republican and equalitarian sympathies, which were blamed for all the evils of the country. 'Ex-Settler', author of *Canada in the Years 1832, -33, and -34,* preferred bush settlements because in longer-settled districts, largely of Loyalist origin, 'nine-tenths of my neighbours will be *Canadian Yankees,* than which I can imagine no character more revolting to a gentleman except it be a yankified Irish labourer'.*

Englishmen [says the English author of *A Few Plain Directions*], who have in general been accustomed to subordination and habituated to a decent, orderly, and respectful deportment, find a difficulty in reconciling themselves to the manners and customs of the *former* republicans, who have a certain vulgarity and contemptuous arrogance united to ignorance and illiberality about them which is disgusting.**

And to this uncompromising indictment he added that Americans of every class, age, and sex had a deep-rooted and deadly hatred for the English and Irish, though the 'conciliatory Scotchman . . . can so arrange his conduct as to make it suitable for

*But John Howison wrote that 'the *ne plus ultra* of vanity, impudence, and rascality' was comprised under 'the epithet Scotch Yankey'. People who had been accustomed in Britain to doff their hats to their betters got new ideas, he said, as soon as someone addressed them as *sir, master,* or *gentleman,* and they were never the same again! A Scot, John Mactaggart, wrote in his *Three Years in Canada* that 'the books of Howison and other authors may be perfectly relied on. . . . What you have heard of the character of the people on this side of the Atlantic is generally true.'

**Or as T. H. Ware put it in his diary: '. . . the *equality* notions which the lower orders in a manner imbibe with the American air they breathe . . . that "Jack is as good as his Master".' (His diary and sketchbook is in the Toronto Public Library.)

all changes and circumstances'. Even John Langton, in no sense
a radical, observed in 1838 that he would like to take a shot
at the Yankees. It must be remembered, of course, that the War
of 1812 was then but a generation away, and that much anti-
American sentiment had persisted from that period; and it was
no doubt the American Patriot raiders over the Canadian border after the Rebellion of 1837 that Langton wanted to take
a shot at.

Joseph Pickering wrote along the same line, being annoyed
by the arrogance and conceit that he found in Americans. He
observed that in their own country it was assumed as a self-
evident fact that 'Americans surpass all others in virtue, wisdom,
valour, liberty, government, and every other excellence', and
they and their fellows in Upper Canada were generally charged
with being given to misrepresentation and humbug, fond of
borrowing without thought of return, and 'shrewd' and 'smart'
in 'taking advantage'—frequently to the point of plain dishonesty.

This characteristic is emphasized in a recently discovered
diary, that of Captain Charles Gifford, who subsequently settled
in Cobourg. Arriving at Cornwall on January 17, 1837, he
began to write his impressions of Upper Canada as he toured
the province during the next six weeks.* After using such
adjectives as 'reserved' and 'distrustful' with respect to Americans, whom he found 'plentiful in the upper province', he wrote:

His bearing is ungraceful but not mean. His thoughts are limited but
practical. He has a head full of wild speculations, and is very fond
of making new inventions, some in fact very ingenious. Any new
invention is generally termed 'a Yankee Scheme'. The character of
the native Canadian differs but little from that of the Yankee, but
any inference that might be drawn would be rather favorable to
the latter.

The Yankee loses a law suit in court without feeling the same
degree of chagrin the old country man would feel, and will ask his
opponent to ride home in his sleigh with as much frankness as if
nothing had happened, comforting himself with the notion that he
can cheat him again the first opportunity he has of trading with him,
which he often accomplishes, more so if he is an old country man. He
cheats his nearest relation as soon as a stranger and justifies himself
by saying 'There is no friendship in trade'. It is my humble opinion
that a great part of the national character of the Yankee is formed by

*The author is indebted to Leon Konorowski for permission to print in the
Appendix, part C, the complete diary—'A few remarks on a Tour in Upper
Canada in 1837'. The quotation herewith is from a slightly modernized
transcription by the owner of the manuscript.

adhering to the admonition of their patron saint Doctor Franklin, who instilled into their minds the love of gain as one of the greatest acquirements of the young adventurer.

The Reverend Isaac Fidler wrote that 'American republicans' were often found 'prowling up and down Canada' in search of quick profits, money-making being 'the only standard of dignity

Toronto Public Library   T. H. Ware

'YANKEE AT REST'

The sketch was made in an American railway car in 1844.

and nobility and worth in that country'. He gives several instances of marriage and desertion for the same purpose, and says that if he went into detail on their knavery, cunning, and similar characteristics* he could furnish a series of tales which would rival Boccaccio's for truth and entertainment. But Americans were admittedly enterprising as well as noted for restlessness, often picking up stakes and pushing farther into the wilderness in hope of eventual gain or just to be on the move.

*A traveller named Mickle noted in his diary in 1852 that the Guelph region had 'few Americans, which is not to be regretted'.

Mrs. Anna Jameson gives an intimate description of an American family of this type. 'Such a group', she believed, 'could be encountered nowhere on earth, methinks, but here in the west or among the migratory Tartar hordes of the east':

They are from Vermont, and on their way to the Illinois, having been already eleven weeks travelling through New York and Upper Canada. They have two wagons covered with canvas, a yoke of oxen, and a pair of horses. The chief or patriarch of the set is an old Vermont farmer, upwards of sixty at least, whose thin shrewd face has been burnt to a deep brickdust colour by the sun and travel and wrinkled by age or care into a texture like that of tanned sail-canvas. . . . The sinews of his neck and hands are like knotted whip-cord; his turned-up nose, with large nostrils, snuffs the wind, and his small light blue eyes have a most keen, cunning expression. He wears a smock-frock over a flannel shirt, blue woollen stockings, and a broken pipe stuck in his straw hat, and all day long he smokes or chews tobacco. He has with him fifteen children of different ages by three wives.

The present wife, a delicate, intelligent, care-worn looking woman, seems about thirty years younger than her helpmate. She sits on the shaft of one of the wagons I have mentioned, a baby in her lap, and two or three younger children crawling about her feet. Her time and attention are completely taken up in dispensing to the whole brood, young and old, rations of food consisting of lard, bread of Indian corn, and pieces of sassafras root. The appearance of all (except of the poor anxious mother) is equally robust and cheerful, half-civilized, coarse, and by no means clean; all are barefooted except the two eldest girls, who are uncommonly handsome, with fine dark eyes. The eldest son, a very young man, has been recently married to a very young wife, and these two recline together all day, hand in hand under the shade of a sail, neither noticing the rest nor conversing with each other, but, as it seems to me, in silent contentment with their lot.

Many of the stores, mills, and taverns of the province were operated by Americans, who were commonly good businessmen. Patrick Shirreff says that Canadians envied Americans their prosperity, though considering them 'a band of cheating and lying democrats'; and that they in turn regarded the people of Upper Canada as 'indolent and dissipated'. When their own West began to be opened for settlement, comparatively few Americans emigrated to Ontario.

For a while Scottish and Irish settlers somewhat outnumbered English, while Welsh are hardly heard of at all.* Yet a Welsh-

---

*'There are also some few Welsh in Canada', wrote William Brown in 1849, 'but as they are unassuming and retired in their habits, I know of no peculiarity which they adhere to as a custom brought from their rugged mountain homes.'

PATRICK YOUNG   SAMUEL STRICKLAND
Young's Point   Lakefield

woman, Elizabeth Gwillim, was the wife of the first lieutenant-governor of Upper Canada, and her diary is among the most valuable historical records of the period 1792-96. The most prominent early provincial land surveyor, Augustus Jones, was a Welshman, and he laid out the York townsite and the course of Yonge Street and other highways. His son by an Indian wife, Peter Jones, became a Methodist missionary and a translator into the Chippewa language. But while many thousands of Ontario residents are of Welsh descent, and there are Welsh farm settlements in the Canadian West, no district of early Upper Canada appears to have been distinctively Welsh; but those who came to Canada brought with them a special interest in mining as well as agriculture, and a fondness for music, art, authorship, and cultural life generally.*

The English settlers in the province were sometimes described as having neat and tidy homes, but the less knowledge of English agriculture they had, it was said, the better for farming in Canada where conditions were so different. English settlers perhaps assimilated themselves more speedily, and they were

*Among others from Wales, or of Welsh descent, are Chief Justice William Dummer Powell of the early period, three modern artists—Robert Harris, W. J. Phillips, and Owen Staples, and Miss Blodwen Davies, author and historian. See also p. 206 fn.

less clannish than Scots and Irishmen. But some of them arrived with no small amount of self-conceit, *bounce,* and *John-Bullism,* which was quickly taken out of them by their experiences, with the help often of rough-and-ready neighbours. John Palmer, a traveller, met two men who had attempted farming in the Upper Canadian backwoods but were on the way back to England. 'It is a damned wild country, full of yankies and agues', volunteered one of them, and they were agreed that there was no place like home. 'Democracy will never go down an old countryman's stomach', wrote another; and he was still more emphatic about it when he found his young sons telling him 'they guess they will do as they have a mind to'.

There were more aristocrats, 'genteel' and cultured people, and other comparatively well-to-do settlers from England than from other parts of the British Isles; and not a few of them came to this country as to a combined fox-hunt and conversazione, accompanied by dogs, rigged out in loud tweeds, patent leather shoes, and even monocles.* Some of the more exaggerated and affected of these were pupil-farmers or 'remittance-men', victims of one of the rackets of the day; and the surprise they received in the Canadian backwoods proved more likely to break than make them. Some survived and rose above their miserable experiences while others were drinking themselves to an early death. Such 'dandies', who appear always to have been assumed to be English, were usually unaccustomed to work of any kind and not inclined to change their way of life. Some of them, observed James Logan in 1836, were shamed into working when they saw that everybody else was busy; but others wasted their funds on horses and dogs, cheated whoever would trust them, and then skipped out to the United States. 'Wherever I went I heard of similar occurrences', writes Logan.

Effective pioneers in general were groups of Englishmen along the 'Back Lakes', like the one on Sturgeon Lake of which one of the best settlers, John Langton, wrote that out of six of them, four 'have been at an university, one at the military college at Woolwich, and the sixth, though boasting no such honours, has half a dozen silver spoons and a wife who plays

---

*Many of the 'aristocrats' who settled near Woodstock were supercilious snobs who squandered their money and land in artificial gaieties and riotous living, aided most willingly by the officers of the Imperial garrison at nearby London. In some instances their own servants—hardworking folk—were shortly owners of their lands.

Courtesy Langton family   Anne Langton

THE LANGTON FAMILY PARTY AT 'BLYTHE', STURGEON LAKE

the guitar'!* Near Lake Simcoe, similarly, there were in the eighteen-fifties a number of retired military and naval officers, referred to by a class-conscious visitor as 'the resident gentry of the neighbourhood'. A great many of this class had left their large holdings 'in despair and disgust at the numerous hardships and privations', but those remaining 'were now owners of substantial homes, with every comfort about them'.

The English officials who had come to the province with Lieutenant-Governor Simcoe speedily grew into a despotic aristocracy in which the minimum *entrée* was membership in the Church of England. John Strachan, aspiring to enter politics, found he had first to change his Presbyterian adherence to that sect; and Bishop Mountain of Quebec seems to have expressed the general sentiment of his church when he called the nonconformist Methodists 'a set of ignorant enthusiasts whose preaching is calculated only to perplex the understanding, to corrupt the morals, to relax the nerves of industry, and dissolve the bands of Society'—by which he presumably meant that the democratic ideas of 'dissenters' were slowly but surely undermining the *status quo*. Yet well after the middle of the 19th

*In addition to the published journals and letters of Anne and John Langton and of Thomas Need, founder of Bobcaygeon, see also 'James Wallis, Founder cf Fenelon Falls and Pioneer in the Early Development of Peterborough', *Ontario History,* Volume LIII, No. 4, by his grandson Hugh Wallis.

From a water-colour in the Artist's scrapbook   Rev. Vincent Clementi

NORTHERN LOON, 1874

The artist, son of a composer who is buried in Westminster Abbey,
was a clergyman in the Peterborough-Lindsay region.

Archives of Ontario   Reginald Drayton

COX'S DAM, 1881

The artist liked to hunt and fish with Indian friends along
the Trent lakes and northward, and took his paints with him.

century attempts were being made in England, as Mrs. Edward Copleston puts it, to transplant 'little communities with all the gradations of squires and peasantry, priests and deacons, with parish doctors and the whole parochial system, to the banks of the Upper Ottawa'. Fortunately no such reactionary anachronism succeeded.

Numerous elderly English* commuted pensioners—soldiers, sailors, personal servants, and the like—some of them state-assisted emigrants, found the change a bitter and often fatal experience. Trying to clear a little land in some remote region, working as well on the roads for half a dollar a day and rations, some sank in despair. 'Many of us have been reduced to starvation', says one, 'and so great has been my distress that I have often wished for death.'

Some died [writes another]; and then there were the poor children and the women—it was very bad for them. Some wouldn't sit down on their land at all; they lost all heart to see everywhere trees and trees, and nothing beside. And then they didn't know nothing of farming—how should they, being soldiers by trade.

Lord Durham said in his famous *Report* that some 3000 commuted pensioners came to Canada in 1832-33 alone, that many were never able even to locate their land, and that some wasted their funds in debauchery and were soon in great want.

The restlessness of military life, in fact, unfitted many a discharged soldier for civilian life. In 1817 Robert Gourlay visited the Perth district just after the main influx of state-supervised military immigrants. About one thousand had been located, and while some were adjusting themselves in agriculture, many—as was also the case with the Loyalists—stayed only long enough to acquire the right to sell their land.

Soldiers in general [commented Gourlay in 1822] choose their trade only to indulge in idleness and give reins to a roving disposition; and after having spent 20 or 30 years in the profession of *gentlemen* cannot easily train into the habits of sober and persevering industry. At the first settlement of Upper Canada it was not uncommon for soldiers to sell their 200 acre lots of land for a bottle of rum. Now-a-days only 100 is granted, and settlers are prohibited from selling till after three years' residence and the performance of certain easy duties. Still, I have been told since coming home by a half-pay officer of the Perth settlement that scarcely one soldier out

*The most comprehensive treatment of nationality and the influence of ethnic groups in the formation of the Dominion is John Murray Gibbon's *Canadian Mosaic* (1938).

of fifty now remains for good. The deserted lots have been for the most part filled up with emigrants from Britain and Ireland.

But here we are interested primarily in those who remained and succeeded, and perhaps the experience of an Englishman from Northumberland, as related by Joseph Pickering, may be taken as not unusual after six or seven years of settlement:

He suffered considerable privations at first, commencing on his lot at the beginning of winter; he had first to build a house and then work out for provisions for the family. He has since built himself another house and barn, dug a well and a cellar, planted an orchard and cleared forty or fifty acres of land, and is now comfortably situated and thriving, although having only 30s. or 40s. left on his first arrival.

Our pioneers rank among the most outspoken and least reticent of people, and there was usually no doubt as to what they meant. Apparently the laws of libel were entirely ignored, as anyone may see who reads their election speeches and comments of one kind or another. All nationalities come in for some harsh criticism as settlers. Some writers claimed that the Irish were not only dirty but revelled in poverty; and that their lack of success was due to indolent habits which they could not or would not break. Some charged them with aping objectionable American manners and customs, and that, like Rip Van Winkle, they were foremost in carousing, cards, and visiting. Their proclivity for brawls and fights was given full vent at fairs, elections, bees, and almost every other gathering. Perhaps Edward Talbot, an Irishman himself, but of that highly objectionable type who hate to see the masses rise, excels all other travellers in criticizing Irishmen, observing that 'of all vapid coxcombs upon earth, an Irish emigrant without education is the most intolerable, the least amiable, and the most preposterous'. A considerable number of Irishmen were located in and around London, near Colonel Talbot's domain, but he disliked them almost as much as he did Scots. Another Irishman, Captain George Hill of Peterborough County, observed his compatriots who had been members of the state-conducted emigration in 1825 to that district:

They have tenaciously preserved the objectionable traits of our national character [he wrote in 1833]: our love of idleness when necessity does not compel us to labour—our improvidence and disregard of the future—our indifference to neatness, cleanliness, and domestic comforts; and, worst of all, our fondness for whiskey.

229

Many of the shanties which they have now been content to exist in for eight years are to this day without any better fire-place than a few loose stones placed against the back logs; and the smoke, unconfined by any kind of chimney, finds a difficult escape through a square opening in the roof.*

Dr. John Bigsby, on the other hand, while travelling up the Ottawa was

much pleased with an Irishman's place who had been three or four years on the spot with a large family of sons and daughters—he himself still in the full force of manhood. . . . He had built a log-house, thirty-five feet long by twenty, in the clear. The ground floor still remained a single apartment, save that a thick green curtain screened the female sleeping-place, while the young men found their lair in the roof by a ladder. The walls were lined with bags of flour, Indian corn, pumpkins, onions, mutton or pork hams, flitches of bacon, and agricultural tools.

It is apparent that centuries of English repression** formed an important factor in the economic and social state to which the people of Ireland had been reduced; and it is similarly obvious that innumerable Irish families rose far above their fellows upon whom harsh contemporary judgments were laid.† A Scottish traveller, Robert Stevenson, wrote home from Windsor that 'the most prosperous settlement I have yet seen in the Western District' was one of 'industrious Irish in the rear of Sandwich, who, though their land was originally wet, have made it highly productive by draining'. Lieutenant E. T. Coke talked with an Irishman in Cornwall who had arrived two years earlier without 'a tenpenny to bless himself with'; but becoming in turn an unskilled labourer, a lumberman, and then a farmer on his own

*But many of these immigrants did much better: see the author's *The Valley of the Trent,* pp. 84-130.

**The period of the settlement of Upper Canada was too late for the inclusion of religious refugees among its settlers. But a large number of descendants of French Huguenots, driven from France in the sixteen-eighties, came to the United States and Canada, where they have tended to retain an independent and non-conformist attitude. The greatest of them all, of course, is Henry David Thoreau, whose philosophy and example have been so influential in shaping the career of Ghandi, British Labour leaders, and broader loyalties of every type throughout the world. The repression which drove the Huguenots from France is described by Geoffrey Adams in 'A Temperate Crusade: The Philosophe Campaign for Protestant Toleration', *Canadian Historical Association, Papers,* 1961. A book on the Huguenot influence in Canada is in course of preparation by G. E. Reaman.

†Among Irishmen prominent in early Upper Canada were Sir John Johnson of Loyalist days and Sir Guy Carleton. Thomas D'Arcy McGee, poet, orator, and patriot, was member of Parliament for Montreal in the first administration after Confederation, and Thomas Moore the Irish poet wrote his 'Canadian Boat Song' in 1804 during a brief visit to the country.

near Williamstown, he was then, 'like all Canadian farmers', very independent in one sense of the word, being his own baker, butcher, tallow-chandler, cider-brewer, sugar-boiler, soap-maker, and, in short, 'a complete jack-of-all-trades'. Highly delighted with his own prospects, he attributed his good fortune to having avoided the handicap of a wife and children!

A. D. Ferrier, *Fergus*

ELORA FROM THE ROSS MILLS, 1845

There were in Upper Canada many Irishmen like Michael Corkery of Ramsay Township, who wrote as follows four years after settlement as a member of the conducted emigration of Irish in 1823:

I came to this country in 1823 from Ireland under the charge of Mr. Robinson,* and received rations for one year. I have now with the exertions of myself and son, cleared upwards of twenty acres of land and have a yoke of steers, five milk cows, two yearlings, besides pigs, poultry, etc., and I consider my lot and crop worth at best £200. Add to this, I am happy and contented.

Perseverance of this type was frequently exemplified by settlers of all nationalities. The founders of Elora were the Mat-

*The state-conducted emigration of Irish to the region of the Mississippi River, Lanark County, in 1823. John Mactaggart says the river's name was Massapi, 'vulgarly termed Mississipi'. The Lanark experiment was followed by a much larger Irish emigration to the present Peterborough and Victoria counties two years later.

thews—father, mother, and nine children—who arrived one day at dusk. They built a shelter of hemlock boughs and a huge fire, but by morning a snowstorm had come on and their cattle had wandered away. But they persevered, and had as their first crop 16 bags of wheat. The nearest market was Galt, so the father and his sons built a pine dug-out 30 feet long, loaded their wheat, and sold it to Absalom Shade, founder of that town, for 50 cents a bushel. They were offered $2.50 for their boat, so they sold it too and walked home.

Scottish settlers retained their national characteristics longest, largely because of their evident desire to settle near others of their nationality.* Several townships and even whole counties were characterised by them, notably Glengarry, Scarborough, Zorra, Lanark, Russell, Vaughan, Esquesing, and Ramsay; and towns like Dundas and Fergus had a notably Scottish flavour. Elsewhere, too, the St. Andrew's Society kept perpetually green the memory of Robin Burns and Auld Scotia, while the St. George's and St. Patrick's societies were much more of an annual affair specializing, respectively, upon Shakespeare and the driving of the snakes out of Ireland. Though characterised by clannishness, Scots were not always a unit among themselves. Especially did Highlanders and Lowlanders engage in disputes, particularly when too much 'Scotch' was drunk in wayside taverns.

To describe the origin of all the attitudes of early settlers would take us far afield. Some people think, says a wag, but others merely revolve their prejudices around in their minds. Whether based upon reason or not, many attitudes descended through several generations. Some people, for example, are more loyal than the Royal Family, regarding representatives as almost objects of worship; others are just the reverse, or loyal with considerable qualification.

The Scots settled in the northern part of Elgin County form a case in point. They inherited some of the ancient antagonism to the English, and were consequently not quite as 'loyal' as others; but there were more important reasons. In that and many another district the evils of heavy drinking were apparent in fights with whiskey bottles and other sordid activities. At the time—just prior to World War I—the Royal Family were

---

*Some Scots came out determined 'to be *lairds themsell*', says John Mactaggart, though probably not with any intention of emulating the vicious conduct of the Scottish lairds who had driven them from their crofts.

known to be somewhat bibulous, as was apparent as well in certain of the governors-general sent out to Canada, and loyalty was weakened as a result . There was, too, the feeling that the Scottish principle of thrift was violated by the excessive cost of keeping up royalty;* and in earlier times it was felt that that aristocratic oligarchy, the Family Compact, was super-loyal as a means to perpetuate their monopoly of power and privilege.** Considerations of a similar type operated to form public opinion in other parts of the province.

Sir John A. Macdonald, William Lyon Mackenzie, and Alexander Mackenzie rank high among Scots in Canada. Two other prominent Scots, John Galt the novelist and Dr. William ('Tiger') Dunlop, were noted propagandists among their nationality for settlement on the lands of the Canada Company, of which they were the chief officials. Contemporary opinions as to Scots in Canada varied, but were generally favourable. While some travellers considered them dirty and their farms and log houses untidy, they were, said others, more civilized than some parts of Scotland from which they had come; and it was everywhere apparent that they worked hard and faced difficulties without flinching.

Almost invariably thrifty and hardy, it could rarely be said that Scots failed as settlers. Gaelic long persisted as the favoured—if not the only—language in some settlements, and the customs and superstitions of the Old Land were venerated. Pipers were obviously popular,† though the head of the McNab settlement up the Ottawa near Arnprior was unique in calling himself *The* McNab and approaching feudal grandeur when he made public appearances with a piper in the van and a retinue of retainers bringing up the rear. Sir James Alexander celebrated St. Andrew's Day in Kingston in 1847, sitting beside

a remarkable character, a Highland kinsman, the chief MacNab. The MacNab was distinguished by a very fine appearance, stout

---

*See John Kenneth Galbraith, *The Liberal Hour* (1960), pp. 187-97. Mr. Galbraith, a native of Elgin County but now American ambassador to India, is among the more incisive thinkers of our time.

**And in that period it was not loyalty to 'Victoria the Good' nor to democracy but to George III, who was for a large part of his reign insane, and to a corrupt oligarchy of ministers whose obstinacy drove the American colonies to revolt and who bungled the early part of the wars with Napoleon; and when George III died the loyalty was to his two dissolute sons George IV and William IV, described by no less a Tory than the Duke of Wellington as 'the damnedest millstones that were ever hanged round the neck of any government'.

†In Stormont County, we are told, the bagpipes 'whustled mony a braw lad to his grave'.

and stalwart, and he carried himself like the head of a clan. . . . He usually dressed in a blue coat and trowsers, with a 'whole acre' of MacNab tartan for a waistcoat—at great dinners he wore a full suit of tartan. On his jacket were large silver buttons which his ancestor wore in the 'rising' of 1745.

After the usual toasts, songs, and speeches a piper of the 93rd Highlanders regaled the company; whereupon

The MacNab called for his bonnet, which was brought him on a silver salver, and putting it on he delivered himself of an oration in his native Gaelic, and after a long pibroch he drank a glass of mountain dew with the piper, who was much flattered.*

We unquestionably owe much of our enthusiasm for education and religion to the Scots. It is recorded that the members of one of Lord Selkirk's emigrations** stood sorrowfully on deck as long as it was still possible to catch a glimpse of the receding shores of their native land, but when Scotland had faded from view they immediately held a solemn conclave for the purpose of organizing the elements of life so dear to them— the home, the school, and the church. With this preparation they transplanted to the American wilderness the traditions of generations of their ancestors.

While English and Irish settlers were often enthusiastic about the transference to the New Land of the clergy and ritual to which they were accustomed, there is something different among Scots, who often made their clergymen their temporal as well as spiritual leaders. In one of the letters of Robert Stevenson he notes that a Presbyterian clergyman from the eastern part of Upper Canada was removing to the western section, accompanied by 'not only his whole congregation but some hundred families besides', and that they would settle as a unit with 'all their old friends and neighbours around them'.†

*There was neither romance nor success in the McNab settlement, however, but continual bitterness, lawsuits, and bad feeling. McNab himself was declared by the courts a public nuisance. Several books have been written about him with varying candour.

**The Selkirk emigration to Upper Canada was ill-fated. Of 111 Scots who settled in 1803 at Baldoon, about fifteen miles north of the mouth of the Thames, no less than 42 died the first season. The settlements of the survivors were laid waste during the War of 1812, and in 1817 only nine or ten families remained.

†A still more remarkable example is afforded by a group of evicted Scottish crofters who set sail for Nova Scotia in 1817 under the leadership of the Reverend Norman McLeod, decided after three years to remove to Ohio via the Gulf of Mexico but were shipwrecked, again built their own vessels and set sail in 1847, under the same leader, for Australia, and finally settled in New Zealand where their descendants are still called the Waipu Highlanders.

Sir Henry Raeburn

THE McNAB

Public Archives of Canada   James Pattison Cockburn

KINGSTON FROM A GROUP OF TREES, 1829

Public Archives of Canada   Sir George Back

CAMP AT GROS CAP, LAKE SUPERIOR, 1842
'Our camp for the night when driven in by the storm'.

In 1856 an Englishwoman noted that English and Roman Catholic Irish settlers commonly 'adhered to the good old English customs—such as the observance of Christmas'; but that in Scottish settlements New Year's Day was in large measure substituted for it, as in Scotland.* Some of the Puritan Loyalists similarly emphasized Thanksgiving Day. The commercialization of the religious festivals, Christmas and Easter, is a modern growth, nor do we hear often of Santa Claus—much less the Easter Bunny, Mother's Day, Father's Day, and all the other efforts to drum up business via maudlin sentimentality. The pioneers had no Christmas trees or cards, and there was certainly no emphasis upon presents, though they sometimes had feasting, decorations, and the Yule log. But if there had been strident advertising few of the pioneers would have been financially able to respond, and strong sales resistance among farmers persisted far beyond the period of their financial stringency; and it was sometimes intensified by the misrepresentations of travelling salesmen.

Dutch and German settlers, almost all of them from Pennsylvania or other sections of the United States, were highly industrious and universally respected. Generally very conservative in dress and habits, they were similarly distinctive in homes, churches, and cemeteries. Dundas County, Waterloo, Rainham, and Markham townships, and towns like Waterloo, Galt, Guelph, Berlin (now Kitchener), and Preston were among those in which 'Dutch' (usually German) settlers were prominent. There was a German newspaper published in Berlin in the eighteen-thirties, and in 1837 it asked for advertisements from merchants in Toronto, Hamilton, Niagara, Beamsville, Brantford, Yonge Street, Newmarket, St. Catharines, Chippewa, Preston, and Stouffville, to serve the interests of German and Dutch residents in these locations. Joseph Pickering noted that those settled near Niagara were 'a sturdy, old-fashioned, and honest race of people'; and he stopped with a particularly industrious one in the Long Point district who had paid for his 200 acres 'by the skins of musk rats he killed in the marshes and sold for their fine furs at 2s. 3d. each'; and he had just built a fine frame house as well. When Governor-General Lord Dufferin visited Berlin in 1874 he said in the course of an address that he recognized

---

*Hallowe'en, an ancient festival in both Scotland and Ireland, was sometimes celebrated in Canada by St. Andrew's and St. Patrick's Societies.

in the German element a contribution of strength to our national Constitution, and a population who, by their thrifty habits, by their hereditary intelligence, by their industry, sobriety, and general good conduct, are likely to aid most powerfully in furthering the prosperity of our common country.*

With much closer connection to Germany were a considerable number of settlers who came to Upper Canada in the eighteen-thirties and later. Many settled in Haldimand County, especially in Rainham Township, which had also large blocks of English and 'Pennsylvania Dutch'.** High taxes, revolution in Europe in 1848, and the Franco-Prussian War of 1870-71 led many more to seek escape to America. Some of them were from Alsace-Lorraine after it became German, others earlier from Germany, and they settled largely in Lincoln, Welland, Haldimand, Bruce, and Waterloo counties. Many of these settlers long retained—and their descendants still retain—a highly conservative if not antique appearance:

We slept at West Flamborough in a thriving district [writes Sir James Alexander], where there are many German settlers distinguished in winter by their heavy and substantial sleighs, their coarse broad-brimmed hats, grey greatcoats with capacious capes, and with beards on their chins. The women in very quaint low caps and primitive-looking dresses.

George Henry adds colourful details in his *Emigrant's Guide*:

It is astonishing, in the time of sleighing in the winter when the roads are good, to see the number of large sleighs with wheat and various kinds of produce coming into the town; and it is altogether a very novel sight. Sometimes will be observed fifteen or twenty of those large box sleds, some drawn by two horses, others by four, all at full trot with their bells jingling, some driven by jolly-looking Quakers, some by the singular sect called Tankards [Tunkers] who never shave their beards—these growing nearly down to their middles—and with their little skimmer hats and long coats have a most extraordinary appearance. Then comes an Indian with his well-known dress, the universal blanket, driving in a load of frozen deer to market, next a Yankee with his load of frozen pigs, all as stiff as the shafts of his sleigh, himself dressed in his homespun suit of brown. All these characters form a very striking contrast.

*The most recent account of the Pennsylvania Germans and their settlements in Ontario is G. E. Reaman's *The Trail of the Black Walnut*. Mabel Dunham's *The Trail of the Conestoga* and her other writings are among our classics of pioneering.
**Germans were Deutsch, pronounced *Dutch* in the pioneer period, hence the confusion.

SMITH'S CREEK (PORT HOPE), 1819

RICE LAKE, 1819

Fothergill, noted also as a naturalist, had a distinctly exotic style.

A not inconsiderable part of the population of Canada West in the 'forties, 'fifties, and 'sixties were fugitive slaves from the United States. In the mid-fifties, for example, there were 1000 negroes among Toronto's 47,000 people, and 800 among Chatham's 4800; while there were 350 in London and 274 in Hamilton. The proportion was larger farther west, Amherstburg having about one-quarter negroes and Colchester Township on Lake Erie nearly one-third. In 'the Queen's Bush', a name originally given to the townships of Peel and Wellesley and the land thence to Lake Huron, escaped slaves were among the earliest settlers while it was still a wilderness in 1846. There was also an early settlement of negroes in Biddulph Township, north Middlesex.

These escapees from the 'land of the free' cleared the forests and farmed like the whites, in some instances on poorer land but frequently mixed with settlers of other nationalities. In general there was no discrimination against them, but where they were most numerous there was a tendency among the whites to be on the lookout for 'sauciness' which might be made the excuse for restrictions; and there were for a time a few separate Coloured schools. A considerable number made no attempt to farm but were small shopkeepers, hotel workers, mechanics, and labourers. They were, of course, less literate than most other settlers and suffered some imposition on that account, but they were in general neither better nor worse as citizens. If they had one predominant characteristic it was a feeling of gratitude that they had reached a better land where servitude and brutality were replaced by opportunity to share the white man's progress and culture.*

With the exceptions noted, plus the persistence for a longer time of the numerous British dialects, all settlers tended to become much alike within a generation. While some came with pronounced class feelings and a sense of their own superiority —like the English 'gentlemen' on the lakes north and northwest of Peterborough—they soon cooled off in the general melting-pot of pioneer life and, like Susanna Moodie, admitted that the superior people in Canada were those who most satisfactorily met conditions here. 'The glories of our blood and state', if

---

*For a remarkable series of narratives of these negroes see Benjamin Drew's *The Refugee, or the Narratives of Fugitive Slaves in Canada. Related by Themselves, with an Account of the History and Condition of the Colored Population of Upper Canada.* (Boston, 1856.)

Courtesy Women's Canadian Historical Society of Toronto

J. W. D. MOODIE, SUSANNA MOODIE, AND THEIR SONS

applicable in the Old Land, were superseded in the New by considerations both more universal and more tangible.

Class distinctions, consequently, speedily broke down, except possibly in the older towns along the front, where the 'gentlemen', 'esquires', and 'respectable'* people tended for awhile longer to keep aloof from 'the lower orders'. On the long-cleared farms and in 'the Bush', among 'the clearings' or in 'the backwoods', these people found themselves levelled in the general

*In its snobbish implications no word has been so overused. William Hazlitt wrote 150 years ago: 'There is not any term that is oftener misapplied, or that is a stronger instance of the abuse of language than this same word *respectable*. By a *respectable* man is generally meant a person there is no reason for respecting. . . . Gentility is only a more select and artificial kind of vulgarity.'

equalitarian feeling. This was the poor man's country, and so-called gentlemen were unpopular. But Great Britain was at the time a hidebound aristocracy, and it is unfair to criticise those whose means, education, and other privileges led them to assume that they were God's chosen people. It is apparent, on the other hand, that most of the cultural life of Upper Canada, in art, music, authorship, and the intellectual life generally, derived from a few hundred of these favoured families. The fault lay not with the privileged classes but with the outworn social system of the Old Land, the lack of any approach to equality of opportunity that 'republicans' and 'democrats' were remedying, however crudely, in the New.

How quickly [observed John Howison, who didn't like the tendency] do mankind discover those things that gratify their vanity! Many of the emigrants I saw had been on shore a few hours only, during their passage between Montreal and Kingston, yet they had already acquired those absurd notions of independence and equality which are so deeply engrafted in the minds of the lowest individuals of the American nation. On accosting two Scotsmen whom I had seen in Montreal, instead of pulling off their hats, as they had invariably done before on similar occasions, they merely nodded to me with easy familiarity. I addressed them by their Christian names and inquired if they had any prospect of obtaining employment. 'This gentleman,' said one, pointing to his companion who was a bricklayer, 'has been offered four shillings a-day at Prescott, but his good lady does not like the place!'*

A few who tried to be exclusive, for example by making arrangements at bees for 'gentlemen' to eat separately, quickly found that such presumptions were both out-of-place and offensive. 'Emigrants of a lower order', observed the Reverend Isaac Fidler, 'are not tantalized by the presence of luxury from which they are excluded.' With somewhat greater exultation, Jem and Jane Powell, who had been Chartists in England, wrote back home:

This is the land of plenty, where industry is rewarded, and not as in England, where some roll in luxury while others starve. . . . No hereditary titles and distinctions such as lords, dukes, and other

*When Charles Fothergill travelled westward along the Kingston Road to Smith's Creek (Port Hope) in 1817 he found democratic feeling carried still further, with 'men' and 'gentlemen' in reverse order. 'The Yankee phraseology', he wrote in his journal, 'is droll enough in some particulars. They call a hawker or pedlar or carrier or any ordinary person whatever a *gentleman*, but one who has really some pretensions to that character they term *a man*.' (The journal is largely printed in the Appendix to Volume Four of the author's *Pioneer Inns and Taverns*.)

nick-names; no fat bishops and state church to supply the rich gentry and fag-end of nobility with large salaries and nothing to do for it.

And that this was not just radical exaggeration is apparent from the fact that, prior to 1832, holders of sinecures and pensions who contributed nothing to the British public service were drawing £1,100,000 annually from the Treasury.*

Even without the influence of American democracy it would have been difficult to retain a privileged position or appearance in a country where, as Archdeacon Strachan put it, hard-working people could speedily rise from 'an extreme degree of poverty' to 'a tolerable degree of affluence'. Beggars and paupers were seldom seen, the exceptions usually being newly-arrived immigrants. All property-owners were politically equal when the vote was based on property, though the franchise was withheld from the rest of the population; and even half a century later the Conservative party was still opposed to universal suffrage. Some radicals, perhaps, became more conservative as their importance and dignity were enhanced by a sense of property, while numerous Tories became reformers when their feelings were outraged by needless suffering and injustice.

Taxes were very light but generally disliked. The main revenue came from customs duties at the ports and along the border, and Upper Canada received two-fifths of what was collected at Lower Canadian ports. Various fees and licences made up most of the balance, except where a landowner chose to pay the cost instead of doing his statute labour on the roads. There were no tithes or poor-rates, a welcome change from their prominence in Britain, and the taxes on improved homes and other 'luxuries' were small if annoying.

Where it was easy to be a landowner, servants were hard to obtain and still harder to keep. Even those brought from Britain were speedily married or on the land, for domestic service was despised. The Irish were found good servants 'when trained', but newly-arrived immigrants formed the usual source of supply; and as land was the symbol of success, male servants and labourers were as quick to obtain it as were the females in

*The reign of privilege and aristocracy could, of course, be exemplified in innumerable other ways, and much later. In an address in Edinburgh in 1876, the historian James Anthony Froude said that twelve noblemen owned half of Scotland, a few hundred half of England, and the members of the House of Lords over one-third of the whole of Britain; and that the owners of these great estates were 'continually devouring the small estates adjoining them'.

acquiring a husband; for this was the general path to independence.

Those who were servants preferred to call themselves *helps,* and as often as not ate with the family, whose head—male or female—might be called *the boss.* Masters and mistresses might be acceptable in Britain, wrote Charlotte Willard, 'but they will not be called so here; they are equals-like, and if hired to anybody they call them their employers'. Or, as John Watson from the pretty parish of Sedlescomb (Sussex) put it, 'I look forward, with a confident and well-founded hope, to the time as not far distant when I shall be a freeholder, and call no man by the degrading name of master'.* Archdeacon Strachan, in giving evidence before an emigration committee, said that immigrants would work in brickyards, in canal-building, or whatever offered, until their earnings were sufficient to buy a yoke of oxen. 'Whenever an Emigrant is able to purchase a yoke of oxen', he said, 'he will not work out again; he considers his fortune made, and employs himself more advantageously on his farm.'

Those who had been suppressed for generations, and often degraded, found these conditions very strange, but they were soon to become accustomed to the new way of life. When they became, in turn, somewhat conceited—even insolent—it was highly galling to their 'superiors', who sometimes claimed that by reserve and dignity, or perhaps by a readier use of language in rebuttal, they were able to keep these democrats or levellers 'in their place'. A few Englishmen, however, after vain efforts to enforce their alleged superiority, wrote home such comments as 'Democracy will never go down an old-countryman's stomach'. Such attitudes of independence were always blamed upon republican United States, but the fact that the labour supply was unequal to the demand had almost as much to do with it.

The trend was to social democracy, however some disliked it. The farm labourer, or 'hired man' as he was usually called in America, became quite an institution. From the 'thirties to the 'fifties his wage was from 50¢ to $1.25 per day, or, by the month, $7 to $12 with board and washing. He was usually treated as one of the family, a common expression being 'If a man is good enough to work for me he is good enough to eat with

---

*'Masters in this country are slaves to their servants', observes the author of *Journal of a Wanderer* with some feeling. 'This is what is called freedom with a vengeance.'

me.' While the wages were not high, from two to four years was often sufficient to enable a hired man to rent or even buy land of his own, especially if he had a wife who 'hired out' as well. A paraphrase of a contemporary account describes the hired man's status as follows:

The typical hired man did the hardest chores and was a reservoir of miscellaneous information, and so was always popular with the growing boys. He would sometimes help with the housework, and could always be depended on to act as a beau for one of the girls. Possibly more often than not he married one of them. Certainly he had an excellent opportunity of deciding which one would make the best wife for a farmer. Then, after he had saved enough to make a down payment on a farm and to provide himself with some live-stock (when the father-in-law did not give the daughter a few head as a dowry), he became an independent farmer and might keep a hired man of his own.*

Rather than embark at once on their own, some settlers worked farms on shares. Sometimes men cleared land for a speculator, receiving in payment largely the produce of the first few years. A landowner might let his land on an 'improvement lease', under which the tenant received all benefits arising from the farm and, in lieu of rent, bound himself to improve it by clearing annually a stipulated acreage. Other landowners might consider it preferable to arrange with a tenant to work the land on shares rather than hire men to develop it. In such share-cropping deals the owner usually furnished oxen, implements, and seed, and in return received half the produce. But by 1860 there were two more usual arrangements: (1) the tenant provided his own implements, stock, and seed and gave the land-lord one-third to one-half of the gross produce; and (2) the landlord provided everything and received two-thirds as his share. Sometimes a man rented a clergy-reserve lot, supposedly paying a cash rent, but, through tardy collection, in effect rent-ing on a credit basis.

But if many rose in the scale of human activity by enterprise and hard work, there were others who not only fell but de-generated. In some outlying parts of present-day Ontario are found the descendants of well-to-do and aristocratic emigrants from Britain, men of considerable culture and distinction in their day. But they had settled in rough and rocky districts, and

---

*Quoted by R. L. Jones in his scholarly *History of Agriculture in Ontario, 1613-1880,* in which may be found much information on the effect of trade cycles and tariffs upon agriculture, and a detailed presentation of the technical problems which were faced by several generations of Ontario farmers.

the hardship and disappointment of the crude life had taken its toll. Today their grandchildren are very different people, but occasionally there breaks out a flash of the gentility and cultivated manners of the men and women who first pushed into the wilderness ninety or one hundred years ago.

Many people, whatever their national origin—and not only in the bushlands—had become almost as wild as their surroundings and way of life. In 1825 Joseph Pickering found in the comparatively long-settled Niagara district that 'some of the people about here have a half Indian appearance: dirty habits, sallow, thin visages, and meanly dressed; living in the woods, surrounded by swamps, they are half hunter and half farmer'. The Reverend William Bell, in travelling in 1817 twenty miles on foot from Perth to minister to remote settlers, found the inhabitants highly peculiar from isolation. Some of them hid or looked at him furtively and with obvious curiosity; almost all, and especially the women, had 'a great talent for silence' as he put it; and the church service in the log schoolhouse 'had certainly a very odd appearance' when these rustic people formed the congregation, the women bareheaded, 'with long hair hanging over their shoulders, suckling children'. 'I could scarcely persuade myself', wrote Mr. Bell, 'that I was not in an assembly of Indians.' During the period of intense settlement about one-third of the population more nearly resembled these isolated backwoodsmen than the dwellers along the front; and while the influence of education and religion and other civilizing contacts gradually improved the status of such people, we have still no small number of the *hillbilly* type in Ontario, as well as others who, largely through hardship and isolation, have become anti-social, criminal, degenerate, or demented.

A large part of the population, and especially immigrants from Europe, were illiterate. It was customary, if correspondence was necessary, to have letters written by the educated few, with messages included to neighbours in the Old Land and wide circulation of letters upon arrival. Many people could not even write their own names and signed only by a cross. Among minor characteristics of interest, many of which were more or less local in extent, the names in common use must be given a place. Where evangelical religion had made a deep impression the children were almost invariably given Bible names. Not only were the usual ones—Matthew, Mark, Luke, Martha, Rebecca, Ruth, Nathan, David—in common use, but many of the more obscure and unusual, such as Ichabod, Lazarus, Levi, Israel, Uriah, Josiah, Asa, Eli, Abigail, and Esther.* There was frequent use of names from *The Pilgrim's Progress,* like Charity, Felicity, Faith, and others which recall the curious nomenclature of Cromwell's Ironsides. Susanna Moodie was struck with the strange names 'belonging to substantial yeomen' near her settlement—she gives Solomon Sly, Reynard Fox, Hiram Doolittle, Prudence Fidget, and Silence Sharman as examples.

I have enjoyed many a hearty laugh [she writes] over the strange affectations which people designate here *very handsome names. . . .* I prefer the old homely Jewish names, such as that which it pleased my godfather and godmothers to bestow upon me, to one of those high-sounding Christianities, the Minervas, Cinderellas, and Almerias of Canada. The love of singular names is here carried to a marvellous extent.

In spite of the levelling effect of democratic ideas and of the life itself there yet remained class feeling. Old settlers often felt themselves superior to new;** half-pay officers were usually convinced of their ascendency over other settlers, whether ex-servicemen or not, and they generally supported the ruling clique which was almost always Tory. Colonel Talbot, who preferred having no equals in his domain, kept the officer class from obtaining land there, but otherwise they were in almost all districts, distinguished, it is said, by their polite though sometimes domineering manners. Even some of the clergy were obsessed with class consciousness and had no doubt that a large part of the population were pre-ordained to rank as 'the lower orders'.

There was, too, especially in the later period, a certain feeling between town and rural dwellers. The townsman, particularly if he were in the upper social or financial brackets, felt superior to farmers, whose rougher clothing and, at times, uncultured manners seemed to set them apart. On their part rural dwellers often evinced dislike for capitalists, who were almost invariably associated with city or town. Rural interests were thought to be subordinated to urban, but this arose in many instances when

---

*The names are from those commonly used in Dummer Township, Peterborough County. The historian of the Long Point Settlement adds many others: Eliphalet, Othniel, Caleb, Abraham, Ephraim, Zephaniah, Ebenezer, Ezekiel; and for women Phoebe, Amelia, Keturah, Mehitabel.

**There was not infrequently admiration implied in nicknames given to the very first settlers: the founder of Paris was called 'King' Capron; Humphrey Finlay and his wife were 'King and Queen of Emily Township'; and 'Father' was often used for an early settler.

farmers felt themselves too busy to attend township meetings or run for office. In towns and villages and the neighbourhood around them there were two main classes, the professional men and large merchants joining to form one, and the labourers, small farmers, clerks, and 'mechanics' the other. Particularly in the earlier period, some of the first and largest farmer-land-owners, frequently men of general culture, long retained a sort of 'landed gentry' position and were commonly leaders in the district and socially inferior to none.

The average farmer's suspicion of town folk arose in some measure from the cheating and misrepresentation to which he was frequently subjected by *sharpers* or *city slickers*. Cash was scarce, and to be wheedled out of years of savings was a most unpleasant but not uncommon experience. The very scarcity of money alone often made the rural dweller penurious and close-fisted, a sufficiently common characteristic to be generally considered, though unjustly, as typical of farmers. By careful management many became prosperous and well-to-do in later life, though not a few, the habit ingrained, continued to hoard their savings into old age, actually finding it painful to expend for their own comfort and enjoyment what they had with such difficulty accumulated.

People who are isolated from their fellows are of two general types: some of them are too shy and self-conscious even to be inquisitive, while others become highly interested in every traveller or chance acquaintance. All of them, as often as not from sad experience, are suspicious of strangers and will impute evil motives to the most ordinary actions. If there are two characteristics most generally noted by travellers in Upper Canada they are inquisitiveness and hospitality. It was seldom indeed that settlers accepted money for meals and a night's lodging.* Instances are not hard to find where clergymen particularly have made lengthy visits at one home, and their hosts felt honoured in their continued presence. There were occasions, of course, where it was felt some advantage might accrue, and older settlers, perhaps from having been imposed upon, are

*Peter Pearce of Norwood, Warden of Peterborough County in 1863 and 1864, was noted, along with his wife, for generosity and hospitality to travellers 'in a manner of which few in later times have any conception or would care to imitate', as Dr. Thomas Poole, historian of the county, put it; and in addition public and religious meetings were held at their home, 'the inconvenience cheerfully borne and all made warmly welcome'. Such people live long in memory, having—in Shakespeare's phrase—raised their own memorial ere they died.

Courtesy Richard Dean

PETERBOROUGH COUNTY COUNCIL, 1863

Peter Pearce of Norwood, twice Warden, is third from the left
in the second row.

said to have been less hospitable than new; but generosity was
certainly a characteristic pioneer virtue. There was, in fact,
one type of generosity—whiskey-treating—that caused a great
deal of drunkenness, for people were very much offended if an
offer of a drink was refused. A whole round of treating was
usual,* and frequently with most unfortunate results. Many a

*Captain George A. Hill considered that old settlers' generosity to new ones
was exaggerated, and that people came to bees more for the whiskey and food
and the expectation of reciprocation: 'Let that humbugging fellow, Sterne,
say what he pleases, hardships and privations will chill the fountain of liberali-
ty in the human breast—it is religion or prosperity that must thaw it.' But in
comparatively recent times Sir James Whitney's administration sought to
control liquor and effect temperance by prohibiting treating. The old type of
bar-room, where patrons stood at the rail together, was much more conducive
to treating than a system of tables and waiters which minimizes contact with
other drinkers and the bartenders.

fight* began with inebriation, and many a wife had to become accustomed to her husband's return from town dead drunk, his horses alone knowing the way to the farm.

But generosity seldom extended to broadmindedness in religion, though prejudice was forgotten in Cavan Township when the Protestant Orangemen (the 'Cavan Blazers') secretly harvested the crops of the one Roman Catholic settler, who fell ill at harvest-time. Further north in Emily, which was solidly Irish Catholic in its northern part and as solidly Irish Protestant in the south, the two factions were traditionally at loggerheads. The Catholics were part of the Peter Robinson emigration of 1825, and they were given tools and rations for eighteen months. The later Protestants, jealous of the aid their neighbours had received, long persisted in the story that 142 Catholic families did no work until all the rations had been eaten, but an emigration report presented to the British Parliament in 1827 told the truth, which was that in spite of widespread death from fever and ague the Catholic pioneers had cleared away 351 acres of pine forest, raised 22,200 bushels of potatoes, 7700 bushels of turnips, and 3442 bushels of Indian corn; that they had sowed 44 bushels of fall wheat for the next season's crop and had made 22,880 pounds of maple sugar; and that out of their own meagre funds they had purchased 6 oxen, 10 cows, and 47 hogs.

When there were few chances to meet and gossip, every opportunity was eagerly accepted. Not only, according to travellers, were people inquisitive to the point of rudeness, but many would exaggerate and misrepresent the facts of any situation in a manner that seemed habitual. They liked to tell their own history, difficulties, successes, and hopes. This characteristic is evident in letters home, which are often coloured and embellished as if to produce envy in their readers as well as astonishment at the writer's enterprise and achievement.

The best example of inquisitiveness is given by Lieutenant E. T. Coke in *The Subaltern's Furlough* (1833):

Having hired one of the four-wheeled carriages known at Philadelphia as a 'dearborn', in the eastern States as a 'carryall', and in

---

*Assault and battery actions were very common in the period of pioneering. As a young lawyer (aged 19) in Picton in 1834, John A. Macdonald, later to be Canada's first Prime Minister, and Dr. Thomas Moore, appeared in court after a fight. Moore was convicted and fined sixpence, while McDonald (so-spelled in the indictment) was acquitted. See 'Minutes of Quarter Sessions, Prince Edward District, April 1, 1834, to Jan. 6, 1835', in the Archives of Ontario.

Utica as a 'wagon', a friend (Mr. B.) and myself started at eight o'clock on the 3rd of August upon an excursion to the Trenton Falls. The road being rough and mountainous and the day excessively hot, we pulled up at a small tavern, eight miles from the town, to give the horses some water. While I was holding the bucket mine host came out, and after looking on quietly for some time without tendering his assistance he observed that we 'had better let the beast stand in the shade a minute or two until it became cool, and then it would proceed more cleverly on the journey'. I understood him immediately, and determining to accept the challenge led the horse into the shade of the house, when the following conversation ensued, much to the amusement of my companion who did not at first comprehend our host's manoeuvre.

Landlord—'You are from the southward, I guess.'

Myself—'No—from Utica.'

'Aye, but you don't keep there, I reckon.'

'No, in the southward.'

'Aye, I guessed so; but whereabouts?'

'Oh! south of Washington.'

'Ah, pretty sickly there now?'

'No, pretty smart.'

'But there's tarnation little travelling now; last fall this here road was quite unpassable, but now I have been fixing it myself, expecting company, and no one comes.'

'You will have them all here when the cholera panic has subsided a little.'

'I don't know that; I heard a gentleman, who had been in the south, say the other day that there was very little money there now; the southerners wouldn't care a fig for the cholera, they'd clear out tarnation soon if they had plenty of money to spare; a'nt it so?'

I had now put one foot on the step of our vehicle, but mine host was not yet satisfied, so he followed me up with—'But you are going to the west, I expect?'

'Perhaps we may.'

'Aye, you came down the canal.'

'Yes.'

'That's fine travelling; that's what I like; you push along so slick, there's no chance of getting one's neck broke as there is aboard those stages on the rough turnpikes; if the boat sinks, one's only up to one's knees in water. You'll see the Falls?'

'We are going there now; which is the way?' So, receiving the necessary directions, we wished this true specimen of an American pot-house keeper good morning and drove on, subsequently finding his parting words prophetic. Though the Yankees are so notoriously inquisitive, yet there is nothing disrespectful in their manner; nor did I ever feel annoyed by their asking such prying questions, generally leading them 'considerably on the wrong trail', as they would say, or else, having satisfied them, commencing a cross-examination, to which they always submitted with good grace.

Many a settler was similarly loquacious in conversation, a method of 'letting off steam' that produced the Sam Slick* humour of the day. Sir James Alexander gives a couple of examples in his lively *Transatlantic Sketches*. An American and a Dutchman had a bet as to who could talk the other out of breath: 'They were locked in a room all night, and in the morning the Dutchman was found on the floor just dead, and the American with strength enough left to whisper in his ear!' Two old cronies were talking and chewing tobacco in the approved pioneer fashion. 'He talks pretty considerable, certainly', said one of them, 'but when he spits I put in.'

The condition of women under the hardships of pioneering is frequently described in letters home and the travel literature of the day, while Anna Jameson, well-known author and feminist, had much to say about it. It was usual for women to work as long and as hard as the men, sometimes from 4 or 5 a. m. to late at night. While there were instances of good choppers among women, it was not usual for them to do heavy farm work in Ontario but to specialize upon milking, churning, spinning, and weaving in whatever spare time remained from housework and the care of children. Female servants sometimes worked in the fields, especially during harvest, and many a settler's wife and daughters aided similarly when necessary; but it is frequently remarked by travellers that women objected to outside work, though keeping the home neat and tidy.

However inferior and unfortunate the status of women** was in pioneer Canada, it was generally much higher than among agricultural labourers in Britain; and that it was as high as it was is due largely to the fact that there were fewer women than men. Whether or not they raised their status by marrying, most girls married and there were few spinsters—'a delicacy of which few mansions can boast', as Edward Talbot indelicately put it. There were, too, large numbers of children, usually considered a distinct asset for they could very early be put to work in a day when schools were lacking or but irregularly attended. 'Have you a numerous family?' Adam Fergusson asked a farmer as he was passing through the country. 'Why,

---

*Thomas Chandler Haliburton (1796-1865), a judge of the Supreme Court of Nova Scotia, is best known for his series, 1837-40, on the shrewd sayings of the itinerant Yankee clockmaker *Sam Slick*. Among his later works were *Traits of American Humour, Sam Slick's Wise Saws,* and *Nature and Human Nature.*

**The subject is treated in more detail in Chapter XII, above.

sir', was the reply, 'I don't know what you call numerous: I've raised nineteen—ten by my first wife and nine by my second'!* Robert Stevenson, in the quaintest and best series of letters which have come down to us from the period of pioneering, describes a visit to his old friend Tam Kennedy, settled 'in a very thriving way' ten miles from London:

When he began farming he bee't to get married, so he got a farmer's daughter from Fenwick, and a handy stirring lass she is, and a grand one for butter and cheese. Their oldest bairn (a lassie) is no six years of age yet, and it's wonderful how useful she is to her mother. It's astonishing how early in this country they make children useful. Boys are set to look after oxen at an age that in Scotland we would be afraid to trust them out of our sight without somebody to look after them.**

Many women and children died, some of them from no other cause than the hardships of the life. Fever and ague, cholera and 'consumption' (tuberculosis) took a heavy toll, and many who survived had a sallow, sickly complexion, their skin dried and wrinkled by the sun and hard work. Women often aged and lost their beauty early, a condition accentuated by the loss of teeth without hope of anything in the nature of plates or other replacement. Travellers' accounts give instances of women pining away and dying from sheer loneliness and 'the want of society'.

From the survival of some of our 'pioneers'—as they are usually called, however inaccurately—into comparatively recent times has come the suggestion, widely accepted as a truism, that in general they lived to a grand old age. Statistics from which the average age of death might be computed are not available, but there is no doubt that it was much lower than in our own times. A glance at tombstones and records of burial indicates that far more people died in infancy or youth than is the case now. It is apparent, too, that men and women in their prime today would have been considered old in the pioneer period, even past the age of labour; and the style of hair and beard lends, from our point of view, an appearance of antiquity

---

*In this respect perhaps Ezra Parney and his son William of Long Point held some kind of a record, for they (not to mention their wives, respectively Elizabeth Slaght and Mary McMichael) had a total of thirty-nine children. 'It takes three wives to bring up a family' runs a pioneer maxim. My grandfather, John Guillet, married three sisters of the Payne family, and the third brought up the fifteen children.

**[Joseph Abbott]: *The Emigrant to North America*. See Appendix B, Volume II, where the letters are reprinted.

to bear out the illusion. This is not to say, however, that there were not many men and women whose rugged constitutions kept them active and alert into the eighties and nineties. To be duplicated in many other districts is this item from the Almonte *Gazette* of April 1, 1887:

Within a compass of a mile, on the 9th of Pakenham, there reside ten old settlers whose combined ages total up the astonishing aggregate of 828 years. We give the names and ages:
    Alex. Lindsay and wife—82 and 80—Emigrated in 1821 and 1820, respectively.
    Walter Wood and wife—87 and 78—Came in 1832.
    John Lindsay and wife—86 and 82—From Scotland in 1821.
    William Clark and wife—82 each—From County Sligo in 1832.
    Mrs. McMann—78—From Sligo County also.

Human sympathy was a common pioneer virtue. In his diary of 1819 Joseph Abbott describes how fire completely destroyed the home of a poor shoemaker, one of his neighbours. The very next day is this entry:

All hands, with the horse, went to a Bee to assist in rebuilding the house burnt yesterday. It was a general rising throughout the settlement—even the women made themselves useful in preparing and bringing provisions to the place. One small party was in the woods cutting down the timber, followed by a couple of hands to line it out; then came the scorers and hewers, and at their heels again the teamsters with oxen and horses to haul it to the place, where five men put it up as fast as it was brought to them; and after a day spent apparently more in fun and frolic than in hard labour, the outshell of a capital log-house, with the exception of a roof, was put up.

And the following day they were back again to put up the rafters, board it, and cut out the doors and windows. 'Some', says Abbott, 'furnished boards, others shingles, a carpenter the door and sashes, and the store-keeper the glass, putty, nails, &c.' So was a misfortune remedied and tragedy averted, and the shoemaker met the cash outlay during the next six months in work at his trade. It was an example of effective philanthropy and practical Christianity.

There cannot be said to have been much in the nature of a distinct national feeling in Canada prior to the Confederation movement, and provincial and separatist feelings were then surmounted only by fear of Fenian raids and American imperialism after the Civil War. The population, however, was much earlier of a solid, independent nature, and much to be preferred to the citizenry of Great Britain and Ireland, where exploitation, rebellion, repression, and pauperism were rampant. Yet only a few years of opportunity and independence in Canada had been needed to transform these very people. Captain Hill addressed intending settlers in a fine passage in his *Guide for Emigrants from the British Shores to the Woods of Canada*:

If you can live in the bosom of your family without constant general society—if you can enjoy the simple comforts of life and leave the hope of its elegancies to your children—if you are rather of an active than a literary disposition, rather mechanical than poetical —if you can delight in seeing the bountiful productions of the earth growing up about you in all the beauty and luxuriance of a new world, and will take pleasure in assisting with your own hands to sow, and plant, and gather them in—if you are determined in purpose and will adopt the motto *'ne tentes aut perfice'*—and above all if you can have patience with the midges and black flies, there will be hundreds to bid you welcome. If you possess only some of these qualifications decide for yourself; but if not one of them belongs to you—stay at home.*

Two backwoodsmen of a special type have their life histories recorded in contemporary travel-books. One of them was known as 'the banished Lord', and he led a Robinson-Crusoe existence over a century ago on Bear Creek, Sombra Township, at the western limit of settlement in the province. Dr. John Bigsby gives a fine description of him in *The Shoe and Canoe*:

I was sitting about mid-day in the shade near my tent on Belle Isle, the sky on fire as is usual at that hour, and the gossamer air trembling over the shiny river. Having been immersed in one of Coleridge's rhymed dreams, I happened to raise my eyes and saw coming down the stream in a canoe a strange-looking person standing upright with a double-barrelled fowling-piece in his hand, while a boy in the stern was paddling direct for our camp. They landed close to me and climbed the little bluff on which I was posted.

A more singular Robinson Crusoe-like figure I never beheld than the elder stranger. . . . Although seldom seen on the St. Clair, this gentleman was not unknown and was called by the squatters 'the Banished Lord'. They knew no other name. His speech and bearing at once revealed that he was an Englishman of distinction. . . .

He was a middle-sized, well-made man, slender and sinewy, as erect as at twenty-five although evidently much on the wrong side of fifty. He had a small, oval, wrinkled face, with the ruddy bloom

*On August 21, 1943, Mr. and Mrs. George M. Douglas of Lakefield, and my own family, after a long walk and much inquiry, located the old Hill farm in Dummer Township, some miles east of Bryson's Landing, Clear Lake. Veteran of Waterloo, first Warden of the district, author, educationist, and township clerk, Captain Hill was buried in a rail-fence enclosure on his rocky farmland, long abandoned except as a sheep run.

LIME-BURNING KILN, DUMMER TOWNSHIP, 1943

The photograph was taken *en route* to the Hill farm. The author is standing at the right, two of his children on top of the kiln.

THE ABANDONED FARM OF CAPTAIN HILL, 1943

The log house of 1831 has been removed in recent years.

of out-door life still lingering on it. There had been a time when he was handsome and very fair. His eyes were grey, bold, and uneasy; the nose rather high and well-formed as well as his lips; and he could not stand steady on account of a little nervous twitch which was always at work somewhere. He had on a rusty, napless, but well-shaped hat with some turns of cord round it. His coat was green, single-breasted, built in the year one, and patched with drabs and greens of all hues and shapes, evidently with his own hands with white thread most unskilfully. Two or three coils of leather thongs hung in his coat button-holes, as if to carry game with him.

The first time I saw him he had no waistcoat, but a coarse clean shirt covered his chest, crossed with a silver watch-guard; but in cooler weather he wore a deer-skin vest up to his throat. His pantaloons were of faded blue calico, fitting loosely and tightened below the knee with leather straps. His foot-wear was the strong mocassin, the best of all for woods and rocks.

His young scamp of a boy was in corduroy and cap, and was soon lying on the grass looking at the sun through his fingers. . . . The secluded life of the banished lord seemed to have blunted no faculty. He was not a hollow-eye misanthrope; but, with a dash of the eccentric, was full of right thoughts, and fitting expressions for them were found at will. As I was on the wing and not likely to intrude into his den on the Bear Creek he was pleased to talk freely with me. He took a gloomy view of the domestic state of Great Britain, and expressed his satisfaction at having escaped from an impending storm. . . .

'There are,' said he ,'vast questions, religious, political, and commercial, to be settled. . . . Property of all kinds is centring in vast masses, while the millions are in the deepest poverty. . . . The people are silently educating for the struggle, and it will take place in my day. Therefore I fled, as have done many others, but most of them into the United States. As I have had in my day a good deal of London life and am passionately fond of field sports, I rushed into the most solitary wild I could find. . . . The change was too violent and sudden for my poor wife, who . . . drooped and wearied in our lone place. . . . She died about four years ago. And now a new and pressing concern has grown up—what to do with two boys and a girl; and, truth to tell, I get stiffer in the joints; so that I am now pondering on a return to civilized life for the education of my children.' . . .

His home was six or seven miles lower down the river . . . but his name I did not learn. His reserve and lofty manner, together with some command of money, had procured for him his bye-name. . . . While not very young he had made a *mésalliance* with a beautiful and gentle girl, who joyfully vowed in an English drawing-room to follow the man of her heart anywhere—across the ocean and into the wilderness; but she sank under the rudeness, the gloom, and strangeness of her new abode. . . . He had been a good husband. His small farm was in tolerable order. His singular dress must have been a whim. He made no companions save one or two good shots

Courtesy *Timiskaming Speaker*

PERCY LEGGITT, 'THE HERMIT OF SAVARD'
A well-known recluse of the Timiskaming area.

who lived ten miles from him; and now and then he had a hurricane tobacco-smoke with a renowned Indian hunter.

At Fort St. Clair he brought me his daughter, ten years old—a handsome, freckled, sunburnt lass, and somewhat delicate in appearance but full of spirits, as she did not know the object of her visit, which was to have a surplus tooth extracted: this, of course, was done—but reluctantly. I do not like pulling at ladies' teeth— they never forgive you; but you are to them an executioner for all time. I suggested to the father the propriety of sending this forest-maid to England, or at least to a good school at Toronto or Kingston, and he took my words in good part.*

The known history of a more unfortunate backwoodsman, Francis Abbott 'the hermit of Niagara', is described in Thomas Fowler's *Journal of a Tour* (1832):

In the afternoon of the 18th June, 1829, a tall, well-built, and handsome man, dressed in a long loose gown or cloak of a chocolate colour, was seen passing through the principal street of the village of Niagara falls, on the American side. He had under his left arm a

*Dr. Bigsby records as well two French aristocrats who did not fit in Canada: 'In the Canadas remarkable persons are continually turning up. The Chevalier and Madame de Brosse are not the only members of the old court of France in the western country. I have repeatedly passed the house (then shut up and going to ruin) of the Count and Countess of K., persons of high consideration in France before 1790, now long since dead. They had no children, and literally shut themselves up in a Swiss cottage which they built on the Niagara frontier. It had a heavy roof, and two wooden galleries running round it.'

roll of blankets, a flute, a portfolio, and a large book, and in his right hand he carried a small stick. He advanced towards the Eagle Hotel, attracting the gaze of the visitors there and others about the place by his eccentric appearance. With elastic step and animated motion, he passed the hotel, heeded not the inquiring gaze of the idle multitude, but, erect, proudly bent his course to the small and lowly inn of Ebenezer O'Kelly. He at once entered into stipulations with his host that the room he occupied should be solely his own; that he should have his table to himself, and only certain parts of his cooking should be done by Mrs. O'Kelly. He made the usual inquiries as to the localities of the falls, and wished to know if there was a library or reading room in the village.

On being informed that there was a library he immediately repaired to the individual by whom it was kept, deposited three dollars, and took out a book. He then purchased a violin, borrowed music books, and informed the librarian that his name was Francis Abbott, and that he should remain a few days at the falls. He also conversed with him upon various subjects, and his language was delivered with great ease and ability. The next day he returned to the librarian, expatiated largely upon the beautiful scenery of the falls, the grand views of the cascades and cataracts, and of that most sublime prospect—the falls themselves. In all his travels, he said, he had never met with any thing that would compare with it for sublimity, except Mount Etna during an eruption. He then intimated that he should remain at least a week; observing, that as well might a traveller, in two days, examine in detail the various museums and curiosities of Paris, as become acquainted with the

Courtesy *Timiskaming Speaker*

'UNCLE TOM'S CABIN'

The log house of another recluse, Louis Marguerat, Tomstown, 1901.

splendid scenery of Niagara in the same space of time. When he was informed that visitors at the falls frequently remained but a day or two, he expressed his astonishment that they should be so little interested in the grand and beautiful works of nature as to spend only so short a period.

After a few days he called again, and again expatiated on the beauties of the falls, adding that he had concluded to remain a month at least, and perhaps six months. In a short time after this he determined to fix his abode upon Goat or Iris Island, and was desirous of erecting a rustic hut for the purpose of abstracting himself from all society and becoming a solitary hermit. The proprietor of this island did not think proper to grant him the privilege of erecting a building for such a use, but permitted him to occupy a small room in the only house on the island. At this time there lived a family in the house, who furnished him occasionally with bread and milk; but he generally dispensed with these, providing himself with other articles and always doing his own cooking. This was his permanent residence for about twenty months. Last winter the family removed, and to those persons with whom he held any communication he expressed his great satisfaction at having it in his power to live alone. For some months he seemed to enjoy himself very much, until another family entered the house. He then concluded to erect a cottage of his own, and as he could not do it on the island, he determined to build it on the main shore. It yet stands about thirty rods from the main fall, on the bank of the river. And he occupied it for about two months.

On Friday, the 10th of June last, he went twice to the river to bathe, and was seen to go a third time, at which time the ferryman saw him in the water. This was about two o'clock in the afternoon. The ferryman did not see him return, and his clothes were observed where he had deposited them. An examination was immediately made, but the body could not be discovered. On Tuesday, the 21st of June, the body was found at Fort Niagara, and on the following day it was removed to the burial ground at Niagara falls, and there decently interred.

Thus terminated the career of the unfortunate Francis Abbott— little known, indeed, even to those near whom he had spent the last two years of his life. Some few gleanings only can be given. He was an English gentleman of a respectable family, of highly cultivated mind and manners. He had a finished education, and was not only master of the languages and deeply read in the arts and sciences but displayed all the minor accomplishments of the gentleman; possessing colloquial powers in an eminent degree, and music and drawing in great perfection. Several years of his life had been spent in travelling. He had visited Egypt and Palestine; travelled through Turkey, Greece, Italy, Spain, Portugal, and France; and had resided for considerable periods of time in Rome, Naples, and Paris. When at the falls, business brought him in contact with some of the inhabitants, with a few of whom he would sometimes be sociable, but to all others he was distant and reserved. At such times his conversation would be of the most interesting kind, and his descriptions of the people and countries were highly glowing and animated. But at times even with those he would hold no conversation, and communicated his wishes on a slate, at the same time requesting that nothing might be said to him. Sometimes for three or four months together he would go unshaved, often with no covering on his head, and his body enveloped in a blanket, shunning all and seeking the deepest solitude of Iris Island. He composed much, and generally in Latin, but destroyed his compositions almost as fast as he produced them. When his little cot was examined hopes were entertained that some manuscript or memorial of his own composition might be found, but he had left nothing of the kind. His faithful dog guarded the door, and was with difficulty persuaded to move aside while it was opened. The cat occupied the place appropriated as his bed, and the guitar, violin, flutes, and music books were scattered around in confusion. There was a portfolio, and the leaves of a large book; but not a word, not even his name, was written in any of them.

Many spots on Iris Island are consecrated to the memory of Francis Abbott. On the upper end of the island he had established his walk, and at one place it was become hard trodden, like that on which a sentinel performs his tour of duty. Between Iris Island and Moss Isle there is embowered in seclusion and shade one of the most charming waterfalls or cascades imaginable. This was his favourite retreat for bathing. Here he resorted at all seasons of the year. In the coldest weather, even when there was snow on the ground and ice in the river, he continued to bathe in the Niagara. At the lower extremity of the island is a bridge leading to what is called the Terrapin Rocks. From this bridge extends a single piece of timber some twelve or fifteen feet over the precipice. On this bridge it was his daily practice to walk. With a quick step he would pass the bridge, advance on the timber to the extreme point, turn quickly on his heel and walk back, continuing thus to walk for hours together. Sometimes he would let himself down at the end of the projecting plank, and hang under it by his hands and feet over the terrific precipice for fifteen minutes at a time. To the inquiry why he would thus expose himself he would reply that in crossing the ocean he had frequently seen the sea boy perform far more perilous acts, and as he should probably again pass the sea himself he wished to inure himself to such dangers.

If the nerves of others were disturbed, his were not. In the wildest hours of the night he was often found walking alone and undismayed in the most dangerous places near the falls; and at such times he would shun approach, as if he had a dread of man. He had a stipend allowed him of about five dollars a week. He always attended to the state of his accounts very carefully, was economical in the expenditure of money for his own immediate use, and generous in paying for all favours and services, never receiving any thing without making immediate payment. He had a deep and abiding sense of religious duty and decorum, was mild in his behaviour and inoffensive in his conduct. Religion was a subject he well understood and

FRANCIS ABBOTT

'The Hermit of Niagara'
Reproduced from an oil painting
of 1872 by R. W. Wallis in the
Niagara Falls Museum, by cour-
tesy of Arnold Sherman and
Francis J. Petrie.

highly appreciated. The charity he asked from others he extended
to all mankind.

What, it will be asked, could have broken up and destroyed such
a mind as Francis Abbott's? What could have driven him from the
society he was so well qualified to adorn; and what transformed
him, noble in person and intellect, into an isolated anchorite, shunning the association of his fellow-men? The history of his misfortunes is not known, and the cause of his unhappiness and seclusion
will undoubtedly to us be ever a mystery. During his stay here he
was perfectly infatuated with the scenery of the falls, and expressed
himself in ecstasies with the romantic retreats of Iris Island. At the
time of his death he was about twenty-eight years of age.

Whatever their difficulties and misfortunes, optimism remained an admirable pioneer characteristic. As they had come
in so many instances from conditions of misery and poverty,
it was not remarkable that anticipation of the future would
be pleasing. In many cases hope was long deferred and con-
templation outran eventual realization, but such is the common
fate of man; and it is apparent that, with all the hardships, the
great majority were better off in the New Land than they could
ever have hoped to be in the Old. No one put it more effectively
than William Singer who, after describing how he had cut himself several times doing unaccustomed bush work, and had
once cut off two toes but had had them sewed on by his em-
ployer, concluded his letter home as follows:

You must not think I dislike the country on account of my misfortunes, for if I was to cut my right leg off I should not think of
returning to Corsley again, for I could do much better here with
one leg than in Corsley with two.

CHAPTER XVIII

CHOOSING A LOT

SOME settlers came to Canada under complete government supervision, while others, having attached themselves to emigration societies, had most of their choices made for them. The vast majority, however, had some control over the location of their new home, and if they had not already decided to settle near relatives or friends there was an important problem to be solved.

It should not be assumed, however, that any large percentage of immigrants were in a position to delay settlement while they investigated and compared the attractions of various districts. In innumerable instances the destination of a chance acquaintance, the fact that a stage was leaving York for one region that day, or the offer of a lift in a farmer's wagon settled for generations the locality in which a man and his descendants were to live. But those who were not in the last stages of disease and misery had probably feelings similar to those of Mrs. William Radcliff, who found that 'the prospect of happiness and independence qualified every sentiment of regret, and reconciled me to the painful alternative we had chosen'.

The 'too prevalent notion', observed Mrs. Edward Copleston in 1856, was that 'all an immigrant in Canada has to do is to hurry on to the west* as fast as possible'. Proceeding to Toronto her family heard that Collingwood must be explored before any one could safely settle down. So her husband visited the place, finding that its chief building was a 'large wooden-framed hotel perched at the very terminus of the railway so that the trains almost ran into it'. But the guests were a rough lot and her husband 'heard the hardest swearing and the most blasphemous epithets and conversation it was ever his lot to have forced upon

---

*That is, Canada West, as Upper Canada had become by the Act of Union, 1840. Canada West became Ontario at Confederation, 1867.

263

his ears'. Someone there told him that Orillia on Lake Simcoe was almost another Brighton, so the family set off for Belle Ewart—'What a name to give to a few wooden shanties huddled together and surrounded by charred stumps, with a Yankee saw-mill the mainstay of its trade!' A 'miserable squalid' tavern put them up until the next steamer sailed for Orillia,* which was found to resemble English Brighton not at all; and she concludes with a remark usually reserved for Americans: that 'all Canadians proper have a great idea of themselves and of all belonging

Toronto Public Library   T. H. Ware

LOG HOUSE, ORILLIA, 1844

to them, and think all they possess, as well as all they do, is inferior to nothing to be met with at home'.

Yet Orillia was 'a pretty little retired village, with some good frame-houses and a few small stores'; though as an election was going on, the inn was a rowdy place and Mrs. Copleston 'quite dreaded sitting at meals with men too much elated to perceive how disagreeable they were behaving', for champagne was being supplied in profusion at the candidates' expense.** The Coples-

*T. H. Ware, who spent a few months near Orillia in 1844, says the village took its name from 'a beautiful red flower which is found in the neighbourhood'. He states that 'most of the Gentry who are settled in this part of the country are possessed of small incomes which they draw from England, & are therefore in a great measure independent of farming; they generally farm no more of their lands than will keep themselves and their cattle; indeed it would be useless to attempt farming to any greater extent as there is no market sufficiently near to make the business profitable.'

**See p. 155 fn. for a more detailed account of the crudities of Canadian elections in the period of pioneering.

tons speedily left the village, spent the winter at a roadside log tavern in 'the Bush' on the way to Coldwater, then spent a few months in Toronto, and, after advertising for a cleared farm near the newly-opened Grand Trunk Railway connecting Montreal and Toronto, finally settled upon one along the St. Lawrence for which they paid £80 annual rent.*

There was interested propaganda in those days as in our own, notably that disseminated by the Canada Company and by certain writers who published emigrant guidebooks or travel narratives which, in effect, jumped on the Company's bandwagon. 'An Ex-Settler', whose *Canada in the Years 1832, -33, and -34* is one of the best of guidebooks, noted that most settlers in those years rushed northwestward to the 'Huron Tract' without once looking right or left, 'and have not been induced by anything more solid than puffing publications from the Canada Company or other equally interested sources'. Not that there was not good land there, but it was 'remote' from the point of view of the times; and some of the miscellaneous holdings of the Company elsewhere consisted of very bad land that must have fooled many a settler.**

Patrick Shirreff was particularly incensed against the Company, and he gave two instances of misrepresentation:

The writers of private letters, the verbal tales of individuals, and the public journals are often called into requisition to laud and misrepresent the country, and people of Britain ought to consider the accounts well before giving them credence. In a Montreal newspaper which lately reached me I observed a paragraph announcing that a yacht club had been formed at Goderich, of which Captain Dunlop was president. At the time of my visit to Goderich, in the end of August 1833, the population were chiefly subsisting on flour and salt pork imported from Detroit. The harbour contained three craft of the smallest size, and I did not see a boat or yacht of any description. The youth of Britain who anticipates displaying at Goderich the uniform of a yacht club, and having the fair sex greeting his triumphant entry into the harbour by the waving of handkerchiefs, may delay his departure for half a century. A steam-boat had appeared off the village in 1833 and could not gain admittance into the harbour for want of water. I did not learn the object of her call, but I am sure all the disposable agricultural produce of the settlement, up to the present time, would not freight a nut-shell.

*And in spite of all her dislikes her book of 1861 was called *Canada: Why We Live in It, and Why We Like It.*
**As for example, near the shores of the Kawartha Lakes, Captain G. A. Hill was among those who were sold land distinctly of a marginal nature, though possibly the Company was not aware of the slight depth of soil that lay beneath the pine forest.

Captain A——, in the township of Blenheim, was told by an agent of the Canada Company that a stage-coach would convey himself and family from Hamilton to the property he had purchased. No such conveyance existed. On representing the imposition which had been practised on him to the managers at York an abatement of price was offered. I saw the correspondence on the subject.

Captain Hill settled in 1831 on a Crown grant in Dummer Township, Peterborough County, and was among a number who had another grievance against the Company, for in 1833 he had purchased from its agent in Cobourg, James Gray Bethune, a 100-acre lot adjoining his own; but when the agent shortly went bankrupt without having forwarded the money to the Company its directors refused to be responsible and repudiated the sale. Hill published in 1834 his small emigration guidebook, and in it he said a good word for the Canada Company; but he subsequently stated in a letter to the *Cobourg Star* that if he ever put out a second edition he would alter very materially what he had said.

The old proverb that distant fields look green applied to the selection of land, and it was apparent, as one man put it, that nothing short of the shores of the Pacific would satisfy some people—if there were any possible way to get there. Choice of a lot was, of course, a difficult matter at best, for as C. Rankin, 'an intelligent surveyor' remarked in 1835, people who had spent most of their lives as weavers could hardly be expected to be good judges of land, particularly when many an expert who was a native of America was deceived by underlying rock and poor soil. And as opinions so widely differed, Dr. Johnson's maxim was perhaps true in this instance as in others, that 'He who chooses quickly will in by far the more numerous cases choose the best'.

Only a writer sensitive to nature could describe adequately the gloom, and at the same time the splendour, of the boundless forest which greeted the pioneer, and there is no better pen-picture than Anna Jameson's as she travelled from Brantford to Woodstock in 1837:

No one who has a single atom of imagination can travel through these forest roads of Canada without being strongly impressed and excited. The seemingly interminable line of trees before you; the boundless wilderness around; the mysterious depths amid the multitudinous foliage where foot of man hath never penetrated, and which partial gleams of the noontide sun, now seen, now lost, lit

Courtesy Coverdale Collection, Manoir Richelieu, Quebec

THE EMIGRANT'S WELCOME TO CANADA

up with a changeful, magical beauty; the wondrous splendour and novelty of the flowers; the silence, unbroken but by the low cry of a bird* or hum of an insect or the splash and croak of some huge bull-frog; the solitude in which we proceeded mile after mile, no human being, no human dwelling within sight, are all either exciting to the fancy or oppressive to the spirits, according to the mood one may be in. . . .

I observed some birds of a species new to me: there was the lovely blue-bird with its brilliant violet plumage, and a most gorgeous species of woodpecker with a black head, white breast, and back and wings of the brightest scarlet; hence it is called by some 'the field-officer', and more generally 'the cock of the woods'. . . . There was also the Canadian robin. . . . There were great numbers of small birds of a bright yellow, like canaries. . . . Sometimes when I looked up from the depth of foliage to the blue firmament above I saw an eagle sailing through the air on apparently motionless wings.

Nor let me forget the splendour of the flowers which carpeted the woods on either side, . . . for in some places did a rich embroidered pall of flowers literally *hide* the earth. There those beautiful plants which we cultivate with much care in our gardens—azalias, rhododendrons,** all the gorgeous family of the lobelia—were flourishing in wild luxuriance. Festoons of creeping and parasitical plants hung from branch to branch. The purple and scarlet iris, blue larkspur, and the elegant Canadian columbine with its bright pink flowers; the scarlet lychnis, a species of orchis of the most dazzling geranium-colour, and the white and yellow and purple cyprepedium (lady's slipper) bordered the path, and a thousand others of most resplendent hues for which I knew no names. . . . How lavish, how carelessly profuse is Nature in her handiwork!

The English author of *A Few Plain Directions* encouraged a highly optimistic—even idyllic—view of what the emigrant might expect in the New Land:

Canada, perhaps, has been represented to him as a gloomy and impenetrable forest, the abode of savage beasts of prey or of Indians even exceeding them in ferocity. Perhaps he has been told that it is locked up by frost for seven months in the year, or buried in snow; and he may have been influenced by these fake or malicious representations. He will, therefore, be agreeably surprised at meeting with the very reverse of such a deformed picture; at seeing a country of an aspect agreeably undulated, watered with fine streams, and possessing a soil as rich and productive as the most fertile parts of the

---

*More than one writer noted that the pioneer forest was most sombre and still and that no birds sang there. There was no linnet, lark, or thrush, wrote the early poet, Alexander McLachlan; and though Canadian birds were

'*surpassing fair,*
Still the song was wanting there'.

**Though the large flowering rhododendron shrubs of Britain and the United States have never grown in Ontario, a smaller species is occasionally seen in the forest and Mrs. Jameson might have come upon it.

A

FEW PLAIN DIRECTIONS

FOR PERSONS

INTENDING TO PROCEED AS SETTLERS

TO

HIS MAJESTY'S PROVINCE

OF

UPPER CANADA,

IN NORTH AMERICA.

Pointing out the best Port to embark at for Quebec.—Provisions and other Things necessary to be provided for the Voyage.—The best and cheapest Method of Travelling from Quebec to Montreal, and thence to Kingston and York, a Distance of 600 Miles, whereby Emigrants may avoid heavy Expenses.—The Method of obtaining Land in the most eligible Districts.—What Property various Descriptions of Emigrants should possess on their Arrival in America.—Advice to Farmers, Tradesmen, Mechanics, &c.—A Description of that fine and interesting Province: its Productions, &c. &c.—Some cursory Remarks on the Manners and Customs of the Inhabitants.

CONTAINING ALSO

A SHORT SKETCH OR JOURNAL OF THE

AUTHOR'S VOYAGE ACROSS THE ATLANTIC,

IN JUNE, 1819.

BY AN ENGLISH FARMER

SETTLED IN UPPER CANADA.

With a Map.

LONDON:

PRINTED FOR BALDWIN, CRADOCK, AND JOY,
47, PATERNOSTER-ROW.

1820.

A RARE EMIGRANT GUIDEBOOK

Old World; at finding that the stately and beautiful forests are so free from underwood and projecting branches that he may take his horse at full speed through any part of them*; and that there are no noxious beasts of prey, no venomous reptiles, and no wild Indians to molest him. . . .

At one time the traveller passes through a narrow strip of cleared land; at another through tracts half a mile or a mile square in a high state of cultivation. He everywhere sees the vestiges of recent clearance in the half-burnt and branchless trunks which have been cut off three feet above the ground, with which the fields are studded.

*This is very different from Mrs. Jameson's 'festoons of creeping and parasitical plants hung from branch to branch'. The truth, of course, lies somewhere between.

269

At every half mile or mile he crosses a beautiful stream of pure and limpid water (for this country is intersected by the finest rivulets in the world), on which is a grist or saw-mill. He is surrounded by fields of wheat, and of Indian corn intermixed with the luxuriant gourd. On either hand his prospect is bounded by the thick and variegated foliage of the forest, except where the majestic St. Lawrence or the light green expanses of the Ontario meets his view through the trees. Above him is a clear and azure sky; he breathes a salutary and pure air; the pine partridge, disturbed by his sudden appearance in its haunts, springs up and perches near him; the humming birds sport amongst the flowers which border the road; and flocks of pigeons, and the blue jays, woodpeckers, robins, and others of the feathered tribe, enliven the scene.

As cleared land along the front was obviously out of the question as far as most immigrants were concerned, they set their course for the woods. The best means of judging forest land as to its potential value for farming was probably the trees which grew upon it, though it was by no means a certain criterion. Some experienced settlers believed that pine trees invariably indicated poor land, but 'Ex-Settler' said that 'some of the best clay I had ever seen in Canada' was almost entirely covered with pine timber. The same man knew of only two trees which he had found an invariable sign of good land—basswood and white elm; and while hardwood trees, such as oak and maple, were supposed to grow on good land, he had sometimes found them on sandy land not worth the clearing.

I believe on good land the timber always splits well [he continued], but this would be rather a roundabout proof to a person hastily traversing a lot; for my part I would go to the roots of the windfalls, of which you will always see abundance, and examine the soil there, which you will be thereby enabled to do to the depth of a foot or upwards. I would see that the surface of the land was level and not in little hills and hollows; that the underbrush was not very thick and tangled; and I would avoid red oak, white birch, iron-wood poles, and young beech; I would also avoid, generally speaking, hemlock and pine.

Joseph Pickering, whose *Enquiries of an Emigrant* is equally good, urged attention to the trees for a very different reason—the availability of plenty of good 'rail timber', such as oak, hickory, ash, cedar, chestnut, pine, butternut, cherry, and black walnut; though he hoped the last two would not be so used but saved for furniture-making. A still more complete classification of good and bad land according to its trees is given by E. A. Talbot in his *Five Years' Residence*:

BERLIN IN 1854

Land upon which black and white Walnut, Chestnut, Hiccory, and Basswood grow is esteemed the best on the continent. That which is covered with Maple, Beech, and Cherry is reckoned as second-rate. Those parts which produce Oak, Elm, and Ash are esteemed excellent wheat-land but inferior for all other agricultural purposes. Pine, Hemlock, and Cedar land is hardly worth accepting as a present. It is, however, difficult to select any considerable tract of land which does not embrace a great variety of wood; but when a man perceives that Walnut, Chestnut, Hiccory, Basswood, and Maple are promiscuously scattered over his estate he need not be at all apprehensive of having to cultivate an unproductive soil.

. . . .

Where the butternut and cherry are [said an experienced settler, J. J. E. Linton] the land is rich, but maple and basswood* with the elm denote the same; if much beech the land is lighter, but a warmer soil. The more 'knolly' the land is (the knolls or small hills being caused by the 'turn up' of the trees in falling) the better the soil. The emigrant, however, will find a superior surface mould at which to try his hand and his plough.

The water supply was a highly important consideration, and the best guidebooks warned emigrants not to take anyone's word for it.

If you inquire [observes 'Ex-Settler' sarcastically] about a lot which happens to have as much water running on it as would fill your hat in twenty-four hours, you are told of 'a never-failing creek' with extensive 'water privileges', and 'great opens for a saw-mill, &c.'; . . . of course I need scarcely say I would look very sharp about water; I have known some people to have been distant from the nearest water two miles, and to have dug forty feet without getting any, and this occurs often in the best land.

Romantic ideas of the soil's excessive fertility—usually blamed upon 'the puffers of the Canada Company'—must be taken as so much humbug, the same writer observes:

Before I went out, whenever I thought of a bush farm it was of rich black loam, splendid clay, land unlooked at since the flood, twenty crops of wheat, &c., &c.—in fact, that you had only to reduce

*But basswood was a soft and unpopular wood in the pioneer period. When the 'Patriots' of 1837, the reformers of the day and the basic leaders for democracy and responsible government, wished to call the Family Compact a bad name they could think of nothing worse than 'a base basswood': 'The backwoodsman', says *Patrick Smith's Almanac for 1834*, 'while he lays the axe to the root of the oak in the forests of Canada, should never forget that a base basswood is growing in this his native land, which, if not speedily girdled, will throw its dark shadows over the country and blast its best exertions. Look up, reader, and you will see the branches—the Robinson branch, the Powell branch, the Jones branch, the Strachan branch, the Boulton twig, etc. The farmer toils, the merchant toils, the labourer toils, and the Family Compact reap the fruit of their exertions.'

Lieut. Philip Bainbrigge

MERRICK VILLE, RIDEAU CANAL, 1838

James Pattison Cockburn

SMITH'S FALLS ON THE RIDEAU, 1829

it in order to make it fit for the common purposes of farming. . . .
A great deal has been said about the 'vegetable mould of centuries!'
—this sounds very imposingly but . . . it is generally from two to
four inches in depth, and its fertility for the first year is wonderful,
but after two or three crops its effects will altogether vanish.

Settlers were warned to avoid swampy land, and it was, of
course, wise to have one's house well removed from low land
if for no other reason than mosquitoes; but 'Ex-Settler' considered twenty per cent swamp a good proportion, for when cleared
it usually drained itself, made a fine meadow, and was the only
land that would produce cedar for buildings and rails. The
coarse grass found in natural meadows, if once burned off, was
succeeded by a better variety of great value to the settler as feed
for stock.

Innumerable settlers were fooled by wild land which was
unrecognizable once the trees had been removed. Much of the
land north of various of the summer-resort lakes, for example, is
now almost useless. Its thousands of small lakes and rivers are
filled with the soil of centuries; its onetime appearance of un-
dulating forest land exchanged for vast areas of unproductive
granite or limestone; its noble oaks and pines replaced by dwarf
jack pine, scrub poplar and birch, juniper, and blueberry
bushes. The descendants of men who helped lumber the region
eighty or ninety years ago exist today on the edge of civilization
in a summer-resort wilderness that, with intelligent treatment,
would never have been such a victim of erosion.

It need not be assumed, however, that all such settlers were
fooled when they selected these pine uplands, nor was all such
settlement a mistake. Some of the most effective pioneers were
primarily lumbermen, and there was a good market for pine
long before the hardwoods were in demand; nor was any drainage needed in these regions, while a good deal of attention had
to be given to it in the clay flats along the front. Even though
such farms were subsequently abandoned it may yet be said
that they served a useful purpose in facilitating the province's
settlement, for at first, in addition to the lumber, most of them
produced good crops of potatoes and Indian corn. Bringing
the analogy closer, sandy Norfolk County, full of abandoned
farms a generation or so ago because unsuitable for mixed
farming, is now a centre of the lucrative flue-cured tobacco
industry.

Lanark and Dalhousie townships, in the Rideau-Ottawa

Photograph by James Guillet

BLUEBERRY RIDGES, MOUNTAIN LAKE, BURLEIGH TOWNSHIP

'It is a vulgar error to suppose that you have tasted blueberries
who never plucked them.'—Henry David Thoreau.

region, as well as many another in which there were extensive
early settlements, similarly abound in rocks and stones, as
Arthur Lang, one of the first members of Ramsay Settlement
near the Mississippi River, wrote in his diary in 1821. But there
were compensations, for in the same rocky region is Lac des
Chats; and the Scots who settled near by considered that with

275

Willis, *Canadian Scenery*   W. H. Bartlett

FALLS OF THE OTTAWA AT LES CHATS

a few villas the district would approach in beauty their famed Scottish lochs—which was quite a concession!

Cheats and racketeers were as prevalent in Canada as in any other country under settlement, and 'Ex-Settler' considered that there were 'no more greedy or unconscionable sharks' anywhere in the world; so he advised the greatest care to avoid victimizing and exploitation. That was one reason to buy land direct from the government, for no one was then especially interested in making the sale; and the title was indisputable as well, the price moderate, and the terms reasonable. Usually such land was sold only at public auction held every fortnight or monthly in each district; and your deed would be forthcoming when you had performed the settlement duties—a shanty 12 feet square erected, a few acres cleared, and the concession line partially opened.

The irregularity, not to say dishonesty, of land-granting in 'Family Compact' days added to settlers' difficulties. The Honourable Peter Russell was particularly noted for granting land to himself in great quantities. Speculators, mostly absentees, obtained innumerable grants, and these with the Clergy Reserves obstructed the building of roads, adding greatly to the bona fide settler's problems. When an official, John Richards, travelled northward from Rice Lake about 1830 he noted 'a great many small openings' along the Otonabee River. They were, he said, 'the relics of former sham settlements', where

absentee owners or their employees had made a fake performance of settlement duties to obtain their patents and then disappeared. And the fraud perpetrated by the absentee owner or
speculator was sometimes returned to him with interest by the
choppers he hired for the purpose, for they were aware of what
was going on, and ran little chance that their work would ever
be inspected:

When the landed speculators made a fresh grab at some wild land,
[writes the Reverend Stewart Darling colloquially in his *Sketches
of Canadian Life* (1849)] they would make a contract with some
of these fellows to do the settlement duties for them, and away
they'd go to the woods with an axe and some pork and flour slung
at their back and a rifle in their hand (for they were mostly half
Yankees that followed this trade). When they found the lot (or if
they made a mistake it wasn't no great matter) they would look for
a place as free from big trees as they could, and then they'd *clear*
it of the brushwood that grew upon it, then they'd cut some of the
saplings into lengths and build what they *called* a shanty, that wouldn't
have covered a calf. Or . . . these rascals would go down the
[concession] line, striking their axes into the trees as they went
along and slashing the brushwood that stood in the way. After this
they would go back and swear that on such a lot, in such a concession, in such a township they had made a *clearing* and built a *log
shanty* or hut, or that they had *cut* the timber on the concession
lines.

And as a result of this racketeering collaboration the men
received their pay, the speculator his deed or *lift,* as it was
commonly called, and the forest lot remained practically in a
state of nature.

At times, and particularly in the eighteen-twenties, land was
both expensive and hard to obtain—a grievance that was an
underlying cause of the Rebellion of 1837. Clergy reserves were
among large blocks held in idleness, but many huge grants had
been made also to government officials and other favoured
persons, who kept them to sell at exorbitant prices. Some sur-
veyors were paid in land and held it for high prices, as it was
often the best for mill sites or villages; and when that practice
was stopped speculators on 'the inside' would get their field-notes
and corner all the best lots, frequently retarding settlement for
ten or fifteen years. A variation was practised when new townships were opened up—to tell all and sundry that you owned
certain choice lots; and then, having frightened others away, to
sell them at five times the cost and rush down to York and become the bona fide purchaser. All such absentee owners, the

LUMBER

1, Lumber Camp.   3, Log Pile by Lake.   4, Felling Trees.
2, Log Train.   5, Lumber Yard and Mill.

LUMBERING AS AN EARLY ENCYCLOPAEDIA SAW IT

curse of innumerable townships, seriously interfered with the proper development of the province.*

'U. E. rights' were often a good buy. They arose from grants to Loyalists' children on coming of age; and lots of 200 acres, normally worth $80 to $100, could at times be bought for less than $20, 'the owners being often of the lowest class and very wretches', as 'Ex-Settler' put it. The difficulty was to hear about the availability of these lots, and it consequently helped to have a friend at court, preferably in one of the government offices.

'Gentlemen' settlers, perhaps with some money and time to spare, were the chief ones who sought the 'better society' that some districts offered. The classes usually listed in this exclusive company include half-pay officers, young surgeons, Church of England clergy, 'private gentlemen', sons of 'respectable persons at home', and graduates of 'the colleges'. Quite a number of these would-be aristocrats were in the vicinity of Woodstock, attracted by Admiral VanSittart and two or three relatives of British peers.** A model township, wrote Mrs. Edward Copleston (closely related to an English bishop), 'should be entirely British in their habits, select in every way, and members of the Church of England', though she admitted that where something of the kind had been attempted it had proved 'most difficult, if not impossible, to carry out'. And many of this type of young man, as an Anglican clergyman, the Reverend Stewart Darling, put it, 'as they found themselves fit for nothing in England', were observed to possess very much the same characteristics abroad, and gave way to the 'most miserable dissipations' and acquired 'wild and repulsive' habits.

But apart from the official set in York, the Newcastle District

---

*Watson Kirkconnell has this to say of the misgovernment of the day: 'An oligarchy at York had almost succeeded in ruining the province in spite of its remarkable natural resources. This pernicious misrule, which had driven 80,000 Canadians across the American boundary in the years 1830-37, was at last revealed to the government through a pitiful little revolt.' (*Victoria County Centennial History,* page 17.) The best exposé of misrule is, of course, Robert Gourlay's classic *Statistical Account of Upper Canada* (1822), but his reward was imprisonment, mistreatment, and banishment from the province. The editor of the *Niagara Spectator*—for the crime of printing a letter of Gourlay's—was sentenced to a fine of £50, to the pillory, to 18 months' imprisonment, and to a debtors' prison indefinitely if he could not raise £1000 security for seven years. Archdeacon Strachan, a leader of the Family Compact, called Gourlay 'a wicked and malignant person who has no regard for the truth'; while Gourlay returned the compliment by describing Strachan as 'a monstrous little fool of a parson—rogue would have been nearer the truth'.

**For further reference to these settlers see p. 227 fn.

had probably a much greater concentration of wealth and fashion and gentility than any other. The district included four counties—Northumberland and Durham and their subsequent offshoots Peterborough and Victoria—and the aristocrats were largely settled near Cobourg and Peterborough and along the famed 'Back Lakes' of the valley of the Trent. Here many a

Edward Caddy

STONEY LAKE IN THE 1850's
The artist was a prominent land surveyor in the region.

gentleman hoped to establish himself as the approximation of a fox-hunting squire, amid grand and rugged scenery that bore out the part. Bexley Township, in the northern part of Victoria County, had as its first settler in 1834 Admiral VanSittart, a cousin of Baron Bexley. The admiral was given a grant of 1000 acres on the shore of West Bay, Balsam Lake, and approached his land by oxcarts via the old Indian trail from Lake Simcoe, parts of which his men had to chop out as they proceeded. His new property was enhanced in interest from its close relation to Indian villages, missionaries, and traders of past centuries— indeed, the stone chimneys of an extensive trading-post were still to be seen in the early 'seventies. The admiral lived in style on his wilderness estate, dressing for formal dinner each evening

W. N. Cresswell

GODERICH IN 1858

and never being without his champagne. His second wife, however, was the daughter of one of his servants, and to her he left his estate. Even in the 'seventies its proprietor was called 'the Laird of Bexley'.*

But if the society in certain districts was 'very pleasing', as some said, the price of good lots was correspondingly high, and in the later period they were usually available only as cleared land. There were certainly not many establishments quite so much in the grand manner as Captain McLeod's near Yonge Street:

Many of the residences on Yonge Street [wrote the Reverend A. H. W. Rose in 1849] are occupied by gentlemen of the highest standing and respectability, as, for instance, 'Dry-nock', the seat of my hospitable friend Captain McLeod which stands some distance from the road, about 18 miles from the city, on the high bank above a romantic lake which forms part of his property, and in the centre of 600 acres of land which he has purchased there and is rapidly converting into an ornamental and productive estate. Such abodes as these, of course, are replete with every comfort which would be presented by a similar residence in England, such as pianofortes, carpets, mirrors, handsome tables and chairs, etc.

The masses, however, had no such thoughts or ambitions. He who arrived with nothing, or whose meagre savings had already been largely exhausted, was advised to hire out as a labourer, preferably in an occupation to which he was in some measure accustomed; and with economy and frugality he could anticipate purchasing his own land or setting up in business within a few years.

You know [wrote Captain Hill] that we come pretty much as a travelling Welsh Merchant does to a market town—with his donkey carrying a pair of panniers; and while one of *our* panniers is sure to be full of young children, the other is filled with anything and everything but money!

Mrs. Anna Jameson, who paid a visit to Colonel Thomas Talbot, describes those who sought land from him as 'groups of strange figures lounging round the door—ragged, black-bearded, gaunt, travel-worn and toil-worn emigrants, Irish, Scotch, and Americans. . . . These he used to call his land pirates'. And she might have added that they were commonly accorded but scant courtesy by the autocratic colonel, and more often than not went away without land, perhaps with his dogs at their heels.

*See also the author's *The Valley of the Trent*, pp. 64-5.

The government agent at Quebec, an official with no axe to grind, was often asked by incoming prospective settlers, 'Where do you advise us to settle in the Upper Province?' His reply suggested that many seemed to think that the farther west they went the better the land got; but he thought that those who were undecided and had the means to enable investigation should go up the Ottawa to Bytown and examine the land there and along the Rideau, much of it offering a desirable district in which to settle. He also suggested the Newcastle District and the Lake Simcoe region.

'Ex-Settler' investigated these, adding the Niagara region and the vicinity of London for good measure, and he concluded that the London district, 'for the last three or four years most run on', was milder, and the land on the average richer; but that communications were poor and the settler was an 'immense distance' from headquarters at Toronto. Lake Simcoe, he found, had a steamship serving the settlers along its banks, and they were only 34 miles from the capital, with frequent stages and wagons on the road; but the soil was somewhat lighter. Near Niagara the land was average, in the Newcastle District somewhat better, and about the Rideau much the same, 'but there is good and bad in all'. All of which was not very useful in influencing choice.

For myself, were I going out again, [he concludes] I would probably, if I had a good deal of money and only wished to enjoy it, choose Niagara; if I sought to farm and to make all land could make I would settle somewhere about the Rideau and Ottawa, and if my object were something half-way between I would take the north-west bank of Lake Simcoe, and from that to Matchedash; but this may be prejudice, as I know it the best and have lived there. Certainly the society is pleasing and the scenery very beautiful.

Goderich and the rest of the Lake Huron shore was considered much too remote by many experts and travellers, but the Canada Company had plenty of supporters for its outlying lands. Joseph Pickering found the soil near Niagara 'excellent for wheat, clover, and grass'; the Long Point district 'a dry sandy soil, . . . not very rich, . . . but will bear good crops' if properly treated; beyond along Otter Creek, 'a fine country' for both farming and lumbering; and the Thames valley, especially the flats, 'the richest land in the province'. But Robert Stevenson found the St. Clair Flats 'the richest I ever saw in any country', with no trees to be logged and burned; and the land was in many places similarly rich east of Amherstburg, though its lowness created swamps which the settlers tried to remove by drainage ditches. But, concluded Stevenson,

The result of all my travels and inquiries is that I would recommend to my friends to settle to the west of Brantford, but not farther west than Chatham. I would give preference to the district of Huron, and next to that the district of London.

In advising prospective emigrants to settle in the townships along Lake Ontario, 'An English Farmer' states that 'the great road from Kingston to York passes through', the soil is 'excellent', the climate 'salubrious', and the land 'well watered by creeks and small rivulets' and 'finely undulated'; and his intimate acquaintance with 'the town of Amherst (commonly called the Courthouse), . . . the village of Cobourgh, . . . the town of Port Hope or Smith's Creek', and Rice Lake—'a most beautiful piece of water—unsurpassed, perhaps, by any lake either in the New or the Old World'—these references suggest that he lived or had lived in the Cobourg-Peterborough region.

There was, of course, danger in giving too much thought to one's choice of land:

You have read or heard [said Captain Hill in his guidebook] of the hungry ass placed exactly between two equal bundles of hay. While he was gloating on one with his right eye the left was fixed on the other; and the consequence was that the poor fellow not only passed the night supperless in the very midst of plenty but got an incurable squint into the bargain.

But there were other important considerations besides the varied attractions of geographical districts, and having come to some conclusion in the matter the immigrant was ready for the next step. The Reverend James Magrath, settled at Erindale on the banks of the River Credit, wrote home to Ireland some highly informative letters on settlement, and thousands of immigrants unquestionably experienced the course of events that he describes in such detail. Having reached York and made inquiry at the office of the Commissioner of Crown Lands, the newcomer, he said, learns that wild land is available at from 5s. to 10s. an acre, but settlement has pretty well filled up 'the front' and he has to travel a hundred miles into the rear townships. He finds, however, that the stage will take him to within ten or fifteen miles of the lots in 'the Bush' that have been recommended.

Hiring a local man at this point, who agrees to provide a

" Thus at the expiration of three or four weeks the Preparations are completed "

THE LOG HOUSE

AN ILLUSTRATION FROM RADCLIFF'S *AUTHENTIC LETTERS*, 1833

Discrepancies in this woodcut of a crude log house of unsquared poles suggest that it was made in Ireland from such descriptions as were available. The roof is of a particularly unlikely type of construction and would have leaked like a sieve. The ox-cart has an Irish appearance, and it would have sunk into the mud of Upper Canada. Some of the more informative letters in the book were those of the Reverend James Magrath.

wagon and serve as guide, he proceeds as far as practicable for wheeled vehicles, and then sets forth on foot. Night overtakes them before they have reached their destination, so in the absence of anything better they sleep on a pile of hemlock boughs near a fire which they hope will drive off the clouds of vicious mosquitoes. The guide is fortunate, for he has become immune to the worst effects of mosquito bites, but the newcomer may get malaria from his experience in the Canadian woods.

Long before dawn, not much refreshed and well bitten, the prospective settler wakes his guide and suggests that they have some breakfast and push onward. A little strong tea forms the breakfast,* and as soon as there is sunlight enough they continue among trees, stumps, brush, and swamp until they find the index

---

*John Mactaggart describes the typical forest meal: 'There, on the bushy hemlock, would we lie down; roast pork before the fire on wooden prongs, each man roasting for himself; while plenty of tea was thrown into a large kettle of boiling water, the tin mug was turned out—the only tea-cup—which, being filled, went round until all had drunk; then it was filled again, and so on; while each with his bush-knife cut toasted pork on a shive of bread, ever using the thumb-piece to protect the thumb from being burned; a *tot* or two round of weak grog finished the feast, when some would fall asleep.'

posts which the guide says are those of the lot he is seeking.*
They walk half a mile or so about it, and then sit down on a log
to think it over. Should he bring his family so far into the backwoods? The water supply seems poor, and the prevalence of
pines, says his guide, is a certain indication of inferior land.
They scramble through the woods two or three miles farther
and locate a lot which seems better, and the decision is made
to go back to York to see about its purchase.

Reader, [wrote John M'Donald in 1821, after some weeks' travel
from Quebec into the Rideau region] pause a little whilst reading
this tale of woe, and consider for a moment the deplorable state of
your unhappy, unthinking, and deluded countrymen, thus exposed
for eight weeks to the noisome exhalations of immense woods, the
excessive and rapid variations of a Canadian climate, and the excessive humidity of an American atmosphere, without any shelter from
the inclemency of the sky, the heavy and unwholesome dews and
the rains and the winds (to which latter there is nothing of a nature
parallel in this country [Scotland]) but such as a few posts driven
into the ground and then wrapped together with the frail branches
of the trees could give—wretched habitations indeed! When the
branches wither they are almost completely open at the sides. Some
who are able cover them with blankets or whatever else they can
obtain on the roof; others have them covered round about. This
will not, however, prevent reptiles such as snakes and lizards from
getting in. I saw a snake myself sucking a frog nigh my tent; but
we killed it and when it got a stroke on the head it shot out its
poisonous fangs. We saw numbers of squirrels running about our
beds, and we were frequently deprived of sleep for the unwholesome
intrusion of oxen and cows, which, straying from their owners, came
close to our tents, and we were much terrified lest they should have
pulled our tabernacles about our ears. The swine would come to
our heads and take away anything they could find, running away
with it in their mouths so that we were obliged to pursue them in
order to recover it. . . .

Each emigrant generally gets two lots to view, and if three set
out together there are 600 acres to be inspected. I thought this would
have almost finished me. . . . One of our companions, a young man,
leaving a wife and family, died after such an excursion. . . . I cannot
but also pity such of my unfortunate countrymen who came hither
in search of a transatlantic paradise, destitute of clothes and money,

*This journey from the front was comparatively easy. Settlers who approached
Verulam Township in the 'thirties—and for half a century afterwards—came
north some 30 miles from Cobourg or Port Hope to Peterborough. If from
Cobourg they went overland by a bush road to Rice Lake, crossed the lake,
and proceeded up the Otonabee River. They then continued by oxcart or on
foot over six miles of miry log-strewn trail to Bridgenorth, and thence by
scow, punt, or canoe up Chemong Lake into Pigeon. At Bobcaygeon the boats
were poled up the rapids or portaged into Sturgeon Lake, on the shores of
which the township lies.

Peterborough Public Library   Caroline Hayward

PORT HOPE IN THE 1840's

Courtesy George M. Douglas

FORD, INDIAN RIVER, COUNTY OF PETERBOROUGH

Public Archives of Canada | Lieut. Sempronius Stretton

YORK BARRACKS, 1804

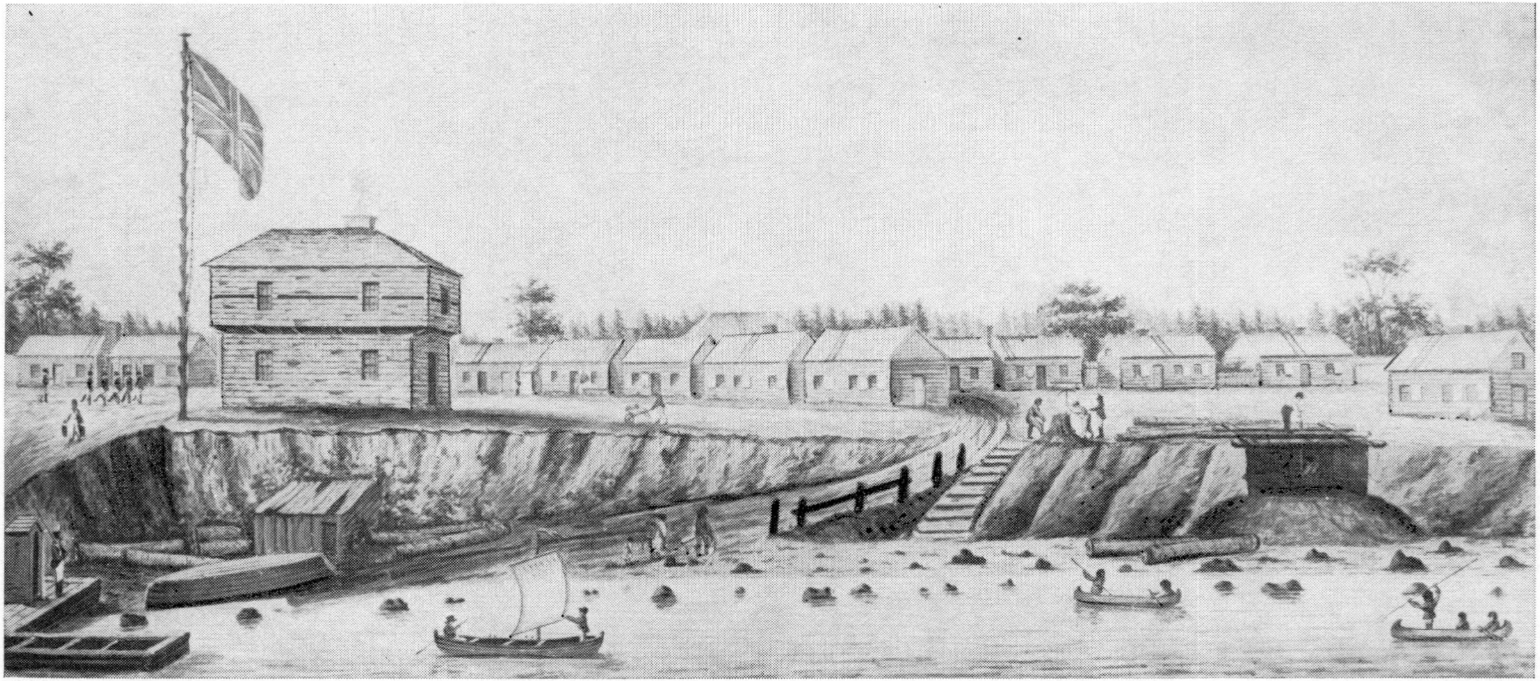

Courtesy Edith Firth

YORK, UPPER CANADA, 1803

Looking east from Jarvis and Palace (Front) streets the main buildings are:

| William Cooper's Toronto Coffee House | Duncan Cameron's House | Dr. W. W. Baldwin's | William Allan's | Peter Russell's | Parliament Buildings | Surgeon Edward Walsh Blockhouse |

A

NARRATIVE

OF THE

RISE & PROGRESS

OF

EMIGRATION,

FROM THE COUNTIES OF

LANARK & RENFREW,

TO THE

New Settlements in Upper Canada,

ON GOVERNMENT GRANT;

COMPRISING THE

Proceedings of the Glasgow Committee

FOR DIRECTING THE AFFAIRS AND EMBARKATION
OF THE SOCIETIES.

WITH A

MAP OF THE TOWNSHIPS,

Designs for Cottages,

AND

A Plan of the Ship Earl of Buckinghamshire.

ALSO,

INTERESTING LETTERS FROM THE SETTLEMENTS.

By ROBERT LAMOND,
Secretary & Agent.

GLASGOW,
Printed by James Hedderwick,
For CHALMERS & COLLINS, &c, WILSON-STREET.

1821.

A RARE EMIGRATION NARRATIVE

because there are five or six months annually of severe frost and snow.

Under such conditions men who became separated from their party were not infrequently lost, sometimes for days. Charles F. Grece considered the matter of sufficient importance to give 'Instructions to Strangers Settling in the Woods or Forests':

It will sometimes happen that people lose themselves in the *Woods.* Cloudy weather operates to deceive but the sun will always direct, by observing its rising and setting from the dwelling place, which Europeans ought strictly to attend to on their first beginning in the forest. Swamps are the most difficult from the thickness of the green timber; in such a case let the person avoid flurrying himself, because fear agitates the mind and leads to frenzy. If fatigued sit down and examine the trees; the north side of large trees is covered with moss; the branches are longest on the south and south-east sides: these will form a compass. Birch trees are the compass for the Indians, their strongest branches pointing eastward.

Should you fall on a river or brook its course will lead to some settlement. The brooks, many of which are little rivers in the spring at the melting of the snow, become dry in summer; but their course may be discovered by observing the way that the growth of wild herbs, grass, and roots of trees lie: their heads will point to the outlet of such waters: the stones will be cleaner on the side next the source than that next the outlet. These observations are easier understood than heights, falls, etc., etc. Sometimes cattle are met with miles from home; by starting them they run from a stranger and generally go home: that will lead the lost person to a settlement. There being little to fear from wild beasts, food is a primary object. As berries are not always to be had any more than nuts, herbs become a consideration. The colts foot, called by the Americans Snake-root, has a leaf formed like the foot of a colt; it is of deep green colour: the roots run horizontally and are of the thickness of a tobacco pipe; they taste like lemon peel. By gathering of that root to eat, a person might exist for some time. This plant produces many lateral roots, it is in greater abundance than most other herbs, it delights in moist situations, and is easy to discover. It is taken as a tea to remove violent colds, when a little sweetened.

But to return to our prospective settler on his way back to York. Before land grants could be obtained the applicant, if a Protestant, took 'the usual oaths of allegiance, abjuration, and supremacy'; if a Roman Catholic the oath of allegiance only. He paid 2s. 6d. Halifax currency for the certificate, and made out a memorial (petition) to the Governor and Council; he appended to it some character testimonials that he had brought with him, and the Clerk of the Executive Council accepted the petition on receipt of another 2s. 6d. fee.

At this time, 1817, the Council met every second Wednesday and applicants appeared personally; and if the applicant's request was favourably received a warrant was given to the Surveyor-General and his name entered on a large map of the township for the lot he had selected. He was then given a 'location ticket' (fee 2s. 6d.). In 1819 the inconvenience of all prospective settlers' having to come to York was remedied by the establishment of Land Boards in each district, with a procedure similar to that of the Land Commissioner's Office at York.

A LOCATION TICKET, 1816

Issued to Peter McPherson, Elmsley Township, County of Leeds.

The location ticket gave the description and location of the 100-acre lot and listed the settlement duties on which a permanent grant depended. Some stated that five acres were to be cleared and cropped, half the road in front of the lot cleared and sown with grass seed, and a house erected. If these duties were not performed within two years the lot might be transferred to another grantee; but if the settler carried them out he could obtain his 'free and common soccage' grant on payment of the patent fee of £5 14s. 1d.

Having now his location ticket in his wallet, the settler collects his family, returns by stage to the settlement nearest his lot, and again hires a wagon, but this time to take his family to a farm whose owner, in return for cash and his wife's help about the house, has made a bargain to keep them and supply provisions for him and his hired labourers while they are building a shanty on his lot and clearing some land.

There is no road to it, so his men proceed with a yoke of oxen and a sled—though it is not winter—for no other vehicle could be brought into the woods. Some of the men go ahead to prepare a bush road, which is done by felling and drawing aside all trees under five inches diameter and cutting a passage through those

Conservation Authorities, Ontario   Snider Collection

SLED RESEMBLING PIONEER JUMPER

of larger size, winding in and out among them as the terrain suggests.

An hour before night they make camp Indian fashion. A ridge pole ten feet in length is placed on two forked sticks six feet long driven firmly into the ground. On one side poles are set obliquely, while the other is open to admit heat from a large fire, as well as smoke to drive off mosquitoes. A thick coat of hemlock branches or bark stripped from nearby trees covers the poles and keeps off rain and dew.

By the time the camp is ready the rest of the party have come up with provisions and blankets, and supper is soon prepared. 'The frying-pan not only supplies successions of savoury pork, but also of bread or paste cakes, not less enticing from the oily drippings of the meat with which they are fried'—no unwelcome supper after a hard day's work in 'the Bush'. The oxen are fed hay or maple branches and tied to a tree, and each man lies down and covers himself with a blanket, his feet stretched towards the fire:

> *. . . Ere long with sleep oppressed,*
> *There we laid us down to rest,*
> *With the cold earth for our bed,*
> *And the green boughs overhead;*
> *And again, at break of day,*

293

Canadian Illustrated News

'FRIED PORK AND FAMILY PRAYERS'

Started on our weary way
Through morasses, over bogs,
Wading rivers, crossing logs,
Scrambling over fallen trees,
Wading pond-holes to the knees;
Sometimes wandering from the track,
And, to find it, turning back;
Scorning ills that would betide us,
Stout hearts and the sun to guide us.*

The party move on some miles farther, erect another camp, and set to work making a clearing for the log shanty. These choppers know better than to leave any trees that might be blown over on the hut, for a man settled near by narrowly escaped death the week before when one crashed over upon his house. Altogether they were busy in the woods for twenty days, for since it was late in the season the settler decided to have them clear enough land to enable him to sow fall wheat without delay.

*'The Emigrant', by Alexander McLachlan, probably the best of Canadian imitators of Burns. He came to Upper Canada in 1840 but was not successful as a farmer. 'The Emigrant' was planned as an epic of backwoods life, but the first part, consisting of seven sections, was all that he completed. It has been suggested that the poetry of McLachlan is 'too close to the life of the working people to be accepted by conventional critics'. (See Margaret Fairley, 'Our Cultural Heritage', *New Frontiers,* Winter 1952.) It was, however, very well received in his own day.

But the cost of all this was appreciable. There was the stage, wagon hire, the guide, the oxen, the expense of removing the family and carrying luggage and provisions, and the lodging for a family of six at the farmhouse for twenty days; then there were the choppers' wages at 50¢ a day and their provisions, the window-frames and iron work, etc., for the house, and the cost of clearing and fencing 10 acres. Altogether he had laid out, including the cost of his 200-acre lot at 10s. an acre, £178.

There was an alternative that many settlers of means preferred to take—the purchase of an 'improved farm' of the same size, on a good road about the same distance from York. Ten acres was cleared and ready for crops, the house complete with domestic conveniences, dairy, wash-house, fowl-house, garden, and other appendages that the bush settler could not expect to have for some years: a *going concern* with almost enough produce for the family and stock. And the sale price was 20s. an acre, or £200, plus about £7 in expenses; or a mere £29 more than the bush farm had eaten up in costs. Good farm land in long-settled districts was, of course, comparatively expensive. When Captain Charles Gifford passed along the Lake Ontario shore in 1837 he noted that it was usually from £3 to £5 per acre; and the higher prices were asked for cleared lots on the main highway, while land near the lake shore or further to the rear brought less.

But there was in those days a consideration that weighed heavily with many aristocrats—the possibility of having to associate with 'inferior' people. Writing in 1833 the Reverend T. W. Radcliff, Church of England clergyman, was pleased that 'by a late and judicious arrangement of the government', people forming groups before they emigrated, or settled, could obtain blocks of land, exclude unpleasant persons, and restrict their settlement to 'attached and intimate individuals . . . pleased with their own society'. His two sons consequently chose bush land in Adelaide Township near London, where their houses were the first erected, their wives the first European females, and there was no danger of contact with 'the lower orders'.

The development of this mutual-admiration society was exceptionally rapid. The men bought their land in July, started work upon it in August, and moved their families in during October. By mid-December the township was settling so fast that they were afraid there would not be room for the relatives and friends they hoped to induce to come out. Some twenty families had settled there, with a clergyman, and had erected a schoolhouse which would serve also as a church until a separate and more commodious edifice could be erected the following summer. Though they were 130 miles from York the land was rich; but the roads were bad, and so were the first potato crops.

Such were the choices of pioneer days—if the settler had funds to take advantage of them. Many purchased a farm in operation, obtained facility of approach, less solitude and privation, and nearness to mill, market, and doctor; preferring these even if the title to their property might prove precarious or doubtful, their liability to the previous owner's debts a possibility, and undesirable neighbours almost a certainty. And in not a few cases such purchasers found to their sorrow that their predecessors had been 'wheat miners' who had impoverished their land by continual wheat crops.

Methods of payment for land were various, but the larger number of settlers were unable to pay cash. A large group of Sussex emigrants, most of them very poor tenants or labourers from the estates of the Earl of Egremont, were placed in a portion of Adelaide Township at state expense. Each received 100 acres at the average price for which lands commonly sold there, the amount to be paid within six years. No interest was charged for the first three years, at the end of which period one-fourth of the purchase money was to be paid; but the remaining three-quarters was payable in equal annual instalments over the next three years, plus interest.

As in other state-supervised emigrations, much else was done for the members. The government erected 'small houses' for them; and the sick had medical care. Road construction was undertaken in the district, in part to make employment available at 2s. 4d. per day and board; and 'in order that the people should not be imposed upon by merchants and others selling provisions' a government store was established in the district. Probably none of them could honestly compare the beautiful farm lands they had left in Sussex to the backwoods of Upper Canada, but an official letter dated September 20, 1832, suggests that most of them were at least better off financially, with eventual independence assured:

Those who have arrived here in the month of July are all very comfortable, and many of them have small crops of wheat in the ground and will be prepared to plant sufficient quantities of maize or Indian

corn in spring to support their families; from which time they will
be quite independent, and will, in the end, become good livers.

The financial terms under which the two Peter Robinson
emigrations of Irish were granted land in the eighteen-twenties
exemplify another type of settlement and payment, for while
they were brought to Upper Canada at state expense they paid
a small annual sum for their 70-acre lots and had the same
settlement duties as other settlers. The annual quit-rent was
2d. per acre payable half-yearly, but the first five years were
omitted from it; and it might be redeemed at any time on payment of 20 years' purchase. The cost of a deed would be about
£2 10s. additional. Thirty acres of neighbouring land was to
be kept ungranted for ten years, and the settler could purchase
it for £10 if he wished. Log shanties were constructed for these
settlers* at about £10 each, but in neighbouring Dummer
Township, settled in 1831, only from $1.50 to $4 each was
expended for the purpose. These latter settlers, many of them
pensioners, received 100-acre lots, and after the first four years
they began paying 1s. per acre per year. Leniency was characteristic of early land settlement under government auspices, but
many had soon paid their total of $80 and received their
titles.**

The point of view that too much could be done for state-
assisted emigrants cannot be dismissed as merely selfishness or
lack of social consciousness. A. C. Buchanan, Emigration Agent
at Quebec, who was prominent in settling various groups
brought out at state expense, voiced this opinion effectively:

I do not admit [he wrote in his *Emigration Practically Considered*]
the policy of taking a half-starved Irish pauper from his miserable
hovel and in the space of a few months not only making him the
proprietor of one hundred acres of land but surrounding him with
domestic comforts he never before witnessed. It is almost too much
for persons in a more improved state of society to endure, and Pat
and his wife Bridget will be amazed and think that we must have
some *pull* in it. I would let them feel and work their way, and their
ultimate success will be more certain. Let the Emigrant have enough
to eat, with a log-hut for shelter, his axe in his hand, and his fuel at

*The author's *The Valley of the Trent* (1957) is the only book in which the
original manuscripts—for many years in the Peterborough Public Library but
now in the Archives of Ontario—are extensively quoted. It is planned to
print a comprehensive coverage of the collection.

**The history of this emigration from Frome, Somersetshire, is assembled in
sequence in *The Valley of the Trent*, pp. 65-72. Included are unusual accounts
of a send-off from the townspeople and the immigrants' appearance when
they docked at Quebec.

LEVI PAYNE (1790-1866)
AND
SARAH, HIS WIFE (1792-1869)
Among the emigrants from Frome, Somersetshire.

Photograph by George M. Douglas, 1910

ORIGINAL HOME OF LEVI PAYNE, 1831
Located on Indian River, Dummer Township.

his elbow; but let his food be of the most economical kind, such as oatmeal, potatoes, fish, Indian meal, and a little flesh-meat. The Irish peasantry do not know how to use flour with economy; and I attribute in a great degree the prevalence of the fever and ague among the late Government Emigrants to their being confined to flour and salt-pork, . . . aliments to which they were unaccustomed.

The Canada Company provides the chief example of settlement on a commercial basis. Patrick Shirreff, who passed through the 'Huron Tract' in the early eighteen-thirties, found the Company unpopular, and of course no mortgage company can hope to be otherwise. The settlers were charged 7s. 6d. per acre, payable with interest by instalments. Purchasers of a specified amount of land were refunded part of their travelling expenses at the time of the second instalment; but by inquiry Shirreff found that at the end of five or six years 'the interest on the unpaid instalments is more than the cleared part of the farm will yield of profit'.

When Shirreff was in Goderich five years after the settlement was commenced he found it contained '40 mean wooden houses scattered irregularly over a considerable space'. Half a dozen of them were near the wharf, and the rest some 200 feet above the level of the lake and partly in a cedar swamp, which was crossed by a corduroy road. Only one of the original settlers still held his land, and many new ones were working on the Company's roads to enable them to meet payments. The Company existed until 1953, mainly to supervise farm mortgages some of which saw their inception a century and more ago.*

Wherever the settlement and whatever the circumstances, there was almost always a loneliness. 'No sound of music is ever heard there', says an early settler in the woods, 'but a melancholy death-like stillness reigns through the forest except when they are agitated by the tempest or storm.' Captain Francis Spilsbury of the Royal Navy was granted a large amount of land in North Monaghan Township for services during the American War of 1812-15.

In 1818 [we are told] he came to Peterborough County to see his domain. His course lay by blazed trail from Cobourg to Rice Lake, thence across that body of water and up the River Otonabee by canoe. On arriving at the shore of Little Lake (now Peterborough) his Indian guide landed and pointed westward to where his land lay. The whole aspect was so dismal—nothing but the charred

---

*The National Trust Company wound up the business of the Canada Company, which had been incorporated in England in 1826.

'spikes' of burnt pine trees and the partially consumed 'slash' of the original forest, interspersed with 'scrub' underbrush—that the captain became disgusted and refused to go farther. . . . The same land now [1884] comprises one of the very finest stretches of highly cultivated farmsteads to be found in the Dominion.

. . . .

It is true [wrote another] that every one who comes here feels at the outset the difficulties of his new and trying circumstances; even the lowest peasant, on first entering his shanty, laments the loneliness of his situation and experiences a sinking of the heart and a longing after his potatoes and buttermilk at *home*; but as his comforts increase he becomes reconciled to his lot, finding himself independent he becomes happy, and experimentally learns that this is really a Paradise to *him*.

And it is astonishing how speedily many a family 'sat down in the Bush' and became to all appearances snugly settled. Dr. John Bigsby actually saw a family experiencing the process along the St. Clair River:

It was a large boat laden almost to sinking with a hearty family of five persons (the parents and three children), with all sorts of lumbering chests and rude furnishings, a long gun, tools, axes, hoes, spades, a dog or two, a few poultry, and a barrel or two of flour and pork. This was a true pioneer family. When I loitered about them, not unwelcome, for a couple of hours, they landed and arranged their goods and went to sleep on matting, snug under the fragrant shelter of pine branches. Two days afterwards I found my friends comfortably housed in an oblong log-hut well caulked with clay.

But others after much suffering were penniless and almost hopeless. Near Niagara John Howison found an immigrant family living in

a kind of cave under a high sandbank, the mouth of which was barricadoed with a chest of drawers, several trunks, &c. A mattress occupied the floor of this wild abode, and two children played gaily with one another upon it. . . . The mother, who continued to shed tears, told me that she and her family were Irish emigrants . . . ; but being now destitute of money they were unable to procure a lodging and knew not where to apply for work, assistance, or information. 'A husband and these two boys', said the woman, 'are all that now remain to me. My little girl died in the ship and they threw her into the sea. Aye, sure that was the worst of all', continued she in an agony of grief. 'Poor babe! she had neither prayers nor a wake.'

Yet even such unfortunates did not blame their sad situation upon the country. This feeling of satisfaction with one's choice is well described by the Reverend Isaac Fidler in his *Observa-*

NIAGARA FALLS IN THE EIGHTEEN-SEVENTIES

tions on the Professions, Literature, Manners, and Emigration in the United States and Canada (1833):

I heard persons in America and Canada frequently expressing how comfortable they were, when the appearance of things around them would not warrant the same conclusion in a stranger. Yet I am quite sure they were so. Mrs. F.—[his wife] felt uncomfortable, and so frequently and loudly complained that I often participated in her feelings when otherwise I should have experienced the reverse. . . . Almost every person I spoke to liked the country who had passed two years in it. They told me that at their first entrance on a change of life and habits they felt so sensibly the want of their accustomed pleasures as to make them wish themselves in their native country and among their former acquaintances; but this feeling soon wore off by the attraction of new habits and the formation of new acquaintances. . . . I must add that I did not meet with one industrious person a short time settled in the country who did not assure me that he was not only reconciled to but even liked it.

And this state of mind was stimulated by thoughts of the depressed condition in which many had lived in the Old Land, and the continual improvement in their lives and properties in the New. Lots on Yonge Street that had been given away in the 1790's were worth a hundred dollars a few years later and from $4000 to $8000 after a generation had passed. In many districts it was estimated that land which was valued at $1 an acre on settlement increased about as much annually for some years, and could usually be sold for many times its original cost. The proximity of large towns, main highways, and railroads often doubled or quadrupled these new values; while the Rideau Canal raised the value of land in that region from 1s. 3d. an acre in 1824 to 20s. to 30s. in 1832. There were to be times of depression, of course, but it was generally found that the farmer, if his progress had not been so spectacular as that of his city cousins, was in a favoured position and withstood bad times better.

CHAPTER XIX

CLEARING THE LAND

A LARGE proportion of all immigrants into Canada came with the intention of farming, either as owners or farm labourers, but for many years they were essentially backwoodsmen rather than farmers, land-clearers not tillers of the soil. This way of life was so different from that of the British farmer that few, even of those who had been used to farming, came with any idea of what they faced. Even the English axe—more like a large hatchet—was of little use in America, and prospective settlers were consequently advised to buy an American axe upon arrival at the place of settlement. Innumerable accidents occurred from their unfamiliarity with its use.

Canadian agriculture reaped highly important benefits from American squatters, a race of people who are seldom given the credit they deserve. They were accustomed from infancy to the use of the axe, possessed of an invincible talent for perseverance, and, as an early emigrant guidebook put it, 'habituated to endure all the privations attendant on such an undertaking'.

One of these men [says A. J. Christie, who was particularly well informed], with his axe on his shoulder, his waggon containing his provisions, &c., and a pair of horses, goes into the wood, where he commences his operations by cutting down trees and building a hut to shelter himself from the weather. This being done he proceeds with his labour until he clears a piece of ground; and after taking one or two crops from it, or perhaps before he sows it, he sells it to the highest purchaser he can find and sets out with the money to buy another uncleared spot, with which he proceeds in the same manner.

Yet these people, many of them 'Americans' or 'natives' only by descent or from having been a few years longer in the country, are not properly termed farmers. Contemporary writers refer to them as 'land-butchers' and 'the most miserable farmers in Upper Canada'. In general they became dissatisfied or restless as soon as their land had been sufficiently cleared for real farming to commence. They had no love for the neat well-tilled farms of the Germans (or Pennsylvania Dutch), but rather a positive dislike for such farming, as well as for the proximity of other people. A backwoodsman near Peterborough in the eighteentwenties, reports an early agricultural journal *The Canada Farmer*,

liked clearing land very much, provided he was the only man in that section who was at it. When he found others flocking in and clearing nearly close to him, or, as he termed it, almost 'under his very nose', he always sold out and moved away further into the woods. And this moving from clearing 'going on under his nose' always took place as soon as his nearest neighbour was within two or three miles of his farm. Such 'civilization and destruction of timber', as he termed it, disturbed the game, and this he could never endure.

Such apostles of Thoreau-like isolation, as they became after a few years of the backwoodsman's work, relished their way of life. A writer in the *Transactions* of the Board of Agriculture of Upper Canada knew numerous men of this type who much

Catharine Traill, *The Female Emigrant's Guide*

'CLEARING THE LAND, AND LOG HOUSE'

The woodcut was probably made in England from a written description, for there are many incongruities in construction and appearance that familiarity with the Canadian scene would have obviated.

Public Archives of Canada   James Pattison Cockburn

NEAR NICOLSON'S RAPIDS, RIDEAU RIVER, 1830
Highly typical of river scenery in the pioneer period.

preferred the rude and rough excitement of chopping, logging, and burning to any more civilized life.

I knew a man of this class, of an iron frame, [he said] who, during a busy lifetime, cleared up a new farm almost entirely with his own hands every five or six years, until he came to ploughing, when he

Archives of Ontario   John Burrows

HOG'S BACK RAPIDS, RIDEAU RIVER
305

became dissatisfied and sold out to purchase new land. He declared that he would not live on a farm that required ploughing.

But some of these men, as might be expected, were rough and tough characters who spent half their time in the woods and the other half in bar-rooms, 'and he is often counted for the smartest chap who is troubled with the least conscience'. Such characters would hire out to do absentee settlers' settlement duties and take the required oath that they had done so, but it was often found afterwards that their work was fraudulently incomplete.

The term *squatter* was, however, used also in the sense of farmers who, from lack of funds or to avoid the difficulties of obtaining land in the regular way, just helped themselves.

Squatters [wrote John Mactaggart in 1829] are those who come to the country for the purpose of becoming settlers; but not having wherewithal to come by a grant of land in a regular way, set themselves down where they think it will best suit them, on unlocated lands or those not in a state of any cultivation. I have frequently thought that the squatters go to work the best of any: they deprive the clerks of the Land-office of all fees—a thing they deserve; and instead of being pointed out farms on *diagrams* where, probably, no such things exist—or if they do are not worth cultivating—they go forth their own surveyor into the wilds, and where they meet with a fine river, a fertile valley, and cool spring well, squat in contentment. Years may roll over before they have a chance of being molested by any one; and should they be they always obtain their farm at a fair value, possession being nine points of the law.

Wandering through the woods [of Lanark] in the winter of 1827 we came upon the track of a sleigh; and as we all believed ourselves far from the abode of settlers we were almost as much surprised as Robinson Crusoe was with the print of a man's foot on the sandy shore of his lonely isle. We followed the track for a mile or two and at length came upon a clearing of about seven acres in extent near the middle of which a neat little log hut sat smoking.

About fifty yards farther on there were a few small houses huddled on each other, but these did not seem to be human dwellings—the grunt of a hog and the crow of a cock proclaimed their purpose. We were met at the door by a man about the age of forty: he was clean dressed and healthy looking; in one of his hands was a child about five years old, and in the other a hatchet; he asked us with a tremulous but kind voice to '*come ben*'. This emotion arose from his not being in the habit of seeing company, as Almack's has it. We all marched in, and there was a snug little cabin with a wife, two more children, some good sleek grey cats, and a very respectable-looking dog. Having broached the rum keg we sat down by the fire and enjoyed the man's narrative over a glass and a pipe.

PROCESS OF CLEARING THE TOWN PLOT AT STANLEY. 1834

Sketches in New Brunswick, 1836

His name was Peter Armstrong, from the town of Hawick, Scotland. He had been fifteen years in Canada, was just a plain working man, saved as much as paid for his passage out, and fought up the water St. Lawrence to a place they ca'ed Perth, and there finding nought ado—*nae country wark*—he just went afar into the heart of the wild woods with his axe, dog, and gun, and after looking about him, fixed on the place where we found him for his abode in this world. There he built a little hut, not the one he then was in but the one that the *pet-deer* had, for he had tamed many deer.

Year after year he wrought away all by himself, read the Bible every Sabbath-day, made a journey to Perth twice every year and bought wee needfuls; at length got a horse and sleigh and cleared about four acres of the woods: this was five years after he had come to the place. He had but few wants, his health was aye good; there was spring-water plenty just aside him, and enough to make a good fire in winter, while with what he caught, shot, gathered, and grew in the yard he lived well enough.

All at once, on one of his visits to Perth, whom should he meet but Tibby Patterson, *wha was the byrewoman at the Laird of Branksome's* where he was once a herd-lad: it is needless to add, they had met far frae hame in a wild land—they had few friends—so Tibby just came awa' with me to the woods and we just took *ane anither's word* on't: that's the way we were married, and here we are, and have been for the last nine years. We are contented, and that is enough; we are not much bothered, and Tibby likes to live in this kind o' way as weel as mysell.*

There were various methods of clearing land. Not uncommon was 'girdling' or 'ringing' the trees, an effective method of choking them to death by cutting out a circle of the outer life-tissue. The appearance of a forest so treated was much like its counterpart in our own times—land drowned by raising water levels for mills, water storage, or hydro-electric development. The great trees, gray and gaunt, with a few only of their larger branches remaining, rose high above dense brush and undergrowth, awaiting final destruction by fire, wind, axe, or more gradual dry rot. Joseph Pickering found this method of clearing common on the Long Point plains, where the trees were often thirty yards apart and easy to plough around. Elsewhere the same result was achieved by girdling all trees above a foot in diameter and removing everything else. The process saved time and labour temporarily, but there were disadvantages. Falling branches from the dead trees formed a hazard for cattle, and

*And Mactaggart was very pleased with the family, whom he called 'Christians of a very high character'. He had met plenty of other couples living common-law, 'but these have all been Yankees—they did not read any Bibles nor sing hamely sangs like Armstrong and his Tibby; they were gloomy, ill-natured, growled a good deal; . . . there seemed to be something gnawing at the conscience.'

the trunks continued to shade a considerable part of the land; and though it was said, it could hardly be credited that the crops were as good as upon properly cleared land.

Another easy and cheap method was 'slashing', which consisted of felling the trees and allowing them to stay where they fell for a season or two. If the land was not immediately needed for crops there was no disadvantage in the method, but the heavy work of piling and burning had to be done some time, and it was the harder from lack of system in the felling.

The Ganaraska Watershed

SQUARING PINE LOGS

John Mactaggart, who undermined his health while working in the 'dreadful' and 'infernal' swamps of the Rideau region, believed that dams might be more effective than axes to get rid of the forests. He said he had seen many places where a 100-foot dam 20 feet high would drown and destroy in eight years the whole timber on 50,000 acres. He recommended the procedure to the Canada Company, then just commencing its settlement of the Guelph-Goderich region.

'Wind-row felling' comprised chopping the trees so that they would fall in rows. But efforts to burn them where they fell were usually only partially successful, and if the chopping was less arduous the *branding* (burning) was more so. The general plan, if the settler wished to get the best results, was to fell one wind-row as regularly as possible, and then a similar row was cut some fifty feet away so that the trees would fall in the opposite direction—in other words on top of the first row. The general result was a number of great ridges of fallen timber which burned so incompletely that a settler seldom resorted to the process a second time. If the trees were cut while the leaves were on, and before the sap returned, the wood dried sooner, the leaves aided the burning, and the stumps were found to rot a year or so earlier. In this way the settler got a better *burn* and it was usually considered, though highly questionable, that 'the blacker the land is burned, the better the wheat crop'.

The size and density of the forests of pioneer times can hardly be gauged by comparison with subsequent growth. Though 200-foot pines that one or two writers mention must be taken as somewhat exaggerated, masts of 100 feet and more—the record is thought to be one of 116 feet from Innisfil Township near Lake Simcoe—were shipped from Quebec for use in the British navy. Such trees would be from three to four feet in diameter one-third the way up from the butt-end, and they probably towered to 150 or 160 feet. John Howison counted 267 rings in an oak he saw felled in Glengarry, but its size was very moderate when compared with others near by which he took to be five or six hundred years old.* As Catharine Traill put it, those who did not have, as she had, an expanse of river or lake on one side of their small clearing in the depths of the forest were

hemmed in on every side by a thick wall of trees, through the interminable shades of which the eye vainly endeavours to penetrate in search of other objects and other scenes; but so dense is the growth of timber that all beyond the immediate clearing is wrapped in profound obscurity. A settler on first locating on his lot knows no more of its boundaries and its natural features than he does of the Northwest Passage.

Much more common than the other methods was the regular felling of the forest and the piling of logs to be burned when dry. Trees up to an eight-inch diameter were usually cut into lengths of 12 or 14 feet after trimming off the branches, while those of

*David Wilkie, author of *Sketches of a Summer Trip to New York and the Canadas* (1837), measured the stump of an oak about ten miles from Hamilton and found it was 23 feet in circumference a yard from the ground, and half as much again at ground level. The rings showed it was about 560 years old. 'The noise was heard for miles round when it was felled', he wrote, 'which three Irishmen accomplished in three and a half hours with chopping-axes—certainly good work.' Oak logs 50 feet long were sometimes squared to 2½ feet. The exultation with which the noblest of trees were destroyed is unpleasant from the modern point of view.

Toronto Public Library   T. H. Ware

MONA COTTAGE, ORO, 1844
The residence of James Scott.

greater size could not be moved if the sections were more than
ten feet long. At least two months was needed to dry the piles.

A preliminary to this—or any satisfactory—method of clearing was the removal of underbrush by a billhook or bushwhack.
Sometimes it was burned ahead, sometimes merely dragged
aside to be used as a crude fence, or as a starter on the tops of
the log-heaps, for the best results were obtained by setting the
fire near the top of the pile. When the fires were lit a strong
wind and good luck would devour the greater part, but the
gathering of the charred remains of the first burning, with the
wet and rotten pieces, was heavy and dirty work. In all such
labour oxen with a yoke-and-bow and a single chain and driver
assembled the larger pieces, while other men worked independ-
ently at the smaller. Sometimes a branding bee was held for
the purpose, and the generation of women are not long dead
who could recall preparing huge meals for a score or more tired
and blackened men.

Sometimes a settler sought a short-cut that might save the
cutting into lengths and collecting into piles. This was to cut
everything down in an indiscriminate mass and set it ablaze as
it lay. Under some conditions this might succeed, but not without great damage to the soil, for instead of intense heat at the
piles it applied all over the land. If the soil contained a good
deal of iron, calcination lessened its fertility; if limestone or

311

calcareous, the destruction of all animal and vegetable matter left no substance for the lime to act upon; while clay soil became indurated by the heat and unsatisfactory for crops. In all types of soil too much ash will render it too alkaline, so such a method of clearing might well make the soil unfit for crops for years. In Muskoka, said F. M. DelaFosse, an attempt to grow a first crop of lucerne failed completely:

> Not a blade of it appeared above the ground [he said], owing to the fact that on that particular part of the clearing there was no soil fit to grow anything. Whatever earth there may have been originally had been either burnt up when the fallow was set on fire, or washed into the lake during the heavy rains. The good old granite bobbed up serenely everywhere.

Settlers in a hurry to get crops sown were also known to try to burn the wood while green. This, of course, was most difficult and necessitated continual burnings, with all the dirty work of collecting and piling and repiling the partially burnt timbers.

Various estimates are given as to how fast and at what cost the clearing of land could be accomplished. James Logan was told that an expert could chop ten to twelve acres in four months; but Samuel Strickland said that if the underbrushing had been done earlier a good workman could chop, cut, and pile an acre in eight days. Six men used to the work, said one guidebook, could chop and burn an acre a day, assuming, apparently, that the trees were dead. One American chopper, said another, could fell the trees on an acre in a week, but could not burn them. A survey made in Glengarry County showed that the average settler had cleared some 22 acres in his first three years. It would seem very unlikely that a man working alone could clear, seed, and fence ten acres in a year, as a highly optimistic writer estimated; the average settler, in fact, would probably have been unable to accomplish half as much. Of eleven pioneer settlers in Norwich Township six were unable to sow any seed the first season, but the other five seeded from four to fourteen acres each.

People of means hired choppers at a dollar a day, or by contract at from $12 to $20 to chop, burn, and fence an acre. John Thomson wrote in his diary that it cost him the latter amount per acre for labour, food, and oxen. Sometimes choppers could be hired to clear land for half the first crop, or if difficult, for half the first three crops. A. J. Christie, observing that the regular method of clearing and burning was the 'most elegant', stated that half the cost might be saved by burning merely the smaller trees and brush, and girdling the larger ones three or four feet from the ground and leaving them to die and fall, whereupon they could readily be burned; but the crop planted amid these trees might not be more than half as good as on fully cleared land.

Some men, becoming expert in backwoods work, not only cleared their own land but afterwards hired out to do such work for others. Several residents of York County, for example, were particularly remembered in after years for their ability to log and chop. James Rogers, son of the founder of Newmarket, spent his entire life, we are told, 'in the work of clearing, chopping, and building houses' for incoming settlers. 'He acquired a fair education for the times', says a reference to Seth Heacock of the third concession of King Township, 'but the clearing of land, making roads through the bush, ploughing among the stumps and stones' were the occupations he had to follow to make a living. Of James Fuller of the eleventh concession in the same township it is recorded that 'although only about twelve years old when his father died, young James showed unusual energy and adapted himself to the work of clearing the farm and making the home for his mother comfortable'. Observing that in Upper Canada two good choppers could cut down in ten minutes 'the finest specimen of pine ever beheld, such as the Old Country eye would think could only be felled with a cross-cut saw', Mrs. Edward Copleston said that 'the temper and edge requisite for the axe is such that the woodsman is as careful over it as he is of his razor, and so treasures it up that he sleeps with it under his pillow to prevent the frost from rendering it brittle.' The chopper who wished to be always at the peak of effectiveness had often *an axe to grind,* but this pioneer saying has come down to us with much more general application.

A combination of methods of clearing, and frequently the hiring of choppers to clear and fence at one time, was usual. The following answers to questions by Robert Gourlay illustrate costs and methods of clearance just before and just after the War of 1812, and in various localities:

For clearing five acres of all timber, and fencing it, £25. For clearing five acres of all under-brush and trees under a foot diameter at the stump, and putting the same under fence, £15 12s. 6d.

. . . .

New land £3 15s. per acre; the first crop generally pays it.

. . . .

313

The cost of clearing and fencing an acre of timbered land £6 5s.; of plains £2 10s. an acre.

. . . .

The common custom of our township [Trafalgar] is to cut down no more at first than the timber which is a foot in diameter measured from about two feet and a half from the root of the tree, and all under that size; and the rest they girdle and kill with the axe. In this state it will produce nearly as good a crop as if all were cut down, and this only costs £1 10s. per acre; the rest of the timber is cut down by degrees for fencing and for fire wood, &c.

Skilled choppers often worked simultaneously at both sides of large trees, or chopped alternately right and left hand, a technique in which precision and co-ordination were essential. Competitions against one another in chopping tree trunks into lengths that could be handled added rivalry and excitement to the work.

Many a farmer went into 'the Bush' for the winter lumbering, a popular means to earn ready cash. Particularly were the young men of the northerly townships sent *shantying*, and in spring and summer many of them remained to float the great masts, booms, cribs, and rafts to market—which might be the nearest sawmill or down to Wolfe's Cove, Quebec, the centre of the square-timber trade to Britain; yet the life was usually demoralizing, created a distaste for regular labour and habits, and unfitted men for more 'respectable' society. The great pine forests of the northern uplands of the Upper Ottawa and the Trent Valley seemed at the time to be inexhaustible, and neither mercy nor good sense was shown by those engaged in the business. In the 'sixties and 'seventies the mills at Fenelon Falls and Bobcaygeon alone had an annual output which at times reached 28,000,000 feet. In the long view such exploitation cannot be defended, but much of the pine country was otherwise sterile, and the industry provided a market for farm produce in summer and employment in almost all seasons.*

In many counties, such as Hastings, Peterborough, Victoria, and Haliburton, the land was purchased largely or exclusively for its timber rights. In some townships three-quarters of the patentees got their land when the right to cut timber, including pine, was included, and many of these did not remain to farm the poor land beneath. Upon removal of the forest the granite regions were found least suitable for agriculture, but the lime-

*See the author's *Early Life in Upper Canada*, pp. 232-251, for an outline of the lumber industry and its more picturesque accompaniments. Less picturesque were the *shebangs* dotted along the rivers, where squaws and whiskey awaited the shanty boys and their winter pay.

Willis, *Canadian Scenery*   W. H. Bartlett

TIMBER DEPOT, WOLFE'S COVE, QUEBEC, 1840

stone country had a soil more chemically favourable. In many districts the inhabitants came to be characterized by moral and physical disintegration; and yet in these districts the school tax was usually very high, for even where it was almost impossible to eke out a living the effort was made to provide a better start for the children.

Government reforestation and watchful care for half a century will be needed to bring such lands back into productivity, for the early lumbermen usually cut down every tree while taking only the best, and recurrent fire served to destroy seedlings and soil at the same time. The only natural recuperation has usually been a growth of scrub poplar and birch, whose wind-blown seed-catkins are scattered over the country. There is general exclusion of the coniferous, whose seeds—where any are found—are largely eaten by squirrels, and such acorns and cherry pits as are dropped by birds find their growth restricted by thin soil.

Winter, otherwise an off season, was popular for lumbering and land-clearing, but new settlers commonly started upon it immediately on arrival, whatever the season. Colonel Thomas Talbot said five acres could be cleared between June and frost, presumably by experienced men; but circumstances alter cases, and a man working alone quite understandably found the dense

INTERIOR OF LUMBER SHANTY, UPPER OTTAWA

MANITOULIN ISLAND LUMBERMEN

Illustrated London News   G. H. Andrews

CLEARING A JAM, 1863

Courtesy Claude Snider

RECORD LOAD OF LOGS, MUSKOKA

Mr. Snider's fine collection of historical photographs was among
the first copied for the Archives of Ontario.

forest discouraging. Anna Jameson received an indignant reply when she told a settler who had cleared only five acres in five years that he was unenterprising in comparison with neighbours who had cleared twice as much in half the time:

Then they had money or friends or hands to help them [he retorted with some heat]. I have neither. I have in this wide world only my-self! And set a man with only a pair of hands at one of them big trees there—see what he'll make of it! You may swing the axe here from morning to night for a week before you let the daylight in upon you!

Mrs. Jameson apologized; but the fact remains that some men were known to log several acres a year entirely alone—without even oxen.

In the absence of any mention of the use of the cross-cut saw in logging, it must be assumed that the trees, no matter how large, were almost always chopped into lengths, not sawn. But five or six contemporary references to the saws indicate that they were available in the period following the close of the War of 1812—they were, in fact, used in America as early as the 17th century. A statistical summary of the 1820 Scottish emigration to Lanark, dated April 12, 1821, lists certain implements 'for general use of the concessions', and among them are '40 whip-saws' and '40 cross-cut saws'. Another reference to the tool is in Ex-Settler's *Canada in the Years 1832, -33, and -34,* in which he says:

Before you depart into the bush, purchase at the nearest large town three or four axes, a grinding-stone, *a cross-cutting saw,* three or four iron wedges, ox chains and bells, hoes, a very few carpenter's tools, augers, shingle and other nails, metal hinges, and two or three common locks; you will require to lay out about fifty dollars thus, and will save both money and time by buying them.

The Reverend William Bell of the Perth Settlement includes the cross-cut saw among 'concession tools', and Robert Lamond, writing of the same general region, says there was one to every fifteen settlers; while John Toshach of Lanark states that both a pit-saw and a cross-cut saw were used jointly by himself and three neighbours. Most of these references, consequently, in-dicate that where available at all it was a communal implement* for the use of numerous families, not an individual farmer's tool;

*One description of its actual use is in Samuel Strickland's *Twenty-seven Years in Canada West* (1853), where he notes its employment to cut tree trunks into 8-foot lengths suitable for splitting by wedges into slabs or planks to use in erecting partitions in his log house; and it may be assumed that only for such exact work was the cross-cut saw used.

Vol. II. No. 6.   TORONTO, UPPER CANADA, MARCH 15, 1865.   Postage Free

The Field.

Logging and Burning.

We now come to the most important of all the operations connected with clearing land. If the logging and burning are badly done, or not finished at the proper season, much difficulty and annoyance will be experienced. The best time to commence is as early in the summer as possible, that is to say, as soon as the land is dry and warm enough for the fire "to run," as it is called. In a good burn the sparks from which the logs extend in all directions. In our last, we insisted on the necessity of throwing the tree tops in the course of the prevailing summer winds. The wisdom of this precaution will now be seen. A fine warm day, succeeding a month or two of dry weather, with a good stiff breeze blowing, should be chosen to burn off the brush. Care should be taken to select a day when the wind blows in the same direction in which the rows are laid. At the leeward side of the fallow, set fire to some old rotten maple stump. This will catch in a moment, and burn like tinder. With an iron shovel, you can carry great pieces of the blazing touchwood from heap to heap.

communicating the fire from heap to heap, you will see the importance of beginning to leeward as directed, for, were you to commence at the other end of the rows, the smoke would soon drive you away, and prevent your lighting the heaps thoroughly. When all is going on well, and the fire is running freely along the ground, you may go to the windward side, and fire the whole line of brush. The entire clearing should be one blazing mass by 11 o'clock in the morning, and before the dews of night fall, there will be a clean sweep made of all the brush, the tree tops, and many of the smaller logs, long lines of smoking ashes attesting the thorough-

ly readily, and ignite all the half decayed timber, while the fire literally "runs" along the ground consuming the chips, leaves, and rubbish, and leaving a clean surface behind it.

It is to be supposed that the chopping has been well and thoroughly done, the trees having been thrown as much as possible into long rows, and the heads forming almost continuous lines of brush heaps, and soon have your fires well going. Always begin at the stump end of the piles of brush, as it is assumed that they have been carefully made by falling the tops from the quarter whence the wind comes. Light as rapidly as possible every brush heap, or row of tree tops. If they catch readily, and burn well, you can miss a wide portion on your return across the fallow with the blazing brands. If difficulty is found in

ness of the work. Next morning, as you survey the smouldering ruins, you will wonder at the extent of the destruction effected. The next step to be taken is raking the ashes, with a view to securing some return from the potash. This is done with a wooden scraper,—the head of which is about two feet long and the handle eight feet. With this you proceed to rake the ashes into heaps, containing from one to two

PIONEER LOGGING AND BURNING

and there is no suggestion anywhere that it was employed in logging.

To save the work of chopping the trees into lengths small fires, in some districts called *niggers,* were occasionally used. These were placed on top of the trunks at intervals which would enable the sections to be handled, and kept burning until they had burned their way through. A settler in Zorra Township, Oxford County, sent back word to the 'auld fowk' in Scotland that he had one hundred niggers working for him; whereupon 'the whole parish was agog with excitement over the Zorra man's wonderful wealth in controlling the services of no less than one hundred negroes'!

What did 'a glorious burning' (as Mrs. Traill calls it) look like? Here is her description:

A magnificent sight it was to see such a conflagration all around us. I was a little nervous at first on account of the nearness of some of the log-heaps to the house, but care is always taken to fire them with the wind blowing in a direction away from the building. . . . If the weather be very dry and a brisk wind blowing, the work of destruction proceeds with astonishing rapidity; sometimes the fire will communicate with the forest and run over many hundreds of acres, . . . consuming all before it, or leaving such scorching mementos as have blasted the forest growth for years. . . .

Of a night the effect is more evident; sometimes the wind blows particles of the burning fuel into the hollow pines and tall decaying stumps; these readily ignite, and after a time present an appearance that is exceedingly fine and fanciful. Fiery columns, the bases of which are hidden by the dense smoke-wreaths, are to be seen in every direction, sending up showers of sparks that are whirled about like rockets and fire-wheels in the wind. Some of these tall stumps, when the fire has reached the summit, look like gas lamps newly lit.

But the 'glorious burning' was often a serious danger, particularly when inexperienced settlers had not taken the precautions usual among old hands at the game.*

My shanty [wrote Captain Hill] had been up some months when the burning of the brush and timber of my clearance was commenced, and it required the utmost exertions of four persons to prevent its being destroyed. The smoke and heat were so suffocating and intolerable that my family was obliged to take refuge for two hours in the cellar; and from the circumstance of the fire having completely surrounded the premises it would have been very difficult to have

---

*A traveller from Guelph to Hamilton in 1851 noticed that bush land was being cleared, but that the burning had got out of hand and the whole country was lit up as the forest burned for miles on either side of the road. (Mickle family Book, Toronto Public Library.)

removed our things to a place of safety had it been necessary to make the attempt. I would therefore repeat the advice to new settlers to chop down and burn off at once at least one acre of the forest immediately about the spot where he intends to put up his house.

There was much disfigurement of the landscape in land-clearing. The easiest way was commonly considered the best, and along beautiful lake shores the trees were more often than not merely slashed down into the water, where they might remain half a century, their roots and trunk an eyesore, and underwater branches a hazard to navigation. People of taste avoided the practice, but for the majority it was, as one said, 'a mighty handy way to get rid on 'em, no chopping 'em up into log-lengths, no piling o' brush, no logging on 'em afterwards, but down with them into the lake and there's an end on 'em'.*

People sensitive to the beauties of nature, like the Reverend William Darling, Church of England clergyman, were saddened to see the vast destruction of wild flowers and shrubs, partic-ularly during the burning. He lists the 'little star-like blossoms of all shades of white and pink and blue' of the hepatica; the 'three-leaved lilies [trilliums] with their drooping bell-flowers of white and purple'; the lady's slipper or moccasin-plant, yellow or white shaded with lilac, 'a singular and often beautiful flower'; the dogtooth violet 'with its yellow Turk's cap'; 'the beautiful leaves and delicate flowers of the bloodroot'; the flowering grass [star flower] 'with its sweet little starry blossom'; 'the wood-anemone, and the wild geranium, and ever so many beside, which, though they may hold no place in the vocabulary of the unlearned, are cherished in the heart and memory of those who love the gentle tribe of the simple field-flowers.'

The settlers' cattle, turned into the woods for their living, ate quantities of wild flowers, but it was logging and burning that devastated the land. Each spring most settlers tried to get 'a good brush burn'.

The fire [wrote Mr. Darling] runs along the ground, consuming the covering of leaves and chips which are thickly strewn over its sur-face, and often setting the piles of underbrush and tree-tops in a blaze without the trouble of lighting them individually. When, how-

*Robert Stevenson was admiring the beauty of a waterfall near Ancaster in 1843, and remarked to a man near by how splendid it was. 'Why yes, mister', he replied, 'I guess it is a very nice water privilege; I wonder no one don't put a mill on it; it shouldn't ought to stand idle.' Stevenson added this com-ment in a letter home to Scotland: 'This glen is really beautiful, but the natives of the country neither ken nor care about these things; they have no notion of beauty but how money can be made of it.'

Catharine Traill, *Canadian Wild Flowers*   Agnes Fitzgibbon

COLUMBINE . . . WHITE TRILLIUM . . . YELLOW ADDER'S TONGUE

The artist was a daughter of Susanna Moodie and niece of Catharine Traill.

ever, the fire fairly begins to 'run', it unfortunately seldom restricts itself to the limits of the chopping (or, as it is called, 'the follow'— a corruption, it is to be presumed, of the English word 'fallow'). It almost invariably gets into 'the Bush', and then away it goes on a journey, sometimes of days in duration and miles in length. To see the woods on fire at night is often a striking sight. . . . The morning, however, reveals a melancholy spectacle—the fallen trees all scorched and blackened—the beautiful foliage of the underwood seared and withered—and the ground, instead of being strewn with leaves and studded with a thousand flowers, covered as with a sable shroud, diversified here and there with patches of white wood-ashes or smoking and smouldering logs. Of course this is dealing in death wholesale as far as the flowers are concerned; and as the same thing is not unfrequently repeated every few years it is easy to see how it comes to pass that they disappear so rapidly.*

But there is one wild flower, known variously as Fireweed and Great Willow Herb, which was the first to reappear— whether in the bombed-out city blocks of Europe or the scorched backwoods of Canada. Pauline Johnson (1862-1913), perhaps the most authentic of Canadian poets, has caught its spirit and its implication to human beings:

Fire-Flowers

And only where the forest fires have sped
Scorching relentlessly the cool north lands,
A sweet wild flower lifts its purple head,
And like some gentle spirit sorrow-fed,
It hides the scars with almost human hands.

And only to the heart that knows of grief,
Of desolating fire, of human pain,
There comes some purifying sweet belief,
Some fellow-feeling beautiful, if brief.
And life revives, and blossoms once again.

What were the agricultural qualifications of the settlers who had to engage in this wholesale felling and burning of trees? A list of twenty-four Scots settled at Perth in 1816 shows that one had been a farm grieve (manager) in Scotland, and seven others farmers or farm labourers. The other sixteen included the following occupations: weaver, dyer, shoemaker, shipmaster, mason, millwright, ship carpenter, schoolmaster, whitesmith, widow, shopkeeper, gardener, and clerk. Yet in 13 months, when all of them reported themselves 'well satisfied', they had chopped a total of 174½ acres, cleared 122½ of them, seeded 72¼ in wheat, 11¾ in oats, and 47¼ in potatoes, etc., although they had but seven oxen among them; they had also made 624 lbs. of maple sugar, sixteen of them had at least one cow, two of these had two cows, and three had three. Eleven months later, when they had been two years settled, the progress in all these categories had proportionately increased. This was a state-supervised emigration, and there was a delay

*Mr. Darling's novelized description of pioneer life was published anonymously in London (England) in 1849 under the title *Sketches of Canadian Life, Lay and Ecclesiastical. Illustrative of Canada and the Canadian Church,* by a Presbyter of the Diocese of Toronto. While upon first glance it appears superficial, it contains much of value that is not exceeded anywhere for fidelity and truth.

Alfred Hayward

RICE LAKE TRILLIUMS

The artist, born near Rice Lake, was world famous for his flower paintings
a generation ago.

of over a year in placing the members on their land, during
which time they lived upon government allowance; and their
eventual satisfaction did not include the details of their transfer
to their new lands, in which there was obviously a good deal of
mismanagement.

It was not to be expected that such a group of settlers would clear as much land, or as easily, as would Americans to the manner born. But the three weavers among them probably effected the transition to choppers more readily than the rest because of their facility in using their hands; and as they had no prejudices as to British agriculture to overcome they speedily followed the farming customs of the new land. Dr. William Dunlop, who travelled widely in Upper Canada, observed that

there is no denying that the weavers from Renfrew and Lanark shires in the Bathurst district are very good and very prosperous settlers, and that the linen weavers from the north of Ireland make the best choppers, native or imported, in the province, as they, to a man, can chop with either hand forward, and by changing their hand they relieve themselves and obtain a rest. This ambi-dexterousness is ascribed by their countrymen, how justly I know not, to their habit of using both hands equally in throwing the shuttle.

Clearing land in the pioneer period did not usually include the immediate removal of stumps, which, as Mrs. Traill says, 'rarely burn out, and remain eye-sores for several years'. To eradicate them was heavy work among the earliest settlers. In the eighteen-forties stumping machines came into use in older-

S. Farmer, *Scugog*

STUMPING MACHINE

settled districts along the front, their owners sometimes contracting to remove stumps, large and small, for 50 cents each. If the stump had not pretty well rotted, its larger roots were usually cut off, and the machine then placed above the stump. The screw attached to the framework was fastened to a chain which was affixed to the stump. Above the machine a long pole fastened to the screw was pulled by ox or horse in a circle, and as the circuit of the stump was made the screw and stump were lifted. The best-known stumping machine was a New England invention which could be obtained in various sizes and of types adapted to the use of two or more men and one or more oxen or horses; and the price varied correspondingly from $100 to $300, a prohibitive price for most settlers.

In general, however, and especially in 'the Bush', it was not considered worth the expense and effort to work at them, and stumps were left to rot until they could be dug out without too much effort, or until an ox-and-chain attached to a main root, or to the three- or four-foot trunk that had been purposely left, was sufficient to rip them out. Cedar, poplar, and birch would usually rot sufficiently in four or five years, but these types were more common as second growth than in the original forest. Hardwood stumps, and especially oak, seldom lasted beyond eight or ten years, but red and white pine sometimes remained solid underground for half a century and more. Early settlers commonly left unchopped such trees as had had their tops broken off by the wind or when others were felled against them, for it was considered that they were no more harmful to crops than were the stumps. Interspersed among a field of stumps, consequently, were numerous scorched *ramspikes* towering above the rest. Stump fences, mute evidences of many an arduous stumping bee, still dot the countryside, but few of them are more than seventy or eighty years old, and some much less.*

James Inches, whose *Letters on Emigration to Canada* is a critique of various emigration 'puffs' that he thought painted much too rosy a picture**—the publications of Dr. William

---

*Further reference will be made to the removal of stumps, especially by machine, in Volume II, Chapter VIII.

**Edward Talbot expressed the same sentiment when he suggested that Captain Stuart's *Emigrant's Guide to Upper Canada* would be more appropriately entitled *The Pilgrim's Guide to the Celestial Regions!* Some writers considered the black topsoil much richer than it really was—'rather too rich for the common purposes of agriculture', as John Howison puts it—and said that the first crops were never as good as later ones; while others ridiculed the notion that a settler had almost to dilute the soil to render it serviceable, and advised immigrants to anticipate much poorer yields than gossip, rumour, and some guidebooks assured them.

Col. H. F. Ainslie

ENCAMPMENT OF THE ROYAL SCOTS AT LONDON, 1842
The dead trees in the background have been girdled.

Photograph by Bob Guillet

DROWNED LAND, LAC SEUL

Dunlop, Adam Fergusson, Joseph Pickering, and 'Martin Doyle' (William Hickey) are especially singled out for attack—quite fairly pointed out that the stumps of the Canadian bushlands were much more of a menace and handicap to agriculture than was commonly stated. Hardwood stumps, he observed, tended to sprout anew each year for some time, and there were shortly new trees; while even if they could be removed in six to eight years, from two to four oxen and several men with axes and crowbars would be needed to cut the roots and pry them out.

Inches noted other disadvantages of stump-filled clearings. Every stump, as he says, is a fine nursery for thistles and weeds, and every hole where one had been had to be filled with earth if an even field was desired. Great stones often came to light after clearing, and there were *cradle-heaps* at the sides of trees that had been unearthed and blown over. Not infrequently, too, the settler came across great mounds of material like wet red sawdust—the rotten but undecayed remains of trees that might have fallen down a quarter or half century earlier. Nothing of use to the farmer would grow on such material, and it had to be carefully scattered as the settler made an effort to level his field for ploughing.

Considerations of beauty did not weigh greatly among the pioneers, and very seldom were small groves or individual giants of the forest left to enhance the setting of the farm. Trees were the settler's enemy, definitely something to get rid of; and even if there had been any sentiment in the matter, fire and wind and erosion would have made such trees difficult to save for any length of time, for the 'immense oaks' and 'noble pines' which survived the ravages of fire could not long stand when their roots became exposed and the support of neighbouring trees was gone. Travellers noticed the indifference of most settlers to any beautification of their 'rude abodes'.

Among the humble dwellings in Upper Canada [writes John Howison, waxing poetic],

> *No roses wreathing,*
> *Or woodbines breathing,*
> *Around the lattice their tendrils spread.*

Nor does the bee, in the stillness of a glowing summer day, hum among the honeysuckle, and, weighing down its flowers, rob them of their luscious treasures for the benefit of him who reared and watered the parent plant.

The truth is, that if taste in such matters was not entirely lacking, as Anna Jameson considered, the difficulties and dangers were sometimes such as to preclude the leaving of groves of large trees, though one objection—that they would attract birds and insects to eat the settler's first crops—is pretty far-fetched. Yet at times some thought was given to appearances, even if ensuing generations would be the chief beneficiaries. Around many an abandoned farmhouse are lilac bushes, honeysuckle, and other flowering shrubs planted in other and better times.

About the intended site of your house [writes 'Ex-Settler'], when chopping and clearing you ought to leave standing a few small trees that promise to spread and be handsome, beech particularly, and have all leaves and 'brush' carefully raked away from about them that they may not be scorched. The beauty of these when they have room to branch out is very great and fully repays you for any trouble they may occasion. . . . I would also plant about my house immediately particularly balsam, butter-nut, and sumach; an energetic person will manage to get a few little jobs of this kind done at the end of a day's work, or an idle man will amuse himself sometimes at them, so that they will not cost much and will add no little variety and pleasure to the sameness of the forest.

Those who hired men to clear their land were often subject to all sorts of tricks and impositions, varying from outright cheating to slipshod and easy methods. Some choppers would notch big trees half way through and then fell others against them to break them off, the result, even if successful, being a mess hard to clear up. Another trick was to leave the felled trees four or five feet from the ground, caught in brush and small trees and dangerous to chop into lengths.* Other careless workmen increased the length and so avoided one or two cuts per tree, severed them only part way through, covered tree tops with brush rather than collect them, and made brush-heaps too small and numerous. For these and other reasons arising out of sad experience, 'Ex-Settler' gave some thought to the preparation of an airtight and foolproof contract which he advised all settlers to follow:

The contract price of clearing and fencing land may, I think, be taken on the average in the old settlements to be twelve dollars an

---

*More than one inexperienced settler was seriously injured by being thrown with great velocity when chopping upon a stump whose roots suddenly snapped back into place. Captain Hill wrote his emigrant guidebook in the spring of 1833 when 'confined to my house, and the greater part of it to my bed, from a severe cut which I gave myself in the foot with an axe, an accident usual enough with young choppers'.

acre, *i.e.,* supposing the wood valueless from its non-proximity to
a town, and in the new ones about fourteen dollars; but in some of
the old settlements it is as low as nine or ten dollars, and in the very
new townships it is as high as sixteen, even at which rate very scarcely will any one be found to take a contract unless it be for a considerable quantity such as twenty acres or upwards. This arises from the
paucity of inhabitants and the difficulty of procuring provisions and
of transporting them in these distant parts; for in order that a contract to clear land may be attended with profit to those who take it,
they must be three or four with a yoke of oxen and must have food
pretty convenient, or a considerable time will be lost in procuring it;
but if the contract be an extensive one it becomes a desirable object
to some of the old settlers from twelve to twenty miles off or more,
who bring up their provisions with their own team and their sons
or neighbours, or more probably, among the new comers, hire as-
sistants to be paid pork or flour, and thus make a market for their
farming produce as well as labour.

However, even at sixteen dollars an acre, though a very high price,
I think this mode of having your first clearing made preferable; for,
of course, the same causes that make contract prices high will
generally make hired labour so, and the additional expense will be
felt in it also; besides, you can proportion the quantity you get done
to your funds. If they be contracted confine yourself to a very few
acres, say three even, or five, crop them according to the season,
and as soon as they are thus completed, set with energy about getting
more done in a manner better suited to your finances. Be very careful to have a written agreement, worded some way thus and witnessed
by some respectable person:

'I hereby undertake and agree to chop, log, burn, clear, and fence
( ) acres for ( ) Esq., on lot numbered ( ) in the ( ) concession of the township of ( ), ( ) district, as this day marked
out by him, for ( ) dollars, being at the rate of ( ) dollars per
acre, and to complete the said work and have it perfected, to deliver
up the said ( ) on the ( ) day of ( ) next, ready for receiving
a crop; and I hereby undertake that the said work shall be done in
a proper and workmanlike maner: that is to say, that all under brush
and small trees six inches through or less shall be cut quite level
with the ground, and all small brush pulled out by the roots, that
all brush heaps, windfalls, and logs shall be burned quite clearly
off, and the whole space inclosed with a fence of good substantial
rails, perfectly sound and only twelve feet long, split out of ( )
wood, ( ) feet high, and consisting at the least of ( ) rails in
height. Dated ( ) day of ( ), &c.'

You may add, if you please, that in case you do not think the
work well done and a dispute arise thereon, the matter shall be
referred to the determination of certain persons—and have a penalty
introduced in case of non-performance of the contract—but this
last is seldom consented to. Don't pay anything if you can possibly
avoid it until the work is done, and not even then until you be

Courtesy Winifred Dalton   John J. Dalton

PARLIAMENT BUILDINGS, OTTAWA, IN THE 1880's

John Dalton took lessons in painting from his mother-in-law, Sarah Ann Carter.

Courtesy Winifred Dalton   Sarah Ann Carter

THE WOODCUTTERS, 1838

A very English treatment of clearing the land on the Lake Erie shore
near Port Maitland, where the artist's father, Colonel John Johnson,
had a grant of 1000 acres.

perfectly satisfied it is done as it ought to be. Examine if the contract has been fulfilled—if it has been done exactly where you had marked it out—if the fence be good, the rails not too thin or too long, for then their own weight weighs them down and they are too weak to bear the climbing over them by persons to which they are unavoidably exposed; if they be sound and not shook with cross splits, and of the wood agreed on. Measure the space and be very particular that the under-brushing has been properly done, for it will save an immensity of time and trouble in the hoeing and harrowing; when all this is quite manifest to you then pay your money and get a receipt.*. . .

When you hire men to chop always get the best you can—a dollar or two a month is well laid out in the difference of speed and execution good hands evince. I would employ Americans for such work, or at least those who had been some years in the country. You will observe the style in which the Yankees use their axes and the skill which they display in throwing down the trees so as to facilitate the piling of them afterwards; they fell the heaviest first, taking care that they shall lie on the ground clear of windfalls; and where they rest perfectly solidly leave them uncut, and throw others sufficient to make heaps at right-angles across them, cutting these latter into short lengths; a couple of men with handspikes afterwards turn them round and roll them close to and all along the whole heavy ones, and heaps are made in nearly half the time they otherwise would be. Yankees also are more expert at logging, splitting rails, making fences, and indeed at any work indigenous to the forest, as why should they not?

Mrs. Catharine Traill has left us a sympathetic description of tree-felling, with the feelings of a spectator unusually sensitive to nature.

There is a strange excitement created in the mind [she writes] while watching the felling of one of the gigantic pines or oaks of the forest. Proudly and immoveably it seems at first to resist the storm of blows that assail its massy trunk from the united axes of three or even four choppers. As the work of destruction continues a slight motion is perceived—an almost imperceptible quivering of the boughs. Slowly and slowly it inclines, while the loud rending of the trunk at length warns you that its last hold on earth is gone. The axe of the chopper has performed its duty; the motion of the falling tree becomes accelerated every instant, till it comes down in thunder on the plain with a crash that makes the earth tremble and the neighbouring trees reel and bow before it.

While some advised against it, the calling of a logging or chopping bee was the common procedure if the settler did not

---

*In a day of illiteracy and independence it is unlikely that many would try to get a written contract signed, much less succeed in enforcing such elaborate terms as 'Ex-Settler', always a perfectionist, recommended.

VIRGIN PINE, NORTH DUMFRIES, 1949

One of the very few remaining in Ontario,
for it was usual to clear the land completely.

CORDUROY ROAD, ORILLIA, 1844

Horses were usually led over the logs,
which were often semi-floating in swamp
country.

hire his work done. A good description of the course of events is by a young *greenhorn* who participated, David Wilkie, whose lively account is in his *Sketches of a Summer Trip to New York and the Canadas* (1837):

On Thursday last I was engaged in performing a very tough day's work. An intimation was sent to F—— that a *Chopping Bee* was to take place on the ground of Mr. Webb, a neighbouring farmer. . . . Having supplied ourselves with the needful chopping axes we set off after breakfast. . . . We arrived in about an hour at the field of action and met fifteen of the backwood gentry, . . . mostly men who employ themselves clearing the woods or turning their hands to anything that promises a good day's feeding accompanied with a fair allowance of grog. . . .

We soon commenced a war of extermination against some of the loftiest trees the world can produce, and in half an hour you might have mourned over many a fallen monarch of the wood. . . . I was even daring enough to challenge one of them to single combat. . . . My opponent and I proceeded thus: we selected a tree of fair dimensions, having a perpendicular stem and standing free of others. We placed ourselves on each side, hatchet in hand, ready to attack our victim on a signal being given. The one towards whom the tree fell was declared the victor—for this plain reason, that his cut must have been deepest. . . . In the course of the day we levelled to the ground many a tree. . . . The oaks of this district are the finest I have seen, but this only forms an additional motive for their destruction. They escape the fire but undergo the inglorious fate of being manufactured into barrel-staves.

The grog I have already mentioned was our only drink during the day, and uncouth as it was the capacious can was many times emptied. . . . Thus passed the play which lasted till about sunset and then came an afterpiece. . . . Instead of shifting the scene the actors shifted their quarters by adjourning to the log-hut of Mr. Webb, whose provident dame had busied herself to some purpose. The festal board was creaking, if not actually groaning, under its substantial load of eatables and drinkables. No ceremony was either thought of or requisite. . . . The soul and body of our feast was pork, tortured into every description of dish; . . . and its simple handmaiden, the potato, was in some of the platters presented to us so buttered, toasted, and shaped that even the shrewd wit of an Irishman might have been taken aback and rendered unable to discover the presence of his beloved root! . . .

At the head of the board sat our landlord on a bag of wool, supported on the right and left by two of his friends occupying chairs, which appeared to be the sum-total in his possession. Down the right side of the board ran a rough-hewn plank, supported at each end by a sack half-filled with corn; and the opposition bench was a broken ladder with similar supports. . . . More noise was made during the process of feeding than there would have been heard at fifty *table-d'hôtes* in New York.*

A logging bee logically followed a chopping, but it was often delayed until summer. A good description is given by James Logan, who visited Upper Canada in 1836 and spent some days in Douro Township, Peterborough Country. After calling upon 'Mr. Traill, whose lady has published an account of Canada', he participated in the logging bee at the farm of another settler, probably James Foulds who was settled on lot 7, concession 9.

There were about six acres to log [he wrote in his *Notes of a Journey through Canada, the United States of America, and the West Indies*], and he had collected about twenty of his neighbours or their servants, as those who could not work were obliged to find substitutes. There were five yokes of oxen, and generally four—but sometimes only three—men to a yoke, with a boy to drive. To the yoke over the necks of the oxen is fastened a long chain with a hook at the end, and this chain is put around a log which is thus dragged to the pile. . . . When the logs, which vary from ten to fifteen feet in length and from one to two and a half in diameter, were brought to the pile we laid them on in a proper manner. After the first layer was arranged the rest of the logs were hoisted on with handspikes; the heaps vary from four to five feet in height, and are not made too large so as to burn with facility. This is a very laborious part of the operation, especially when the logs are heavy; and if they should slip you are in danger of getting your leg broken or even of losing your life. We worked hard all day from nine, and logged about three acres. At one we had dinner in the barn, masters and servants together without distinction.** Two young Englishmen were present, but did not assist and were therefore laughed at. They disliked the country after three years' trial and were on their way home. In the evening we had a dance and were otherwise agreeably entertained until one in the morning when we walked home, but were entangled in a wood where we groped about for two hours, although the distance we had to go was only half a mile.

There were variations in a bee called by Samuel Strickland, and the piles were burned the same evening:

*On another occasion Wilkie was entertained at a 'sparking bee', often an aftermath of a day's work. Pretty girls with 'smooth shining faces' and 'clear and glistening tresses', a bright moon but no other light, and games with romantic forfeits which seemed to be specially aimed at him—these dangerous circumstances led Wilkie, after a good deal of kissing and petting, to excuse himself before he lost his heart entirely! (See his *Sketches*, pp. 182-6.)

**This was not always the case. At the raising bee of Captain John Thomson, Medonte Township, several 'being gentlemen . . . messed in the dining room, while the others, landed proprietors but no gentlemen, lived in the kitchen'. This caused bad feeling among 'certain Yankified personages', and only by a good deal of subsequent mixing was the 'bad impression' removed. (Thomson diary, April 22, 1834, Archives of Ontario.) See also Volume II, p. 342.

As soon as the ground was cool enough I made a logging Bee, at which I had five yokes of oxen and twenty men, four men to each team. The teamster selects a good place to commence a heap, generally against some large log which the cattle would be unable to move. They draw all the logs within a reasonable distance in front of the large log. The men with hand-spikes roll them, one upon the top of the other, until the heap is seven or eight feet high and ten or twelve broad. All the chips, sticks, and rubbish are then picked up and thrown on the top of the heap. A team and four good men should log and pick an acre a day when the burn has been good.

My hive worked well, for we had five acres logged and set fire to the same evening. On a dark night a hundred or two of these large heaps all on fire at once have a very fine effect and shed a broad glare of light for a considerable distance. In the month of July in the new settlements the whole country at night appears lit up by these fires.

If great care were not taken serious accidents occurred during logging. 'One of the principal farmers of the settlement killed by a tree falling upon him' is an entry in the diary of Joseph Abbott. Particularly where trees were girdled was there danger, for they sometimes fell without the slightest stimulus or warning, and especially in the spring after alternate frost and thaw. Cattle seemed to sense the danger, removing to open spots during storms.

Susanna Moodie found logging bees 'the most disgusting picture of a bush life: . . . noisy, riotous, drunken meetings, often terminating in violent quarrels, sometimes even in bloodshed'; and she considered that very little was done, considering the outlay for food and drink, and that two or three hired men would have done twice as much work and done it better. But before their land was ready for sowing fall wheat they had to 'endure a second and a third repetition of this odious scene'. In a clever parody her husband's verses indicate the usual course of events:

> *There was a man in our town*,*
> *In our town, in our town—*
> *There was a man in our town,*
> *He made a logging bee;*
>   *And he bought lots of whisky*
>   *To make the loggers frisky—*
>   *To make the loggers frisky*
>   *At his logging bee.*
>
> *The Devil sat on a log heap,*
> *A log heap, a log heap—*

*'Town' was a common abbreviation in the pioneer period for 'township'.

CHOPPING BEE, TOWNSHIP OF DUMMER, 1882

Held on the farm of Robert Payne, Sr., this bee consisted largely of Paynes and Battens.

A red-hot burning log heap—
A-grinning at the bee;
And there was lots of swearing,
Of boasting and of daring,
Of fighting and of tearing,
At that logging bee.

In later years, and especially in certain districts, bees were held without liquor, a reform due to the influence of Temperance and Total Abstinence societies. But so great was the general dissipation and so little the work accomplished that 'Ex-Settler' advised immigrants that they should

never call a 'bee'. You have, no doubt, heard of 'bees' of men and oxen coming to you, working gratis—cutting down the logs—hauling them and putting up a building, &c., &c., all in one day; but beware of this harum-scarum drunken work. A gentleman or any respectable man has no business with it—the idle riff-raff are they who will surely come, getting drunk, eating up all your pork and flour, and fighting like Irishmen; and, if they work at all, put up some ugly botched thing you will pay others to take away. Hire men for every thing, or set your work out by contract.

At the close of the century, when pioneering was largely a thing of the past, whiskey-drinking had become generally frowned upon, but E. A. Owen said in a well-considered statement that this was not so much an improvement in the conduct of people as a betterment of the times.

We drink less whiskey than they did [he wrote], not because we are better men and women but because we live in a better age. Then it was the fashion to drink whiskey*, now [1898] it is not. Then it was deemed a universal tonic for every weakness of the flesh, and was considered indispensable in the daily transaction of business; now we look upon old king Alcohol as a deceiver, a mocker, and a destroyer. If our forefathers had seen the old tyrant in the brighter light of our times they would have shown him less favours than we do, for their convictions of right and wrong were stronger than ours, and they were more courageous in giving their convictions practical effect than we are.

The advice to avoid bees was followed by Joseph Abbott, whose diary gives the details of logging on his farm—even how he rather forcefully dissuaded his labourers from working on Sunday:

---

*Owen gives authenticated examples of old-time whiskey purchase and use up to *half a gallon per day per person* over a period of months, and he concludes that these facts are sufficient proof that whiskey must have been *'cheaper* and *purer'* than it was when he wrote (1898). It might be added, that if used in such quantities without death ensuing, it must have had a much lower alcoholic content.

Reginald Drayton

MAJOR ANDERSON'S OLD TRADING-POST, RICE LAKE, 1880
Located on the north shore near the Indian village of Hiawatha.

Courtesy Helen Marryat   Rev. M. A. Farrar

HASTINGS-ON-THE-TRENT
Mr. Farrar took lessons from J. M. W. Turner, the great English landscape painter.

May 19th.—At the same work with two extra hands; for 'logging', as it is called, cannot be carried on to advantage with fewer than four hands, or five if the timber is heavy, as the teamster would have to assist in rolling up a log when the logs got high, and thus not only lose time with his team but keep the men waiting till he drew in another log, which he ought to have had ready on one side while the last was being put up on the other. A log pile consists, when the trees are at all of a uniform size, of five logs on the ground, four on the top of these, then three, two, and one; and when they are not uniform two are substituted for one, or sometimes three for two; and when crooked pieces are met with, which is very seldom, the holes which would be left by their lying alongside of straight ones are filled up with large chips, thick ends of branches, and pieces of old rotten logs which have not been consumed when the fire had been 'run through' the slash to consume the underbrush, and as more than sufficient quantity always remains, the residue is then thrown upon the top of the pile or against the ends; the pile is then set on fire. Generally two or three days' work, or more, is burnt at once; fifteen heaps is about a day's work for five men.

The morning after, two men go to every pile and roll up the burning embers closer together with handspikes, and again about six or eight hours afterwards; this occupied our time till the evening of the 21st, when I paid my two extra hands at the rate of two shillings a-day and discharged them.

May 22nd.—Drew together into one heap a few remaining brands, as we term the burnt log ends left after the pile has been all but consumed, gathered up the ashes, and carted them home.

May 23rd.—Sunday—My men wanted to go in the morning to brand up the pile we had set on fire the night before, which they said was generally done in the backwoods where they came from. I thanked them for their attention to my work and endeavoured to convince them of the impropriety of such conduct, but I fear with little success. I then told them I would much rather see them getting ready to go to church, which, from the black and begrimed state of their clothes, being the same they had worn the day before, they did not seem inclined to do, and asked with some astonishment and in a deprecatory manner if I wished them to go to church *every* Sunday, when I told them that to neglect this duty without sufficient cause, of which I must be the judge, I should consider tantamount to a notice to quit my service. They submitted to my wishes, but one of them thought me a hard and cruel task-master; that one, however, is now a serious, orderly, and regular attendant at church and a communicant, and attributes all his subsequent success in life, as well as his reformation of conduct, to such trifling instruction as I was led to give him on such occasions; thus a word in season is sometimes like bread cast upon the waters, which may appear after many days.

The rather ghastly appearance of recently burnt rural clearings was somewhat different near towns or in populous districts.

There the timber might be squared, some of it sawn into boards, the smaller trees cut up into four-foot firewood, and only the brush burned. The scene in such regions would be of stumps, burning brush, and piles of wood. But apart from the use of a few logs for farm buildings, or the sale of the best if the settler lived near a sawmill, the only revenue the backwoodsman obtained from the wholesale destruction of the forest was from wood ashes, unless he had limestone at hand from which lime could be burned. By no means all settlers made the effort to gather and store the ashes, though in the early period there was a ready market. Some were contented if they merely picked up a few bushels to exchange for whiskey or make into a little soft soap.

Those who were thrifty carefully collected the ashes as soon as possible after the second burning, for a rain would spoil them. A wooden scraper with a two-foot head and an eight-foot handle was recommended for gathering ashes. Usually they were stored in a log shed until winter, when they could easily be transported in barrels to the nearest ashery or store. Later, as roads improved, an 'ashman' came with a wagon and bought them. From 4d. to 6d. a bushel in goods could be obtained for them, or about one bushel of wheat for fifteen of ashes; but the Winchester measure for wheat was only half the size of the bushel used for ashes. J. Abbott says he received £15 for two barrels of potash he had made, but the process was a laborious and difficult one and it took the ashes from four acres of forest to make the 1000 pounds of potash that he sold. James Dobbie wrote home from Lanark in 1826 that a neighbour, Robert Affleck,

has a potash kettle of his own, for which he paid in ashes, and while on the road I passed two barrels from his house on the way to Brockville (sixty miles), for which he would get about £10. They also make their own soap. It was white, but softer than that sold in Glasgow.

In the heyday of the trade there were two main types of ashes —pot and pearl—but the heavy cost of transport, together with the advance of chemistry, gradually lessened the trade after 1835, and eventually ended it altogether. Thereafter many farmers continued to extract the lye and, by mixing with grease, manufacture their own soft soap. This was often women's work, and the utensils needed were a barrel or a section of a hollow log, an earthenware vessel, and an iron kettle. Hay at the bottom of the barrel served as a sieve, through which lye

Courtesy J. M. McCrea

PIONEER STONING MACHINE

A collection of the McCrea models of pioneer buildings
and processes is in the Royal Ontario Museum.

Conservation Authorities, Ontario

STONE PILES IN CULTIVATED FIELDS

The result of heavy work on lot 15 concession V of Bentinck Township.

seeped into the earthenware pot as wood ashes and water were
poured in at the top. The lye, boiled with fat, produced the
soap.*

*More detailed descriptions of the making of soap and potash, as well as the
processes of lime-burning and charcoal-making, are given in Volume II,
Chapter XII.

It is said that white clover was usually the first plant to spring up on newly-cleared land, to be followed by greensward, as wild grass was often called. But the more useful grasses such as timothy, herdsgrass, lucerne, foul meadow, and red clover had to be sown. In many districts cleared land was found almost useless because of underlying rock, while in others great boulders were bared as the topsoil washed away. Joseph Abbott described in his diary the difficulties of moving them, as well as an ingenious 'stone drag' that he made to facilitate the process:

April 23rd.—Blasting a few large boulders in the corn land, which had been drilled by contract at three halfpence an inch, and drawing them off with the oxen on a stone drag, a machine made of plank about three inches thick, split out of a crooked ash tree and hewed even with a curve of about six inches in its whole length (five feet), its breadth being about two feet and a half, the planks dowelled together and a small piece of scantling pinned on across the ends and along each side to keep it firmly together and to prevent the stones from rolling off. We made it in about four hours.

April 24th.—Finished getting off the stones, although we had two of them to blast over again, or at least portions of them which were too large to move. Hard work—all went to bed very tired.

Most settlers removed the stones much later, when they became more noticeable after the stumps had been removed and ploughing commenced. Many a man devised some machine or method for lifting the heaviest, but in general a stoneboat or wagon hauled them away. Stone fences and great piles of rocks still testify to the hard work, oft repeated, of making rocky fields useful for agriculture, and quite frequently they are most prominent on farm land long since abandoned.

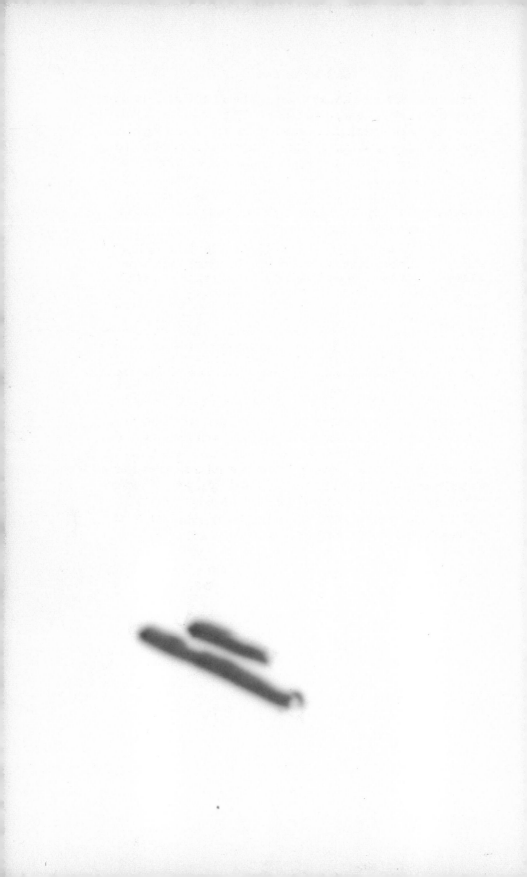